DATE DUE

BRIDGENORTH		
JUL 1 4 2001		
AUG 1 8 2001		
SEP 2 5 2001		
JAN 1 2 2002 JUN 1 8 2002		
JUN 2 8 2002		
JAN 0 6 2005 MAR 2 6 2005		
SEP 2 1 2005		

Bloodlines

BLOODLINES

The Rise and Fall of the Mafia's Royal Family

Lee Lamothe and Antonio Nicaso

HarperCollins*PublishersLtd*

Bloodlines:
The Rise and Fall of the Mafia's Royal Family
Copyright © 2001 by Lee Lamothe
and Antonio Nicaso.

Photographs courtesy of the authors
except where noted.

www.harpercanada.com

HarperCollins books may be purchased for educa-
tional, business, or sales promotional use.
For information please write:
Special Markets Department,
HarperCollins Canada,
55 Avenue Road, Suite 2900,
Toronto, Ontario, Canada M5R 3L2

First edition

Canadian Cataloguing in Publication Data

Lamothe, Lee, 1948–
Bloodlines : the rise and fall of the mafia's
royal family

Includes index.
ISBN 0-00-200034-2

1. Cuntrera family.
2. Caruana family.
3. Mafia – Italy – Sicily – Biography.
I. Nicaso, Antonio
II. Title.

HV6453.I82S635 2001   364.1'092'2458
C00-932353-8

01 02 03 04 HC 4 3 2 1

Printed and bound in the United States
Set in Sabon

Contents

CUNTRERA - CARUANA - VELLA FAMILY TREE

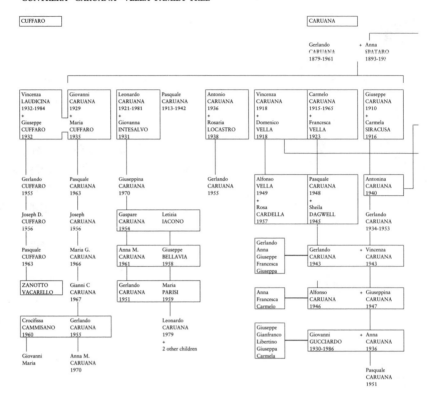

CUFFARO

CARUANA

Gerlando
CARUANA
1879-1961
+ Anna
SPATARO
1893-19?

| Vincenza LAUDICINA 1932-1984 + Giuseppe CUFFARO 1932 | Giovanni CARUANA 1929 + Maria CUFFARO 1935 | Leonardo CARUANA 1921-1981 + Giovanna INTESALVO 1931 | Pasquale CARUANA 1913-1942 | Antonio CARUANA 1936 + Rosaria LOCASTRO 1938 | Vincenza CARUANA 1918 + Domenico VELLA 1918 | Carmelo CARUANA 1915-1965 + Francesca VELLA 1923 | Giuseppe CARUANA 1910 + Carmela SIRACUSA 1916 |

Gerlando
CUFFARO
1955

Pasquale
CARUANA
1963

Giuseppina
CARUANA
1970

Gerlando
CARUANA
1955

Alfonso
VELLA
1949
+
Rosa
CARDELLA
1957

Pasquale
CARUANA
1948
+
Sheila
DAGWELL
1945

Antonina
CARUANA
1940

Joseph D.
CUFFARO
1956

Joseph
CARUANA
1956

Gaspare
CARUANA
1954

Letizia
IACONO

Gerlando
CARUANA
1934-1953

Pasquale
CUFFARO
1963

Maria G.
CARUANA
1966

Anna M.
CARUANA
1961

Giuseppe
BELLAVIA
1958

Gerlando
Anna
Giuseppe
Francesca
Giuseppa

Gerlando
CARUANA
1943

+ Vincenza
CARUANA
1943

ZANOTTO
VACARELLO

Gianni C
CARUANA
1967

Gerlando
CARUANA
1951

Maria
PARISI
1959

Anna
Francesca
Carmelo

Alfonso
CARUANA
1946

+ Giuseppina
CARUANA
1947

Crocifissa
CAMMISANO
1960

Gerlando
CARUANA
1955

Leonardo
CARUANA
1979
+
2 other children

Giuseppe
Gianfranco
Libertino
Giuseppa
Carmela

Giovanni
GUCCIARDO
1930-1986

+ Anna
CARUANA
1936

Giovanni
Maria

Anna M.
CARUANA
1970

Pasquale
CARUANA
1951

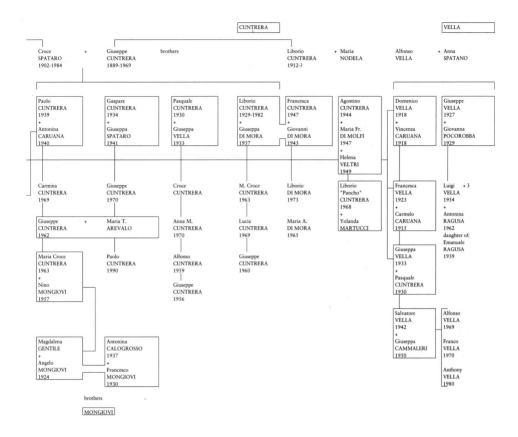

THE CARUANA - CUNTRERA CONNECTIONS

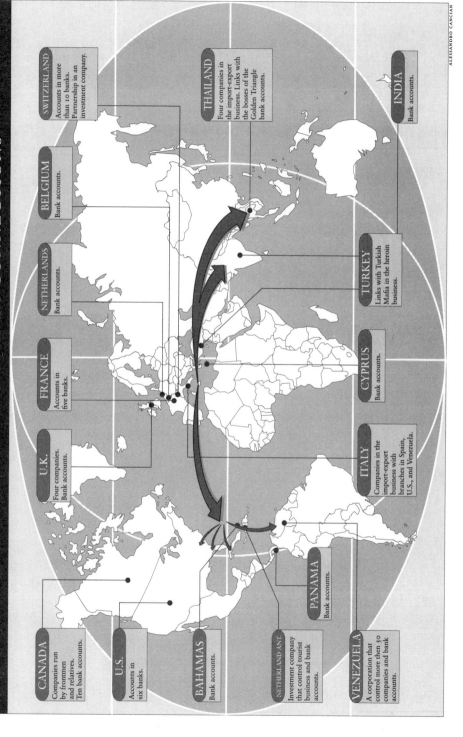

SWITZERLAND
Accounts in more than 10 banks. Partnership in an investment company.

BELGIUM
Bank accounts.

NETHERLANDS
Bank accounts.

FRANCE
Accounts in five banks.

U.K.
Four companies. Bank accounts.

THAILAND
Four companies in the import-export business. Links with the bosses of the Golden Triangle bank accounts.

INDIA
Bank accounts.

TURKEY
Links with Turkish Mafia in the heroin business.

CYPRUS
Bank accounts.

ITALY
Companies in the import-export business with branches in Spain, U.S, and Venezuela.

CANADA
Companies run by frontmen and relatives. Ten bank accounts.

U.S.
Accounts in six banks.

BAHAMAS
Bank accounts.

NETHERLAND ANT.
Investment company that control more then 50 companies and bank accounts.

PANAMA
Bank accounts.

VENEZUELA
A corporation that control more then 50 companies and bank accounts.

ALESSANDRO CANCIAN

Introduction

The face of the Caruana-Cuntrera criminal organization is the face of the future: globalization instead of regionalism, cooperation instead of conflict, alliance instead of antagonism. Using a blend of traditional mafia values and modern technologies, the Caruana-Cuntrera organization has, over a century, become an almost perfect criminal enterprise.

The constant rebirth of criminal conspiracies among many members of the clan can only lead to the conclusion that it's a criminal dynasty, with sons replacing fathers, down through generations. Indeed, a close friend of Alfonso Caruana, who led the organization in the 1990s, casually noted: "Growing up within the walls of a Mafia family he had very little choice in the matter. . . . If he hadn't been a Mafioso he could have been a successful businessman; he was more modern-thinking than most Mafiosi." This from a Canadian Mafioso, himself of some repute. And Alfonso Caruana himself once said: "My father was Mafioso, my grandfather was Mafioso."

While traditional respect was a basis of the Caruana-Cuntrera's operations and personal conduct, it was their focus on cooperation and corruption that brought them relatively secure success in the underworld. Turf wars are unprofitable and a waste of energy. Energy can be better spent infiltrating financial systems, corrupting politicians, and sharing the wealth. As Alfonso Caruana himself said: "If you shoot, you make enemies. If you share, you make friends." This belief allowed the Caruanas and Cuntreras to operate for a century, seldom bothered by law enforcement—and then usually by accident. Their persistent corruption of governments, notably in Venezuela and Mexico and, to a lesser extent, in Europe and North America, allowed them to remain one step ahead of the law. When they felt too much attention coming their way, or if they were tipped off that they were under close investigation, they vanished and re-appeared in a similar form in a faraway place.

The nucleus of the Family is melded by blood, the outer shell is hardened by marriage, and encompassing all are the layers of corruption, co-option, and co-conspiracies. Secrecy and discretion are the watchwords of all the clans tied to the Caruana-Cuntrera.

The thicket of relationships, after a century of intermarrying and forming other familial ties, is almost impenetrable. Caruanas and Cuntreras appear, then disappear, and as often as not never blip again on the radar. In researching this book the authors often found "lost" Caruanas or Cuntreras—often believed dead by law enforcement officials—living quietly productive lives in out-of-the-way places. One "lost" Caruana about whom no one seemed to know anything, was found by accident, in a cemetery, his date of death the only clue to his fate.

Our success in drawing together the intermarriages and familial relationships has admittedly been mixed. The "wicker basket" infrastructure of the Caruana-Cuntrera (and Vella, Cuffaro, et al.) appeared at first to be a problem that could be solved by logic and meticulous cross-checking and referencing. Between spreadsheets, index cards, wall charts, and scraps of paper it appeared we had the family members tracked and positioned. As late as the final edit of the book, when facts were checked and the details nailed down, we found another Caruana floating on the edges of the story and had to scramble to include him. Our feeling of discomfort was somewhat allayed when, in a late interview with a close associate of this powerful organization, he mentioned a family member's "cousin." No, we said, he's his uncle.

"No, no, his cousin, I think his second- or third-cousin. His mother is married to the brother of his father's . . ." A lengthy explanation ensued, ending with ". . . so that's what, his third-cousin, right?"

Presented with the Canadian, American, and Italian family trees he was suddenly enlightened: the fellow he thought was his closest friend's cousin turned out to be an uncle, barely older than the cousin himself.

The basis of the organization was its perfection of the traditional Mafia role: placing itself between supplier and client, a position sophisticated organized crime groups have occupied since their inception. Rather than controlling, for example, the cocaine trade, the Caruana-

Cuntrera endeavored to control the trade routes. The genius of the organization was its ability to provide financial and political services—money laundering, corruption—to the criminal organizations through the washing of money and the penetration of legitimate sectors.

And it wasn't just corruption that allowed the organization to flourish. In the case of Canada, it was lax legislation and the Charter of Rights. Alfonso Caruana often said he "felt safe" in Canada, even in the face of international warrants for his arrests. He was aware of the protections that the Canadian judicial system offered, particularly because he was a Canadian citizen. He steadfastly refused to enter the United States under any circumstances, a country with a less merciless justice system and a more adequately funded law enforcement.

At the end of his reign he refused to use banks, having been once burned by the paper trail commerce in the "over-world" leaves; instead, he entrusted several millions of dollars in cash to a chain of couriers who bulk-carried the money out of the country.

Working from tens of thousands of pages of documents, audio tapes, video tapes, and interviews with underworld figures, journalists, and police officers in several countries, we, at the end, find that we've surfaced only a portion of the story of the Family. We have read and listened to hundreds of hours of conversations—some relating to criminal activities, but the bulk of them everyday discourse of men and their families—and what we found was, in addition to a truly global criminal syndicate, a world populated by men and women who are alarmingly normal in most respects of their lives.

When writing a book, the last thing you write is what comes first: the foreword. It isn't until the end of the project that you find, having started with a pretty general list of questions, that each question itself brought more questions than answers. And many of those questions are unanswerable. The Caruana-Cuntrera family turned out to be complex to the point of being almost incomprehensible. Where we were able to get some clarification about the interrelationships from those close to the group, none within its heart were willing to discuss even the most innocuous details. They have carried from rural Sicily the most basic of the closed family traits: the exclusion of outsiders to the inner structure of their clan. While this is a stumbling block on the road to knowledge, it is also what makes the Caruana-Cuntrera worth examining. If they weren't secret, they wouldn't be of any real interest. And if they talked, could they be believed? The seriousness of the family membership was summed up by a friend of Alfonso Caruana's: "He's not a *'quaqua-raquà'* (lightweight) . . . he's a man of firm principle, a family-oriented man. He will never turn as informant. . . . Defection is not part of his culture and he cannot trade on his own blood."

The globalization of organized crime is very real. But it has unfortunately been inflated, not necessarily in its size or power, but in its presentation. There are Mafia families working with Eastern European organized crime groups; there are Triads working with motorcycle gangs; there are Colombian cartels working with Yakuza cells. They operate in every country where there's a "client" market for their goods and services. Sometimes, as we discovered researching an earlier book, there are three or four distinctly separate criminal organizations working together, often for lengthy periods of time in several jurisdictions.

However, the current presentation of this global phenomenon is to show a darkly sinister force taking over the world, much in the manner of the cardboard characters populating adventure comic books, shaven-headed creatures with the power to destroy the world with the press of a button. In this book there's a small but important scene in which Alfonso Caruana, Oreste Pagano, and Antonio Scambia—respectively a Sicilian Mafioso, a boss of the Neapolitan Camorra, and a member of the Calabrian *'ndrangheta*—arrange a South America-to-Italy cocaine network.

This meeting has been documented in books, magazine articles, and police intelligence reports as the creation of an international crime conglomerate. The world was to be flooded with cocaine now that the three major Italian-based criminal organizations had met and divided up the global drug trade. The meeting took on a grainy image of men wearing dark glasses and dressed in dark suits who met in shadowy boardrooms lined with bodyguards, broken shafts of light pouring through high windows. The world, we were told, had a chilling new criminal threat.

The facts are a little less dramatic. Three men came together in a hotel on Margarita Island and chatted. None wore suits, none had legions of bodyguards, none had a map of the world and a pointer to show trade routes. When the three men concluded their business, a pipeline for cocaine had been formed. Three existing organized crime groups had reconfigured themselves and embarked on a business venture. Perhaps uniquely, a money-laundering component had been added to allow each of the partners to repatriate their profits, but otherwise it wasn't any more than what it actually was to the naked eye.

It would do well to remember it was "three men" who met, not "three multi-national crime lords bent upon addicting the world as part of a sinister plot." The steady reduction of organized crime figures into single-faceted, single-minded characters makes them monsters we expect we'll be able to recognize as being different from the rest of us. Monsters who somehow stand apart and separate from us. And that's how they hide: we watch for the gargoyles, never realizing they look just like us. But they're not monsters, although they may do monstrous things. They dote on their children, they fret over their own mortality—all seem to have some medical condition—they philosophize on life, they pump their own gas to save a few pennies a liter. They're funny and angry and they're buried under huge responsibilities. They are the heart of organized crime in this new century.

As long as we believe they're monsters they can never be defeated. They'll frighten us from the shadows with their fabled superhuman omniscient powers. They'll defeat our resolve with their legendary mythical prowess. We'll become—if we haven't already—of the belief that the battle against the organizations is already lost.

And this leads to a paraphrase of assassinated Sicilian magistrate Giovanni Falcone—words that should be our mantra: "The mafia was born of men and it can be destroyed by men."

In the words of a member of the Caruana-Cuntrera family: "Why can't people realize we're just a family like any other family?"

This book is the story of how an "untouchable" criminal organization was dismantled. It wasn't destroyed; it may have been slowed down a little by the jailing of half a generation of half a Mafia family. And it wasn't done with a massive budget or special powers. It was done by men and women chipping at a rock with laws that aren't sharp enough, funding that materialized seemingly by accident, and a strange kind of attitude that makes one wonder if they only took down the Caruanas out of spite for their own bureaucracy.

Finally, some notes on the making of this book.

Mafia with a capital "M" refers to the Sicilian Mafia; mafia with a lower case "M" refers to generic criminal organizations; the American mafia is La Cosa Nostra, or LCN.

We have collaborated on several projects in the past, and bring to this effort differing—but not opposite—points of view and attitude. Throughout the making of this book we have debated, often enthusiastically, our interpretations of events and the significance of data and research. We attempted to stay to the line, but where opinions and analysis diverge, every effort was made to present a balance.

And "Bloodlines" was created to be two books: one, the story of a specific mafia family over a specific period of time, and the other a vehicle for research on organized crime. We've used sidenotes, some of them lengthy, to give context to events within the story. We hope this method will allow one type of reader to follow a specific story, and another kind of reader to veer off the narrative. And both types of readers to enjoy it.

LEE LAMOTHE
ANTONIO NICASO

Prologue

"The Mafia's Rothschilds."[1] This is how an Italian newspaper in 1989 described the Caruana-Cuntrera crime family. It's an apt analogy.

There are a number of significant similarities between the powerful Mafia organization and the international European bankers. One is the driving ambition within each family to rise from abject poverty and strife to immense wealth and influence. The two family dynasties have similar dynamics and used similar means; that the former is so thoroughly criminal and the other not is perhaps a matter of accidental opportunity and the indifference of circumstance.

As Mayer Amschel Rothschild rose from the Jewish ghetto of Frankfurt to become an international financial magnate, so too did the Caruana-Cuntrera family rise from their dirt-poor existence in western Sicily to become international money brokers. As Rothschild was able to exploit the Napoleonic wars that changed the alliances and allegiances of Europe to amass huge financial reserves, the Caruana-Cuntrera organization was able to exploit the global wars among crime syndicates to gain control of the narcotics trade and provide channels for laundering billions of illicit dollars.

On his deathbed, Rothschild ordered his heirs to marry among themselves "in order to keep the capital intact." Whether the patriarchs of the Caruana-Cuntrera family were given the

> Alfonso Caruana, for example, married his first cousin, Giuseppina Caruana (b. 1947); his brother Gerlando married her sister Vincenza Caruana (b. 1943). Both women were daughters of the Caruana brothers' paternal uncle, Giuseppe Caruana (b. 1910). Giuseppe Caruana thereby was both uncle and father-in-law to the Caruana brothers.

same advice is a matter of conjecture; certainly subsequent generations took that path, an endogamy with few precedents in the history of the Sicilian Mafia.

Like the Rothschilds, the bosses of the Caruana-Cuntrera family sent their male children to schools around the world—from London to Lugano, from Montreal to Caracas—to receive a first-class education and enter the realm of business. And like the dynasty of bankers who, with their fortunes, influenced the political and military strategies of the rulers of their age, the Caruana-Cuntrera family was adept at fostering contacts with local politicians, bankers, lawyers and judges, government ministers, and even heads of state. Insinuating themselves into a country's power structure—whether it be in Venezuela, Italy, or Canada—was imperative to the success of their international criminal enterprise.

"More than the strength of intimidation and association, they use their brains," explains Alberto Maritati, a former Italian deputy national Mafia prosecutor. "They guarantee services: drugs and money-laundering techniques."[2] According to Maritati, respect, especially outside of Italy, is not obtained through *omertà*—the code of silence— or violence, but with professional business practices and high-level international connections.

The evolution of the Caruana-Cuntrera organization from criminal with underworld ties to criminal enterprise with widespread political and financial connections was recognized publicly in an article published on June 5, 1998, in *El Nacional*, the most influential newspaper in Venezuela. Quoting an anonymous Italian diplomat in Caracas, the article confirmed what many had long suspected: "Here many men of straw operate on behalf of the Caruana-Cuntreras, who in turn have connections with party leaders, congressmen, judges, and other public officials."

The Caruana-Cuntrera represent an untypical group in the Sicilian Mafia. Members of the family left Sicily in the 1950s and 1960s and formed Cosa Nostra colonies in North and South America. Then, slowly, with a mind-set different from that of the ravaging Mafia clans they left behind in Sicily, they set themselves apart and became a true criminal enterprise, driven not by honor but by profit, and most of all by a thirst for power and absolute respect. The ambition of the Caruana-Cuntrera wasn't meant to challenge the highest levels of the Sicilian Mafia—who looked askance at their evolution with a mixture of greed, envy, and admiration—but to nurture a kind of early globalization and to set off a campaign to form strategic alliances.

The Caruana-Cuntrera decided to become managers—power brokers—and began to build bridges with the most powerful criminal organizations in the world: in Italy, the United States, Canada, Turkey, Thailand, Mexico, Brazil, and Colombia. They had something to offer: primarily self-contained, they could move drugs by the ton and invest the colossal revenues in legitimate ways by using offshore banks and other sophisticated financial systems, found particularly in Canada and Switzerland.

> The recruit is taken to a secluded location (which may also be a private home), in the presence of three or more men of honor of the family, and then the oldest informs him that the goal of "This Thing" is to protect the weak and eradicate abuses; afterward one of the candidate's fingers is pricked and the blood is spilled onto a sacred image. Then the image is placed in the hand of the novice and set on fire. At this point the novice, who must endure the burning by passing the sacred image from one hand to the other until it is completely extinguished, swears to be loyal to the principles of "Cosa Nostra," solemnly stating, "May my flesh be burned like this sacred image if I do not keep faith with my oath."—from *The Sicilian Mafia, The Business of Private Protection* by Diego Gambetta, from statements by Tommaso Buscetta

In short, they created a modern Mafia of their own, different from the traditional one with its initiation ceremonies, hierarchies, vendettas, and well-defined territories. The sheer closeness of the core members eliminated the need for many of the outside services other criminal enterprises required; it is even in question as to whether members of the Caruana-Cuntrera engaged in the traditional ceremony of blood.

It's a Mafia that, wherever it operates, forges alliances with the politically and financially powerful and disdains the powerless.

As a Mafia organization, the Caruana-Cuntrera is a whole unto itself, a self-reliant entity that travels the corridors of international crime as easily as the old Mafiosi traveled the paths and dirt roads of rural Sicily a hundred years ago.

1

In April 1995, Enio Mora was admitted to Northwestern General Hospital in Toronto suffering from chest pains.

In Canada's underworld, the powerfully built Mora had carved out a particular niche. He was neither fish nor fowl, given that he did not boast the Sicilian or Calabrian or Neapolitan heritage shared by most members of traditional organized crime. Instead he came from a family in Sora, a city in Italy's central province of Frosinone, where several of his relatives operated in an informal mafia-like organization. Mora was proud of his wide circle of friends, including American La Cosa Nostra members, leaders of Canada's 'ndrangheta clans—the Calabrian mafia—and Sicilian Mafiosi on both sides of the U.S.-Canada border and at home in Italy.

"I have a lot of friends—maybe some friends are not too friendly, but they're friends, they're part of my life," he often said. "They can call it a mafia or whatever they like; I go out every day and I make money to put food on my family's table. How I do it is how I do it."[1]

And he did it, he admitted candidly, through gaming and "banking," but never from the drug trade, which he described as "a fucking swamp for pigs." He also admitted that some of his associates were notorious drug traffickers, but he shrugged it off: "How they put food on their family's table is their business. I don't ask."

Mora, at forty-seven years old, had so far escaped arrest, despite several police investigations and attempts to deport him to his native Italy. Primarily a gambling house operator, loan-shark, and extortionist, he was at one point implicated in an international heroin ring, but he convincingly and successfully explained it away as an elaborate scam to deprive an undercover officer of his money: "They wanted to give me their money, [so] I took it."

He was suspected of involvement in several murders and beatings, and he had a reputation as a tough guy. Once, during a robbery at a gaming house he operated, he was shot. He lost part of his leg, and so earned the nickname "Pegleg." One of the two men who'd robbed the game was later murdered by a shotgun blast through the window of his basement apartment. The murder was never solved, but Mora commented on the killing: "Basement apartments are dangerous places: drafty, infestation, no privacy. A man should own his own home, his land."

At a hearing to deport him, he was read a list of local and national crime figures and asked if the names were familiar; he readily admitted to knowing all of them, making no apologies. Some of the men named had been previously charged with organized crime offenses, ranging from heroin trafficking to extortion and gaming. Some ultimately became victims of a gangland war that, when the shooting was over, found Mora on the winning side as the representative of the John Papalia crime family, the Ontario branch of La Cosa Nostra, with connections to Buffalo, New York.

As Mora was recovering in hospital in 1995, he became one of the targets of a secret Toronto Police intelligence operation dubbed "Project Pipe." Another target of the probe was Agostino Cuntrera, a prominent member of the Sicilian underworld who was often seen meeting with Mora. Wiretaps revealed that the men were discussing investment in a Cayman Island bank.

As part of Project Pipe, Toronto Police Detective-Constables Bill Sciammarella and Tony Saldutto had authorization to wiretap several telephone lines, notably those in Mora's home. During the third week of April, Mora, from his hospital bed, was talking to his wife, Giuseppina.

Project Pipe remains an active police investigation relating to a money-laundering sting that deprived several prominent organized crime figures of millions of dollars. The name comes from the discovery of a pipe bomb at the home of a university professor in Guelph, Ontario, as a warning to his brother, a crooked investment broker, who was suspected of taking Mafia money and fleeing Canada.

Agostino "Dino" Cuntrera (b. 1944) is a resident of Montreal, Quebec. He is variously described as the number-one member of the Caruana-Cuntrera in Montreal, or as the number-two man in the city, operating under Mafia godfather Nicolò Rizzuto. Cuntrera was sentenced to five years in prison for conspiracy in the 1978 murder of underworld figure Paolo Violi. Agostino Cuntrera is a cousin of brothers Pasquale, Paolo, Gaspare, and Liborio Cuntrera, the first "true" generation of the Caruana-Cuntrera family's international narcotics empire.

They discussed family matters, how the children were doing, and engaged in general household chitchat.

"We're supposed to go to that wedding this Saturday at Sutton Place," Giuseppina said to her husband.

"Yeah, yeah."

"We should tell someone we cannot make it."

As the conversation continued, the couple mentioned that one attendee would be Agostino Cuntrera.

Sciammarella and Saldutto, when they received the "dailies"—transcripts of the day's interceptions—noted the comment about the upcoming event. The detectives went to the Sutton Place Hotel and were told that the bride was to be Francesca Caruana, and the groom Anthony Catalanotto.

Anthony Catalanotto, married to Alfonso Caruana's daughter, Francesca, has no criminal record. The 1985 U.S. Department of Justice/Federal Bureau of Investigation Report states: "'La Cosa Nostra in Canada' shows two men named Catalanotto as drug suppliers to Canadian Sicilian Mafia members in the 1970s. Police files show no relationship between Anthony Catalanotto and the Catalanotto family members noted in the American law enforcement reports."

Weddings, funerals, baptisms, and other family events are intelligence-gathering opportunities for criminal investigators. At an 'ndrangheta funeral in 1980, for example, a photograph of the group of dour men carrying the deceased's coffin provided an insight into who was at the power-center of several Calabrian mafia families operating in Ontario. These family events allow investigators to update their photo files, trace license numbers for new addresses and affiliations, and see who's walking with whom. Often the gathering is used by members of far-flung criminal outposts to get together and catch up on gossip.

The Caruana-Catalanotto wedding, because it was mentioned by Mora on Sciammarella's wires, seemed to have important intelligence potential. The name Caruana was notorious in international drug trafficking and money laundering on several continents. But there are many families with the name Caruana, many of them law-abiding citizens.

Sciammarella and Saldutto notified three of Canada's experts on traditional organized crime: Staff-Sergeant Larry Tronstad of the Royal Canadian Mounted Police (RCMP), RCMP Sgt. George Capra of the Combined Forces Special Enforcement Unit (CFSEU), and Detective Ron Seaver of the Ontario Provincial Police (OPP). They then telephoned the

Montreal Urban Community Police Anti-Gang Squad and asked if they had information about anyone who might be attending the wedding who had the name Caruana. They were told that an Alfonso Caruana was wanted by Italian police and was believed to be the current head of the Caruana-Cuntrera organization.

The Toronto Police Mobile Support Services—expert in mobile surveillance—was notified; intelligence teams were set up; and hotels in the downtown core were canvassed for known organized crime figures, several of whom were found to have booked rooms for the occasion. Informants were casually interviewed about the event.

Sciammarella and Saldutto obtained charts of the Caruana-Cuntrera family tree from investigators in Italy and determined that the fugitive named Alfonso Caruana had a daughter named Francesca.

By Saturday, April 29, 1995, the Sutton Place Hotel was under police surveillance from every angle. As dozens of cars—luxury sedans and upscale sport-utility vehicles—arrived after making their way from the small, elegant St. Margaret Mary Church in Woodbridge, Ontario, just northwest of Toronto, Sciammarella and Saldutto cruised the area, collecting license plate numbers. A video post was set up on an upper floor of a government building across from the hotel.

The day was cool and very windy; women in sleeveless dresses hurried through the front doors of the hotel as their tuxedoed escorts dropped them off. Liveried doormen tried to organize the sudden rush of cars. Alfonso Caruana's daughter and her new husband arrived in a white stretch limousine decorated with white flowers. The rest of the wedding party traveled in vehicles festooned with gold bows. Shivering, the bridesmaids, wearing full-length peach-colored dresses, rushed into the warmth of the hotel.

Familiar faces from past and present criminal investigations were seen moving into and around the hotel as the bride and groom arrived. Francesca Caruana wore a stunning wedding dress with a long train; her headpiece was a jeweled tiara. Anthony Catalanotto, tall and beefy, escorted his bride into the hotel.

As Montreal Mafia boss Vito Rizzuto arrived,

Vito Rizzuto (b. 1946) is the son of the Rizzuto family's patriarch, Nicolò "Zu Cola" Rizzuto (b. 1924). The elder Rizzuto is an internationally known drug trafficker and the man behind the 1978 Mafia coup in Montreal in which the Paolo Violi regime was ended.

American actor Steve Guttenberg, unaware he was passing through a real-life drama, slipped from the revolving doors, casually dressed and smiling widely.

The father of the bride arrived in a black Mercedes and took gift bags from the trunk. Dressed immaculately in a tuxedo, his hair black with hints of gray, he made his way into the hotel. Well barbered and moving with ease and confidence, he looked like a man without a care in the world.

Sciammarella and Saldutto spent the following Monday and Tuesday running checks on the license plate numbers and scouring the photographs and videotape. By Tuesday they'd identified the owner of the black Mercedes sedan driven by the father of the bride. It was registered to Francesca Caruana, who lived at 38 Goldpark Court, in Woodbridge, a town made up of middle- and upper-middle-class dwellings, home to a large Italian-Canadian population.

The two detectives began working the phones, leaving messages at several investigative agencies, including the RCMP in Montreal and the Federal Bureau of Investigation (FBI) in Washington and New York.

A land title search of 38 Goldpark Court showed that the residence was owned by Giuseppe Cuntrera, Alfonso Caruana's nephew, and his wife, Maria Teresa Arevalo. The tenants were listed as Alfonso and Giuseppina Caruana.

Three different Giuseppe Cuntreras would be identified during the Caruana-Cuntrera investigation. They are Giuseppe "Little Joe" Cuntrera (b. 1962), the son of Mafioso Paolo Cuntrera (b. 1939), now in prison in Italy; Giuseppe "Big Joe" Di Mora Cuntrera (b. 1960), son of Liborio Cuntrera (b. 1929) who died of cirrhosis of the liver in 1982 in England, where he had been in charge of the Caruana-Cuntreras' United Kingdom heroin operations; and Giuseppe "Venezuelan Joe" Cuntrera (b. 1956), son of Mafia boss Pasquale Cuntrera (b. 1930), currently serving a prison sentence in Italy on drug and Mafia-related charges.

The U.S. Justice Department/Federal Bureau of Investigation Report, *The Caruana/Cuntrera Sicilian Mafia Organization Racketeering Enterprise Investigation Intelligence Profile, 1991,* lists Giuseppe "Little Joe" Cuntrera as a "Member." He was "recently expelled from Aruba."

Giuseppe "Little Joe" Cuntrera has never been accused, charged, or convicted of any crime. According to documents filed with the Ontario provincial government for a Private Investigation & Security Guard license, he lived until 1989 in Aruba, where he managed Club Visage. He also

5

managed two Toronto-area restaurants—Pat & Mario's and Crawdaddy's. He is Alfonso Caruana's nephew (his father, Paolo Cuntrera, is married to Antonina Caruana, Alfonso Caruana's cousin and sister-in-law). Giuseppe Cuntrera was granted his private investigator's license under the Atlas Security Personnel Service Inc. of Mississauga, Ontario. He was licensed to carry a firearm under the provincial government's Private Investigators and Security Guards Act. He received a diploma certifying that he had completed "The Basic Law and Combat Handgun Course" with a 99 percent score on his shoot. He currently resides in Toronto.

Giuseppe "Little Joe" Cuntrera's father, Paolo Cuntrera, is in the file as a "Key/Dominant Figure. . . . He is a brother of and right-hand man to Pasquale Cuntrera. Has had residences in Agrigento, Sicily; Montreal, Canada; Sao Paolo, Brazil; Aruba; and currently resides in Caracas." A year after the report was compiled, the Venezuelan government deported Paolo, Pasquale, and their brother Gaspare Cuntrera to Italy to face Mafia-association charges.

Giuseppe "Big Joe" Cuntrera, the son of the late Liborio Cuntrera, is also the nephew of Pasquale and Paolo Cuntrera and is Alfonso Caruana's cousin.

A report from the Raggruppamento Operativo Speciale (ROS) dei Carabinieri di Torino sent to Canadian law enforcement in 1996 lists Giuseppe "Peppe" Cuntrera (b. 1962), son of Paolo Cuntrera and Antonina Caruana, in its index of members of the Caruana and Cuntrera families.

RCMP reviews of financial records during Project Pilgrim show Giuseppe "Venezuelan Joe" Cuntrera 1956 ("son of Pasquale Cuntrera") was the recipient of checks traced through Alfonso Caruana–controlled bank accounts. He has never been accused, charged, or convicted of any crime.

In 1998, during a police raid, RCMP Sergeant Reg King discovered a bag containing $200,000 cash in the ceiling of the Shock Nightclub, of which Giuseppe "Little Joe" Cuntrera was part-owner. The money was seized; no charges were laid against anyone at the nightclub.

The Cuntrera name was also well-known in police intelligence circles, often named in conjunction with Caruana as part of "the Caruana-Cuntrera," a shadowy and mysterious group of drug traffickers and money launderers who had migrated across the world like modern-day criminal gypsies. And the Cuntrera name was well known in Canadian police files in connection with murders, extortion, and other organized crime activities.

At 3:15 p.m. on Thursday, June 13, 1995, Montreal RCMP Sergeant Dan Legault called Detective Sciammarella and reported that there was an Alfonso Caruana identified on the Canadian police information system. This Alfonso Caruana was wanted for extradition to Italy— where he was known as "The Ghost" because no one in authority had ever seen him—after having been sentenced *in absentia* on Mafia and drug offenses. A copy of the Interpol warrant A-632/12-1993 was sent to Toronto.

CAUTION: This person is considered to be violent and armed. OCCU-PATION: Businessman. COUNTRIES LIKELY TO BE VISITED: South American countries. LANGUAGES SPOKEN: Italian, Spanish, Sicilian dialect. SUMMARY OF FACTS OF THE CASE: Caruana is accused of membership of a Mafia-type criminal organization known as the "Cosa Nostra". The members of this criminal association use firearms, threats and coercion (including subjecting people to "Omerta"—the law of silence) to commit their crimes against persons and property and to traffic in drugs and weapons for gain. There is sufficient evidence to conclude that Caruana belongs to the dangerous organization headed by the "Cuntrera" Family and the "Caruana" Family, who have been involved in international drug trafficking (especially in heroin) for many years. It has been established that Caruana Alfonso deals in particular with transactions relating to the purchase of drugs, and reinvests the profits. The offences were committed in Palermo, Sicily, and in other Italian towns and abroad, from 1977 onwards. REASON FOR NOTICE: Wanted on arrest warrants No. 1268A, issued on 12th February 1983 by the judicial authorities in Rome, Italy, and No. 306/86, issued on the 23rd September 1986 by the judicial authorities in Palermo, Italy, both for Mafia-type conspiracy and drug trafficking. EXTRADITION WILL BE REQUESTED FROM ANY COUNTRY. If found, please detain and immediately inform Interpol Rome (Reference 123/C2-Sez. 1/433684/2-2/GI of 17th December 1993) and the ICPO-Interpol General Secretariat.

The FBI revealed that it knew the name Catalanotto, noting that a family with the same last name owned property in New York State, described as a possible meeting site for organized crime figures. The home address in New York City for the Catalanotto family was two doors down from that of Gerlando Sciascia, a senior member of the Bonanno La Cosa Nostra family.

Yet another phone call, this one from RCMP Sergeant Dan Tentamenti of the Proceeds of Crime unit, notified Sciammarella and Saldutto that Italian authorities were involved in a major international narcotics investigation that had identified Alfonso Caruana as "the main supplier of narcotics for many organized crime families based in Italy."

A package of information from the Italian authorities was forwarded to the detectives: the data showed that 11 tonnes of cocaine and US$20 million had been traced through Switzerland, Holland, Venezuela, and the United States, all linked to the Caruana-Cuntrera family.

In Italy, news of the possible capture of Alfonso Caruana, one of the most wanted Mafia bosses in the world and now identified as "the number-one man in the Caruana-Cuntrera organization," was met with cautious optimism. If police forces on two continents had failed to find and arrest Alfonso Caruana, how could it be as easy as two constables monitoring a wedding?

And in fact there was some question as to whether the man pictured on the Interpol warrant was the same as the sleek, graying, bespectacled gentleman who attended his daughter's wedding. The Interpol warrant showed a pre-1993 picture of a dark-haired subject with the coarse features of a peasant. As well, it stated that the "wanted" Alfonso Caruana was likely living in South America.

Detective Sciammarella studied the Interpol warrant, compared the photo to the dozens taken at the Sutton Place, and couldn't say definitively that the men in the photos were one and the same.

The Alfonso Caruana investigation cooked away on a back burner, as Sciammarella and Saldutto worked other cases. Communications and information gathering continued with the Italian government agencies and slowly it began to become apparent that "The Ghost" may have finally been located. On January 26, 1996, the RCMP sent a memo to Dennis Fiorido, the Rome liaison officer, providing an update on the hunt for Alfonso Caruana, pointing out the similarities between the two Caruanas: same daughters' names and ages.

"At the present time investigators of "O" Division (RCMP Ontario) are attempting to physically identify Caruana, but no recent photo exists at this end. If Italian authorities have a fairly recent photo of subject it would be of great help."

Information continued to pour in. A computer check of Alfonso Caruana in the Canadian law enforcement system instantly kicked him back: "Male, European, 01–01–46; age: now 50; five foot six inches, brown eyes. Caution: Violence, off(ensive) weapon, drugs, also known as Alfonso Vella . . . armed and dangerous. Special Interest: Do Not Divulge Interest to Subject. Wanted in Italy for drug trafficking . . . do not arrest based on this info; if located advise Interpol Ottawa immigration authorities."

The Revenue Canada Customs & Excise Passenger Targeting Unit had similar data on file: "Subject may be a DEA (Drug Enforcement Administration) suspect; prior criminal record . . . prior drug conviction overseas; wanted by Italian authorities for Mafia conspiracy and trafficking heroin . . . Extradition will be requested. Subject considered violent/armed . . . Subject is suspected to be associated with currency/narcotics violations."

By September the CFSEU was convinced their Alfonso Caruana was the same as the one wanted in Italy. On the 18th a memo was sent to Interpol Ottawa: "Please be advised that Alfonso Caruana is now residing in Ontario. Please provide background on subject and the current status of outstanding warrant."

Although still cautious about the success of the Canadians in finding Caruana, Inspector Paolo Palazzo of the *Ragguppamento Operativo Speciale* (ROS), the organized crime section of *Carabinieri* (the Italian paramilitary police), flew to Canada from Turin, Italy.

He attended a meeting at the Newmarket, Ontario, RCMP offices with Sciammarella, Saldutto, RCMP Inspector Ben Soave, RCMP Sgt. George Capra, and OPP Detective Ron Seaver, a veteran of several Italian organized crime cases.

Inspector Soave was the head of the Toronto Integrated Intelligence Unit. He was well known in Italy and had worked as the RCMP liaison officer in Rome, where he'd collaborated with the best of Italy's Mafia investigators: the late magistrate Giovanni Falcone; the chief of the

Italian State Police, Gianni De Gennaro; and the director of the financial crime section of the Italian State Police, Alessandro Pansa. De Gennaro and Pansa had been the first officials to investigate the Caruana-Cuntrera organization.

Inspector Palazzo told the detectives that the Italian government was in the process of asking Canada to extradite Alfonso Caruana to Italy, where he not only faced a twenty-one-year and ten-month prison sentence but was wanted on new charges for operating an international drug and money-laundering conspiracy. He revealed that several monitored telephone calls placed by suspects in Italy had been logged during the ROS investigation to the home of Anthony Catalanotto, now known to be Alfonso Caruana's new son-in-law.

Palazzo produced a photograph of Alfonso Caruana he'd brought with him from Italy. Standing on the deck of a boat, the man wore sunglasses and looked fit and relaxed.

Bill Sciammarella took one look at the picture and immediately shook his head: "That's not the guy we're following."

Siculiana and Castelvetrano, western Sicily

The criminal dynasty of the Caruana-Cuntrera put down roots in the late 1800s, in the towns of Siculiana and Castelvetrano in the western Sicilian provinces of Agrigento and Trapani. Although some of the Caruana clan—notably Alfonso Caruana—were born in the town of Castelvetrano, the group became known as the Siculiana Mafia.

Sicily, particularly the western rural area at the turn of the last century, was ripe for Mafia domination. Peasants and the poor were no more important than bales of hay or heads of cattle. Injustices were as common as the daily bread.

At the time of the unification of Italy in 1861, a class of middlemen emerged who managed estates in southern Italy for the absentee land-lords and controlled the peasant farmers. They were aggressive and intimidating—frowning, serious men who wore their caps crooked upon their heads, their cartridge boxes and short-barreled shotguns across their chests, riding donkeys through the countryside with an arrogance born of the transference of the power of the aristocracy. What at that time was called *campiere* (armed guards) or *gabellotto* (tax collectors), later became *Mafioso*. And among these privately hired goons, a Mafia of romantic ideals emerged to champion the rights of the weak and poor, to bring balance to a life severely weighted against the common man. Even today, old men recall the long-gone days, the days before heroin and money laundering and machine guns and bombs, before arti-ficial wealth and power—the days when the Mafia was, it is said, "a thing of beauty, of love," when murder was a privately held affair, a calmly plotted shotgun blast in the darkness, or a hot-blooded knife fight in a bar.

In a region dichotomized by two classes—the landlords and the peas-ant farmers—the Mafia became the middle class, setting themselves up as representatives of the disenfranchised. But in truth, they exploited both the rich and the poor.

Later, this situation was recognized as not only a criminal problem but also a political one. "[The] Mafia is not a shame for Sicily," said Sicilian member of parliament Giuseppe De Felice in 1900, "but for the Government that supports it."

As in many small Italian towns, the village square in Siculiana is the promenade where people gather and socialize. Couples who are court-ing stroll close together but do not touch, followed at a distance by their mothers and other female relatives; men discuss the crops and weather and politics; and gossip is conducted in whispers lest inflection or tone offend. The etiquette of survival is this: don't say aloud what you can whisper; don't whisper when you can gesture; don't gesture when you can pass a glance.

Siculiana, like much of Sicily, is a place where trust and faith erode the farther you stray from the family hearth. The elderly sit here grim-faced and have the appearance of people awaiting something—some fate, some passage. They have the faces of retired spies, minds stuffed full of fatal deeds and the knowledge of dark events and uncharted histories.

"No one here knows the Caruanas and the Cuntreras," a sun-weathered man says. "They've been gone too long. But every year they send money for the feast of our patron saint. When they can help somebody, they do it without hesitation."

Others decline to discuss the clans. Typically they say, "*L'omo chi parra assai nenti guadagna.*"—"The man who speaks a lot gains nothing." And "*Questa bocca è fatta per mangiare.*"—"This mouth is for eating."

The last time the Cuntreras appeared in town was in the 1970s, at the Feast of the Holy Crucifix, which is held annually on May 3. A wooden sculpture of Christ on the cross is carried through the streets by *forzati*—strong men wearing traditional red neckerchiefs—as fireworks are set off on Mount Meli behind the town.

Inside the main church, the memory of Alfonso Caruana's father, Carmelo, and Pasquale Cuntrera—a senior member of the Cuntrera family—is forever preserved. Carved on a brass plaque on a pew, their names are visible even today.

Indeed throughout the pews are plaques containing names of men who were key in creating the international heroin trade: Spataro, Cuffaro, Lo Presti, Indelicato, Mira. And the history of the Siciliana family's involvement in the drug trade is also apparent in the town's cemetery, where beautiful stone-cut chapels are dedicated to several family members, including Alfonso's father, Carmelo, and his murdered uncle, Leonardo.

The Caruanas were last seen in Siciliana in 1977. On October 10 of that year, Gerlando Caruana and Maria Parisi were married. Gerlando Caruana (1951) is the son of Leonardo Caruana, Alfonso Caruana's uncle. The ceremony was witnessed by former Italian agriculture minister Calogero Mannino, who signed the marriage certificate.[3] Like other successful people who leave small towns and later return, they flashed their newfound wealth and status. They were free with their money, giving funds to the local soccer club and wearing expensive clothes.

Former mayor Paolo Iacono admits that some of the Caruanas and Cuntreras are from Siciliana: "But this town has nothing to do with them. Some of them were born here, this cannot be denied, but for the rest, everybody went his own way. Here the father-in-law of Pasquale

Cuntrera, his brothers-in-law, many cousins of his, are living. All of them respectable people."[4]

This is the Sicily of stark contrast, of genius—the Sicily of many Mafia bosses—but also the Sicily of Leonardo Sciascia, Luigi Pirandello, Giuseppe Verga, Salvatore Quasimodo, Elio Vittorini, and Giuseppe Tomasi di Lampedusa, some of the leading lights of world literature.

It's the Sicily of rugged beauty, the Sicily of riotous colors: the yellow of the stinging esparto, the greens of the carob trees and wild thyme, the bleached whites of sea lilies and pinks of tamarisk and wild orchids.

But Siculiana is also just ten miles from Agrigento, an area that has provided much of North America with its crop of Mafiosi, particularly since the Sicilian Mafia first set out to control the international drug trade.

Most of Siculiana's five thousand inhabitants angrily reject the town's reputation as "the financial soul of the Mafia," much as the residents of Corleone, south of Palermo, reject their town's notoriety as the most murderous place on the island.

Not surprisingly, Paolo Iacono is displeased with the town's distinction: "According to newspapers and TV, in Siculiana we are all Mafiosi; for you this is the world capital of drug dealing and money laundering."

But that Siculiana is the source of many of the world's most active Mafiosi drug dealers can't be denied. Heroin traders from Siculiana and surrounding towns were active long before the Caruana-Cuntrera family became an international powerhouse. Western Sicilian-born traffickers were considered ideal for the emerging Italo-American gangsters in the days of the formation of La Cosa Nostra. Coming from pure Mafia stock, secretive by nature, cunning by blood, Siculiana-born Mafia members were single-minded in their pursuit of profit.

Early files, now dusty and yellowing, from the U.S. Bureau of Narcotics (the forerunner of the Drug Enforcement Administration [DEA]) show the emergence of the primitive Siculiana family in the 1930s. Nicola "Zu Cola" Gentile, born in Siculiana, emigrated to the United States in the early 1900s. A small-time drug trafficker, Zu Cola was involved in several crimes in Italian communities in the United States. In 1937, he was charged with dealing heroin, likely as part of the growing drug ring of infamous American gangster Charles "Lucky" Luciano.

Granted bail, Zu Cola fled back to Italy, where he became a prominent member in the Agrigento Mafia of Don Giuseppe Settecasi.

When the Allies landed in Sicily in 1943, Zu Cola provided intelligence and advice to assist the American forces. He was one of the Mafiosi who benefited when the Allied forces set up a civil administration to rule the island. Many were arbitrarily named mayors of villages and given other positions of power, from which they were able to conduct black-market operations. In later years, Zu Cola's power was such that political parties fought each other for his assistance in getting out the vote.

In 1946, Lucky Luciano was sent back to Italy from his prison in the United States, apparently as a reward for assisting the Allies in their landing during the war. Luciano quickly began setting up a heroin network from Sicily to the United States. Most of the heroin came from morphine refined by Corsican networks. Luciano, who had a legion of contacts throughout Italy—many of them among the wave of Italo-Americans deported by American authorities during the war—is believed to have gone into business with Zu Cola.[5]

Another Siciliana Mafia member, heroin trafficker Giuseppe Mira, was based in Palermo. A friend of Zu Cola's, Mira was involved in the Caneba network, an organization that, throughout the 1950s, smuggled heroin into the United States by using contacts in Canada. Mira's primary contact in Canada was Settimo "Big Sam" Accardo. Mira, according to police documents, supplied him with large amounts of heroin for almost ten years.[6]

A meeting recorded in the Bureau of Narcotics files during those early years shows, possibly for the first time, the name of Caruana: Mira was observed in Milan with Carmelo Caruana, who was Alfonso Caruana's father. The men were, it was later discovered, supplying suitcases full of heroin to Settimo Accardo.

The identities of the people who brought the most infamy and slander to the town of Siciliana are well known: the Caruanas and the Cuntreras. They are the people who built an unfinished, bunker-like villa that stands near the town like a monument to greed and avarice. They are the people who, with patches on their pants and a few dollars in their pockets, left a homeland forsaken by God and man and emigrated throughout the world, to Europe and North and South America. They are the men who were to accumulate vast power and huge fortunes as they rose to high positions in the international criminal underworld, and who lived and worked above even the Mafia.

From farmers and local bandits, over a thirty-year campaign, the Caruanas and the Cuntreras emerged onto the global stage as brilliant financiers, criminal billionaires, with a genius for infiltrating the highest echelons of financial and political institutions on three continents.

Also, members of the Siciliana family—Liborio Cuntrera, Giovanni Caruana, and Nicolò Rizzuto—later showed up as an offshoot of the famed French Connection case. Recently, journalist Tom Blickman, who wrote about the Caruana-Cuntrera's activities in Aruba, interviewed an elderly man in Siciliana who told him "he was approached by a Cuntrera to 'lend him his son,'" the implication clearly being it was to use the youth in drug trafficking.[7]

It was at the beginning of the last century that the Caruanas and Cuntreras began forming the nucleus of the intricately woven criminal structure that would make them the power center of the Siciliana family. Gerlando Caruana (b. 1879–d. 1961) and Giuseppe Cuntrera (b. 1889–d. 1969)—respectively the grandfather of Alfonso Caruana and the father of Pasquale Cuntrera—married two sisters, Anna and Croce Spataro. These two marriages yielded the first generations of the Caruana-Cuntrera clans that would grow to global prominence.

Gerlando Caruana and Anna Spataro had seven children: Giuseppe (b. 1910), Pasquale (b. 1913–d. 1942), Carmelo (b. 1915–d. 1965), Vincenza (b. 1918), Leonardo (b. 1921–d. 1981), Giovanni (b. 1929), and Antonino (b. 1936). Giuseppe Cuntrera and Croce Spataro had five children:

While the first recorded generation—Gerlando Caruana (b. 1879–d. 1961) and Giuseppe Cuntrera (b. 1889–d. 1969)—exercised individual and joint Mafia-like powers in western Sicily, their sons Leonardo Caruana and Pasquale Cuntrera habitually engaged in traditional Mafia activities, ranging from cattle rustling and arson, to murder and extortion.

Liborio (b. 1929–d. 1982), Pasquale (b. 1930), Gaspare (b. 1934), Paolo (b. 1939), and Carmelo (b. 1942–d. 1943). This is the first generation of Caruana and Cuntrera to take an international role in narcotics trafficking.

At this point in the history, the family structure is definable. However, intermarriage within the Caruana-Cuntrera has resulted in a complex family tree with relations not just between the clans, but between generations.

Carmelo Caruana, Alfonso's father, married Francesca Vella; Francesca Vella's sister, Giuseppa Vella, married Pasquale Cuntrera, making Carmelo Caruana both Pasquale's first cousin and his brother-in-law. Domenico Vella (b. 1918), brother of the Vella sisters, also became part of the Caruana family when he married Carmelo Caruana's sister, Vincenza Caruana.

Carmelo Caruana and Francesca Vella had four children: Gerlando (b. 1943), Alfonso (b. 1946), Pasquale (b. 1948), and Anna Maria (b. 1950–d. 1968). Gerlando and Alfonso Caruana married their first cousins, sisters Vincenza (b. 1943) and Giuseppina Caruana (b. 1947), the daughters of their uncle Giuseppe, making Giuseppe their father-in-law as well.

To further complicate matters, Vincenza and Giuseppina Caruana's sister, Antonina, married their cousin, Paolo Cuntrera.

The Vella family, with its own complex network of intermarriages, forms an important underpinning to the Caruana-Cuntrera organization. Fifteen separate families are married into the Vellas, among them numerous individuals named in literally dozens of Italian, American, Canadian, and South American narcotics investigations. The Vella family tree shows relationships going back to the original Caruana-Cuntrera-Spataro marriages. An early Italian police document shows thirty-six families made up of hundreds of people in the Caruana-Cuntrera-Spataro-Vella orbit.

All these complexities would puzzle law-enforcement agencies for decades throughout the twentieth century. But at its beginning, the Caruana-Cuntrera story is relatively simple, revolving around two men living in Sicily in the early 1900s.

As young men, Gerlando Caruana, who in 1910 was thirty-one, and Giuseppe Cuntrera, ten years younger, worked on the sunburnt lands of the aristocrat Baron Nicolò Briuccia Agnello, whose family moved from Segnefari (Cefalù) to Siculiana in 1797. Gerlando Caruana and Giuseppe Cuntrera were, by all accounts, tough-minded men who fought ruthlessly and successfully for the most highly sought of prizes: respect. At a time and in a place where power exceeded riches as the ultimate of a man's worldly attainments, to live a life without respect was to live the life of an animal. The respect they craved was not born of criminality but earned through a day-to-day manifestation of self-sufficiency, the ability to be independent and in control of one's own destiny. The two men are remembered as having acquired their respect not with violent outbursts and public exhibitions but with a quiet and private subtlety.

It was inevitable that their sons, Giuseppe Caruana (Alfonso's uncle) and Pasquale Cuntrera, would emerge as men of honor, through their own deeds but also because of the added cachet of their fathers' power.

Many years later Alfonso Caruana, while not admitting to being a Mafioso himself, proclaimed, "My grandfather was Mafioso; my father was Mafioso."[8]

Among the old gentlemen who, in those years, spent their days in the town squares of Agrigento and their evenings playing cards in the cafés was the elegant but modest Don Giuseppe Settecasi.

From Agrigento—at the center of the pre–World War II drug trade—Don Settecasi maintained far-flung contacts throughout the Sicilian Mafia, and even overseas. In the 1950s, it was Don Settecasi who supplied Sicilian traffickers for Lucky Luciano's heroin networks. For the Mafia of Siculiana and surrounding towns, the nucleus of the Sicilian Cosa Nostra universe was the Agrigento power base of Don Settecasi.

Throughout most of his career—until he was murdered at eighty years of age during the 1981–83 Mafia war for control of the international heroin trade—Don Settecasi went virtually uninvestigated and untroubled as he sent his emissaries throughout the world. Hiding his power from slow-moving international police forces, he took advantage of the corruption rife throughout Sicily.

A report that might have firmly placed Settecasi as a powerful Mafia statesman at the center of the international drug trade—a report based on conversations held with Canadian Mafia boss Paolo Violi, recorded over hidden microphones placed in a bar in Montreal, Quebec, in 1974—was ignored by Agrigento authorities and was filed away in the

"The transcription of that conversation, taped in Montreal, anticipated by years the information about the new structure of the Sicilian Mafia that was later provided by State witnesses in the 1980s," Judge Aldo Rizzo testified before the Italian anti-Mafia Parliamentary Commission in 1986. "The terminology used in Montreal would become familiar only after Tommaso Buscetta turned informant in 1984." According to Judge Rizzo, had the Montreal transcript been uncovered sooner it would have allowed the Italian magistrates to have conducted the first Maxi Trial several years earlier.

(Tommaso Buscetta [1928–2000] was a prominent and important member of the Sicilian Mafia. After becoming one of the first *pentiti*—turncoats—to testify about the inner workings of Cosa Nostra and its role in the international drug trade, Buscetta provided authorities with much of their initial intelligence about the Caruana-Cuntrera organization and its key position in the underworld. Buscetta died in April 2000 while in the U.S. witness protection program.)

back of a desk drawer for several years. On the tape, Violi is heard meeting with a man named Carmelo Salemi, who was visiting from Agrigento. Salemi brought a letter of credentials from Settecasi. During the taped conversation, Violi asked Salemi about the situation in Sicily. Salemi, in answering, used a number of terms—*capomandamento* (district boss), the *commissione provinciale* (Mafia provincial commission), and the *commissione regionale* (Mafia regional commission)—that at that time in Italy were barely known outside Cosa Nostra. He also identified Giuseppe Settecasi as the new boss of Agrigento province.

As a young man growing up in Agrigento, Don Settecasi was aware of the Caruana-Cuntrera families in the nearby town of Siculiana. The power and greed of the two clans was legendary throughout Agrigento province. Periodic waves of arson and murder led to the arrest of several of the families' members, but all were later released when evidence proved too weak or witnesses vanished.

As the Siculiana clan grew in strength and power, Don Settecasi took them under his wing, and when it was time for them to go out into the world, it was Don Settecasi's guidance and connections that facilitated their exodus from Italy.

During the rule of Mussolini and the Fascists, public records show that Giuseppe Caruana, Alfonso's uncle and later father-in-law, was rounded up on June 21, 1931, with several other men who were suspected of being members of the Mafia. Giuseppe was twenty-one years old. In keeping with the Fascist regime's practices, although there was little if any evidence against him, he spent some time in jail. Five years later he was accused by Sicily's General Inspectorate of State Police of criminal association; he was again released by a judge who found there was insufficient evidence in the case. In 1957, Giuseppe Caruana left Sicily and moved to Brazil, where he established himself in Rio de Janeiro as the first boss of the Siculiana family outside of Sicily. He returned to Siculiana temporarily in 1961.

As a young man, Pasquale Cuntrera, son of patriarch Giuseppe Cuntrera, followed a similar path. He was arrested on December 19, 1953, in Castelvetrano on double homicide, robbery, and arson charges. The judge acquitted him on January 18, 1954. Like his cousin Giuseppe Caruana, Pasquale Cuntrera moved to Brazil, returning to Siculiana only briefly in the 1960s.

Palermo, Sicily

Mafia families in Sicily made up a wide patchwork of organizations of various sizes, some operating in almost complete isolation. Old grudges, some as minor as an argument between two men from a past generation, would occasionally flare up. A broken fence that allowed farm animals to graze on a neighbor's land could lead to a glance of disrespect, a jostling in a lineup for feed, or even physical violence. This made day-to-day life precarious. Larger issues, such as the extortion of a victim under protection of another family, could lead to months, if not generations, of conflict.

The city Mafia and the country Mafia often regarded each other as inferior. The country Mafia, generally the families in western or central Sicily, had little use for the urban kind, who bought politicians and grew rich at the expense of their "Tradition." The city Mafia believed that the country Mafia were backwards, living in a time past, with no recognition of the broader power that could be acquired through penetrating the financial, industrial, and political sectors.

In October 1957, a delegation of the American La Cosa Nostra visited Sicily to discuss the international drug trade with their Sicilian counterparts. The head of the delegation was Joe Bonanno, leader of one of New York City's five families, and he brought with him several high-ranking Americans, including the underboss Frank Garofalo and the rising star in the family, Carmine Galante. The Sicilians were led by Mafia boss Don Giuseppe Genco Russo, who was accompanied by some of the élite of the Italian underworld: Lucky Luciano, Salvatore "Cicchiteddu" (or "Little Bird") Greco, Palermo-area boss Gaetano Badalamenti, and Salvatore and Angelo La Barbera, brothers who were emerging as powerful forces in heroin production and trafficking. In all, there were about thirty men at the meeting, including Don Giuseppe Settecasi and Tommaso Buscetta, who, sickened by what was to come, would later turn State's evidence.

The purpose of the summit was to formalize a relationship between the families in Sicily and the families in the United States. Essentially, the Sicilians would supply heroin to the Americans, and the Americans would control the sale and distribution. At the meeting, introductions were made, alliances were formed, and members of each group were assigned tasks to facilitate the scheme.

In the middle of the four-day meeting, Joe Bonanno, Garofalo, and Galante had dinner at Palermo's Spanò restaurant with several Mafiosi, among them Lucky Luciano, Gaetano Badalamenti, and Tommaso Buscetta. Luciano, who had been in the United States during the formation of La Cosa Nostra Commission, set up to avoid bloodshed and strife among U.S. crime families, extolled the value of such a body: dialogue instead of murder, cooperation instead of confrontation. Decision-making, however, remained at the top, with rules that would streamline and bring order, peace, and profit to the diverse families.

Badalamenti and Buscetta both liked the idea. For several months after the Spanò dinner, together and separately, they visited and lobbied the families across Sicily. Remarkably, they achieved a consensus, and the *Cupola*—the Commission—was born.

The creation of the *Cupola* resulted in six years of relative calm. Territorial disputes were ironed out between the families, inter-family rivalries were adjudicated, and meetings were regularly held to resolve minor differences before they exploded, as they had in the past, into major bloodbaths.

But the frenzy to step into the international drug trade led to a breakdown in the power of the *Cupola*. Everybody wanted a piece of the action. Steadfast notions of honor and cooperation fell by the wayside as an increasing number of families began setting up heroin networks and making their own independent connections.

Two groups emerged as the primary powers in the Sicilian heroin trade: the Greco family of Ciaculli (a Mafia enclave near Palermo), and the La Barbera brothers, the new breed of Mafiosi, younger men with modern weapons and a ruthlessness that was to become the hallmark of the modern Cosa Nostra.

On June 30, 1963, a bomb was left in a car parked in front of a garage in the town of Villabate; the blast killed two pedestrians. Later that day, *Carabinieri* officers received an anonymous call that another bomb had been placed in a car parked near the center of Ciaculli. The police found the car near the home of Salvatore "Little Bird" Greco, who, in addition to being the head of his family, was also the acting president of the *Cupola*.

When the *Carabinieri* arrived, they spotted the bomb in the back seat and soon defused it. But only seconds later an even more powerful device, made up of an estimated 200 pounds of stick dynamite hidden in the trunk, detonated, killing seven *Carabinieri*. For at least fifty yards around the blast site, the only recognizable items were a *Carabinieri* officer's beret and a finger with a wedding band on it.

The government's response was strong and swift, and unprecedented for Sicily, whose criminal problems had long been ignored by the national government in Rome. The army commander, General Aldo De Marco, unleashed his troops on the island, ordering wholesale roundups of anyone even suspected of being involved in organized crime. By the hundreds, Mafiosi were taken into custody. Police and soldiers were given *carte blanche* to procure information, and stories of torture and illegal confinement soon spread. Known Mafia districts were sealed off, and helicopters dropped squads in to root out suspected criminals. Overnight, Sicily became an armed camp of searchlights, barking dogs, and crashing doors. Streets were choked with armored vehicles and checkpoints. The government introduced and passed an anti-Mafia law in less than a week. The *Cupola* was shut down, and Mafia activities became almost unheard of as the bosses went underground.

Cosa Nostra members scattered—some back to their villages, others to the Italian mainland, still others to North and South America, where they planted the roots of an international drug trade that has lasted now for almost forty years.

Feeling the pressure from the Italian government, dozens of Caruana-Cuntrera left Sicily and spread throughout the rest of Italy, in Europe, and North and South America.

In 1965, Pasquale Cuntrera was ordered to leave Sicily by the Palermo Court of Appeals. He went into forced residence in Penne, a small town near Pescara on the Italian mainland. A month later he fled exile and secretly emigrated to Canada, where he joined his cousin, Agostino, and his three brothers—Paolo, Gaspare, and Liborio—who were living in Montreal. He later left Canada for Caracas, Venezuela.

Next, the Agrigento court sent Giuseppe Caruana into forced residence in Ronciglione, in the province of Viterbo in central Italy. Giuseppe remained in exile for nine months; then, having obtained a special permit to attend the marriage of his daughter Vincenza to his nephew Gerlando Caruana in Siculiana, he fled to Brazil. One of the last decisions made by the *Cupola* was to allow Giuseppe Caruana to leave Sicily and move his entire operation to South America.

With family members almost all outlaws living in self-imposed exile across the world, a Mafia war behind them, and an uncertain future in front of them, it was only a matter of time before the clans focused on their destiny.

Alfonso Caruana was at this time seventeen years old. His family had left his birth town of Castelvetrano in 1955 and gone to Siculiana briefly before moving to Agrigento and, a year later, back to Siculiana. His father, Carmelo, was learning the drug trade under the helpful eye of the boss of Agrigento, Don Giuseppe Settecasi.

By 1968 there wasn't much left in Sicily of the old Siculiana families. The primary players were forming satellite organizations in other countries and fitting themselves into the international heroin trade. Those family members who didn't care to stay behind and shore up what remained of their local operations made plans to follow the expatriates.

2

Alfonso Caruana was born on New Year's Day, 1946, a year of great historical importance in Italy. A referendum was held that year in which 54 percent of voters decided to do away with the monarchy. King Umberto II di Savoia was sent into exile in Portugal and a constitutional assembly was formed. Women were given the vote; criminals were granted amnesty. Enrico De Nicola was elected provisional president of the Italian Republic.

Twenty-two years later, in 1968, Italy was undergoing yet another time of change. The counterculture of the west was beginning to make inroads into traditional Italian society and culture. Authority was being challenged. Students protested and rioted at universities. And not all the upheavals were man-made. In mid-January a violent earthquake struck the Belice area of western Sicily, leaving hundreds dead and 150,000 homeless. Six towns were completely destroyed in Agrigento and Trapani provinces. Chaos reigned.

By 1968, Alfonso Caruana was thoroughly a "made man" of the Mafia. He'd come of age in a time of unrelenting brutality and had himself been the architect of much of it, as had his father and grandfather before him. And like any successful father's son, his vision was broader and farther reaching.

Alfonso Caruana looked at the deteriorating situation of his life in Sicily, which he had once called a "beautiful thing." He saw the seemingly endless rounds of murders and betrayals and revenge killings, the continual government harassment, and he told his friends, "There's a storm brewing here."

He began making plans to relocate.

By the late 1960s, many Siculiana family members had already made their way to Canada, and others were preparing to make the transatlantic move themselves. A strong family base was set up in Montreal, consisting of brothers, uncles, and cousins. Marriages were regularly taking place, new children were being born into the clan, and the quickly growing Siculiana family was putting down deep roots. Where earlier in the century long ocean voyages had been the only route available to immigrants, the new wave crowded themselves onto jetliners.

At 4:25 p.m. on Friday, August 2, 1968, the major tragedy of Alfonso Caruana's life struck.

Alitalia flight 660, a DC-8, was preparing to land in Milan en route from Rome to Montreal. There were ninety-five people on board. Heavy fog and driving rain reduced visibility to zero, passengers later said. A powerful down-draft forced a shudder through the four-jet airliner; it suddenly dropped and crashed into a wooded hillside six miles from Milan's Malpensa Airport. The aircraft plowed through the heavy trees, cutting a path 150 feet long. When it came to rest, shredded by tree trunks but still mostly intact, most of the passengers managed to escape before the motors caught fire and fuel ignited, sending flames flaring across the entire aircraft. Twelve passengers died in the inferno.

Among the victims were Alfonso Caruana's mother, Francesca Vella, and his eighteen-year-old sister, Anna Maria Caruana. Alfonso's brother, Pasquale, who was emigrating to Canada, survived and walked away from the crash. He spent some time in a local hospital recuperating and then continued on to Montreal.

Alfonso Caruana, friends later said, was completely devastated by the loss. The close ties of the Caruana family were precious and guarded, even by Sicilian standards. He'd lost family and friends to murder—it was, after all, a hazard of his lifestyle—but the arbitrary death of innocents was something no son or brother could prepare himself for. Years later, when his first daughter was born, he would name her Anna Maria, for his lost sister, and he would name his other daughter Francesca, after his mother.

The *Leonardo da Vinci* was built by Italian Lines as a replacement flagship for the ill-fated *Andrea Doria*, which had plunged to the bottom of the Atlantic off Nantucket in 1956. The 761-foot *da Vinci* liner, built at Genoa, was designed with the ability to convert from steam turbines to nuclear power. She weighed 33,300 tons. In June 1960, she was completed and was able to make the crossing from Europe to North America in about nine days. First-class passage cost $390, and tourist $235.

A luxurious ship, she had six swimming pools, splendid dining rooms, and plumbing in each cabin. Her passenger lists include the celebrities of the time: Paul Newman, Tony Curtis, Gore Vidal, Janet Leigh, Elizabeth Taylor and Richard Burton, Prince Rainier and Princess Grace of Monaco, as well as cardinals and politicians.

By 1965, two larger and splashier ships, the *Michelangelo* and the *Raffaello*, overtook the *da Vinci* as the choice of the rich and famous. She went into a subtle but steady decline and became more accessible to the average person, the equivalent of a seagoing bus.

Among the passengers making the crossing in September 1968, headed for Montreal, was Alfonso Caruana, still grieving from the deaths of his mother and sister.

Later in life, Alfonso Caruana often said he "felt safe" in Canada. Even in the face of several profitable and attractive enticements by canny American police to lure him into crossing the border to conduct business, he preferred to operate in or from Canada.

His loyalty to Canada isn't surprising. On September 12, 1968, when he presented himself to immigration officers at Halifax, Nova Scotia, as an electrician, he had, he said, one hundred dollars in cash. Twenty-five years later he owned mansions around the world, had hundreds of millions of dollars in bank accounts on three continents, and was the head of an international family-run criminal organization. He jet-setted among Montreal, London, Caracas, Zurich, meeting with bankers and the world's most powerful Mafiosi. He had almost exclusive control of several key drug-trafficking routes from Asia and South America. He had connections to members of several international crime organizations, ranging from the Camorra in Naples to the Somchai narcotics organization in Thailand, from the Colombian cartels to the Turkish mafia and the Calabrian *'ndrangheta*.

But in 1968 he was, by all appearances, just one of hundreds of thousands of immigrants emigrating from the poorer regions of southern Italy, striking out into the world to improve his lot in life. He was young and unmarried. He said he had family in Canada—his older brother Gerlando, who'd arrived the previous year. An immigration file—number 205459—was opened, and he was passed without incident into Canada. Caruana failed to mention that his younger brother, Pasquale, had arrived a month earlier, or that several related members of the Siculiana-based family—notably Giuseppe Cuffaro and Salvatore Vella—were also residing in Canada and making their own destinies in the underworld.

Don Giuseppe Settecasi had outposts of his own in Montreal and Toronto, run by the Zizzo family of Salemi. The power of American La Cosa Nostra families extended into several Canadian cities, most predominantly in Ontario and Quebec, where major Canadian and American centers were linked by corridors: Detroit and Windsor, Buffalo and Toronto, New York and Montreal.

Alfonso Caruana quickly made his way to Montreal, where he found a criminal and family infrastructure in place.

The 1950s and 1960s were boom years for organized crime in Canada, particularly for heroin traffickers. Montreal was the Paris of North America, home to gangsters of many nationalities. The mafia controlled most criminal activity in the city, including gambling and bootlegging— "Activities that later came under control of the government," retired American La Cosa Nostra boss Joseph Bonanno ironically recalled.[1]

In the underworld, Calabrians and Sicilians had operated in an atmosphere of mutual respect and cooperation. This had held true since the 1930s, when the various components of the American La Cosa Nostra got along. Calabrians such as Albert Anastasia and Frank Costello rose in an organization dominated mostly by Sicilians. It was a world where courage, boldness, and faithfulness—in a word, *ominità*—determined the quality of a man.

The mafia was also in control of several other criminal enterprises: extortion, prostitution, drug trafficking, and loan sharking—all producing profits that allowed the bosses to corrupt police and politicians. When, in 1955, the Montreal police searched the house of Frank Petrula, one of the enforcers under the Bonanno family in Montreal, they found a notepad detailing payments of $100,000 to defeat the incumbent mayor, Jean Drapeau. Petrula's notebook also showed the names of media personalities who had accepted money for smearing Drapeau's campaign. That compromising notepad seized from Petrula's home soon disappeared, like so much other evidence linking mafia bosses to political power centers.

During those years there was also an investigation by Justice François Caron into allegations made by Montreal's former deputy chief of police, Pax Plante, who denounced connivance between police officers and mobsters. Many police officers were removed from their posts, including Chief Albert Langlois and his predecessor, Fernand Dufresne.

Montreal in 1968 was a thoroughly cosmopolitan, corrupted, and corruptible city, a gateway to the United States for heroin. Several drug organizations—Corsican, French, and American—were active in the city, using the docks, the Montreal–New York corridor, and body-packed couriers to make drug shipments. Almost every major international drug-trafficking investigation—whether Canadian, American, or Italian—would uncover a Montreal connection.

The Montreal underworld was primarily under the influence of the Cotroni crime family, headed by Vincenzo Cotroni, a former wrestler, extortionist, and strong-arm man who had been appointed by the New York Bonanno family as their representative in the province of Quebec.

Tommaso Buscetta, one of the first Sicilian Mafia defectors, concisely summed up the Canadian situation: "The Cotronis worked in collaboration with the Bonanno family in New York, whom they consulted on matters of importance. Their relationship was much like that of a subsidiary company in a neighboring country, which had a great deal of independence but would defer to the parent company on matters of policy. Montreal had all the necessary qualifications to become a mafia capital: it was close to the United States, in particular New York; it had a large Italian immigrant population, although mainly Calabrian rather than Sicilian; and it was the main route for the shipment of heroin into the United States from Europe. Also, Canada's historical relationship with France had made it an attractive refuge for French and Corsican gangsters from Marseilles."[2]

Cotroni's underboss was Luigi Greco, a prominent Sicilian underworld figure who had started his career as a gangland strong-arm in the 1920s. He'd evolved into a specialist in corrupting police and politicians and was one of the first to recognize the strategic importance of Montreal's position as a gateway into North America for narcotics and other contraband. His contacts, initially with Sicilian-born American criminals in New York City, came to include important drug traffickers overseas. He traveled with Frank Petrula to Italy in 1951, where he reportedly met exiled American mafia boss Lucky Luciano, to whom they "offered up Montreal." Five years later the fruits of this overseas venture were apparent when it was estimated that 60 percent of the heroin entering North America passed through Montreal.[3]

In 1972, Greco died in an accidental fire at his pizzeria. When Cotroni named Paolo Violi as his underboss, problems began. In spite of his strong roots in the 'ndrangheta, the appointment of Violi was seen in hindsight as a strategic error by Cotroni. And the bloody events of the next six years would lend credence to the theory of the delicate balance of a Calabrian-Sicilian split.

Violi had come to Canada in 1951 at the age of twenty. His entire past history was steeped in the 'ndrangheta of southern Italy. His father, Domenico, was a member of the Calabrian mafia and would later be refused admission to Canada, settling instead in Parma, Ohio. Violi's marriage to Grazia Luppino—daughter of highly respected Hamilton, Ontario, 'ndrangheta boss Giacomo Luppino—fulfilled a family connection that led to the heart of Ontario organized crime, and with it, ties to the Buffalo La Cosa Nostra family of Stefano Magaddino.

Violi made the beginnings of his reputation as a criminal in Canada when, four years after arriving, he shot a man to death in Toronto. He admitted to the shooting, pleaded self defence and was freed. In 1970,

The ensuing battle for control of Montreal has raised several theories. Possibly it was a turf war for the rackets in the city; another theory suggests that the Cotroni-Violi organization disdained the drug trade. But intelligence reports clearly noted that the Cotroni-Violi were already deeply immersed in international heroin trafficking with the Sicilians. A U.S. Justice Department report from 1985 names Leonardo Caruana, Alfonso's uncle, as the Cotroni organization's contact in Sicily in the 1970s. The link between the Montreal family and the Siciliana family traffickers was Vincenzo Cotroni's brother, Frank Santo Cotroni. Frank Cotroni's links to the American La Cosa Nostra were at the highest levels: he regularly met with Joseph Todaro Sr., who would become the head of the Buffalo organization, and Phillip Rastelli, who would later head the Bonanno family in New York City.

with Vincenzo Cotroni, he attended a meeting with legendary underworld banker and gambler Meyer Lansky in Acapulco, rubbed shoulders with the élite of the Bonanno La Cosa Nostra family in New York, and earned a reputation as "a dual man": one persona, the public one, was a fatherly mediator who dispensed advice within his community; the second was someone who flew into rages, kicking and punching at those who angered him.

His personality and appearance were described by Mafioso Antonino Calderone, who met Violi during a visit to Catania, Sicily, in the early 1970s: "He was a braggart, a big, fat man who didn't seem to have much upstairs."[4]

As he rose in the Cotroni organization, Violi quickly began to make enemies, particularly among the Sicilian faction, who had been quiet under Luigi Greco's mature hand but chafed at Violi's aggressiveness.

In Montreal, Alfonso Caruana quickly aligned himself with members of the Sicilian wing of the Cotronis. He kept primarily within the business and social circles he knew. Operating from a pizzeria, he associated with others in developing the Siciliana organization, his own relatives, the Cuntreras, the Cuffaros, the Zambitos, and the Guaragnas. He rarely came to public or police attention, but he was clearly working behind the scenes to facilitate drug networks with his *paesani* in Sicily and in New York.

In 1969, a year after Alfonso Caruana arrived in Canada, Mafia boss Tommaso Buscetta visited Montreal, where Salvatore Catalano, an Italian-American connected to the Bonanno family, had recommended he look up the Cuntrera and Caruana brothers. (Buscetta's visit wasn't all business. In addition to discussing the heroin trade, he was recovering from a particularly nasty bout of gonorrhea.)

Introduced to the Caruanas and Cuntreras as "a man of honor" from Sicily, Buscetta later recalled, "I understood I was meeting with other men of honor. . . . Nobody would dare introduce a boss that way to someone who does not belong to Mafia."

Buscetta stayed at Pasquale Cuntrera's home for eight days, meeting with Giuseppe Caruana, who was visiting from Brazil, and learning the routes and methods the Siciliana family used to get their heroin into the United States. Several years later he told his police debriefers that the Caruana-Cuntrera were "the biggest exporters of heroin to the United States from Canada."

Buscetta also met with Giuseppe Bono, the boss of the Bolognetta family in Palermo, who supplied Pasquale Cuntrera with his drugs. But he had little time for the Cotroni-Violi organization and, except for some social occasions, confined himself to the Siciliana group.

Outwardly, Alfonso Caruana remained above the tensions generated by the deteriorating Calabrian-Sicilian situation. By all accounts, Caruana lived quietly, operating a series of small businesses, bringing heroin from Europe through Montreal and south into the United States. Until Cotroni died, the Sicilians—including several from Siciliana—maintained a low profile, allowing the Cotronis and Violi to invite increasing law-enforcement scrutiny. Whenever they could, however, the Sicilians would take a poke at the Cotroni-Violi power structure, often sending the angered bosses to New York for guidance and support. Several instances occurred in which the Sicilian faction, completely bypassing the Cotroni-Violi, smuggled heroin through Montreal, acquiring it through their own secretive channels from Sicilian bosses, including their old mentor Giuseppe Settecasi. On the American side there were, within the New York families, like-minded Sicilians who operated on their own, or would pay minimal tribute up the ladder to their own bosses. When the Cotroni-Violi later heard of the treachery, they sent emissaries to New York, hoping to get permission to discipline the Sicilians in their own family. Their complaints generally fell upon deaf ears, although if it looked like things might get out of hand, La Cosa Nostra would send a mediator to Montreal to shuttle between the two factions.

The main player in the tensions between the Cotroni-Violi and the

Sicilian wing was Nicolò Rizzuto, whose family had been in Montreal since the early 1950s. Born in 1924 in the village of Cattolica Eraclea in western Sicily, Rizzuto was steeped in Mafia tradition and strongly connected through family ties. Although long part of the Cotroni mafia family, Rizzuto had little patience for the Montreal power structure, and in particular for Paolo Violi. He was particularly angered with Violi's edict that the Caruana-Cuntrera couldn't operate independently in Montreal. Violi told him: "Without our permission, they can do nothing."

And Rizzuto didn't have much use for Vincenzo Cotroni's appointment of Violi. Rizzuto and his Sicilian cohorts believed their own power came from their blood, not from Americanized mafiosi in New York City and along the Eastern seaboard. Rizzuto was well set up in the international heroin trade and made a lot of money for a lot of people.

In retrospect, many intelligence analysts believe that the Caruanas and the Cuntreras were using Rizzuto as a cat's paw to bring down the Cotroni-Violi organization: "They were whispering into his ear: 'How can you let this *Violi* tell you how to operate?'"[5]

But no matter who was pulling the strings behind the scenes—whether it was the Rizzutos exercising their independence, or a Machiavellian plan by the Caruana-Cuntrera—by 1971 things were getting out of hand. Word of the problems in Montreal reached Sicily, and soon thereafter Paolo Violi hosted a meeting at a cottage north of Montreal. Among the Sicilians who attended were Giuseppe Cuffaro, money manager for the Siculiana family; Leonardo Caruana (Alfonso's uncle), who would later be expelled from Canada and eventually be murdered in Sicily; and Pietro Sciarra, a Siculiana-born Mafioso with a reputation as an enforcer, who himself would also be assassinated. Nothing was resolved at the meeting; indeed, less than a year later, police wiretaps heard evidence to suggest that the strife was escalating, including Vincenzo Cotroni saying that Rizzuto should be kicked out of the family. In another recorded conversation it was suggested that Rizzuto should be made to "disappear." The peacemakers from the American La Cosa Nostra made trips to Montreal to try to calm the situation down, but no agreement could be reached. Don Giuseppe Settecasi himself visited the city, but he was unable to negotiate a settlement.

Violi vocalized his main complaint against Rizzuto's independent style: "I told him he goes from one thing to the other, here and there, and says nothing to nobody. He does things and nobody knows nothing."[6] During a visit with mobster Natale Evola, a leading member of the Bonanno family, Violi angrily said: "Rizzuto must be given a lesson; he's doing whatever he wants, accounting to nobody." Evola listened patiently to Violi's rantings, but told him: "At present we can't do anything."[7]

The Caruana-Cuntrera did nothing to ease the situation. In fact, they regularly absented themselves on business trips. For a while, in 1974, Alfonso and his brother Gerlando left the scene entirely to join their brother, Pasquale, in Caracas, where they opened up a number of companies. But even in their absence, there were signs that they were in fact actively exacerbating the Rizzuto-Violi feud by carrying out their activities without informing Violi or Cotroni, dealing instead directly with American mafiosi and the families in Sicily. At least one strategy meeting was held near Montreal to discuss the Siculiana family's activities. While delegates came from Toronto, Agrigento, New York, and Montreal, they made a point of not notifying Paolo Violi, but they made certain he was later told about it.

"The Cotronis were just getting pounded in those days," an underworld source said. "Dope was flying into Montreal and out again and the Cotronis, except for Peppe [Vincenzo's brother, a notorious drug smuggler], they knew nothing until the gossip filtered up to them. Then they went ballistic. The Americans had to say on the one hand, 'Oh, those bad Sicilians,' but on the other they were getting the product they needed down there. A lot of people had a lot of respect for Vic [Vincenzo], and as long as he was the big boy, the Sicilians had to be careful not to push it too far. Violi wanted to kill Rizzuto, but he couldn't get permission from New York."[8]

Things were, he noted, "shaky, but not too out-of-control." Where Vincenzo Cotroni was a quiet-speaking, calm man, his second-in-command, Paolo Violi, was seen as a loud country bumpkin, trading on his marriage into the Luppino family and the muscle provided by his brothers.

The spark that changed Montreal from a Calabrian/American–influenced criminal structure to a thoroughly Sicilian one—and ultimately brought the Caruana-Cuntrera and the Rizzutos to power—came in 1972 when the Quebec government called a commission of inquiry into organized crime.

Fearing the inquiry, and aware that Violi was negotiating his assassination, Rizzuto fled to Caracas, Venezuela, where he linked up with his old friend and partner, heroin trafficker and fugitive Mafia boss Tommaso Buscetta, with whom he operated a company that exported powdered milk. He told Buscetta: "Violi wants to kill me."[9]

Others on the Sicilian side of the Cotroni-Violi family were also feeling the heat. Pasquale, Paolo, Gaspare, and Liborio Cuntrera went to Caracas to live and set up a power base. Alfonso Caruana returned to Siculiana, where he remained for eleven months, handling family affairs and arranging heroin routes, before moving to the seaside town of Ostia, just outside of Rome, and then in 1975 to Brazil and Venezuela.

Back in Canada, however, the Quebec inquiry completely bypassed the Caruana-Cuntrera. Cotroni was called in, and he testified at length, but his answers had no substance and were obstructive and not responsive. In 1975 was sent to jail for just one year on contempt charges. In his place, he left Paolo Violi.

Underworld players began preparing for the worst.

On April 22, 1974, Paolo Violi was visited at his ice-cream parlor by three men: Pietro Sciarra, Giuseppe Cuffaro, and Carmelo Salemi, a prominent Mafia boss from Sicily. What happened during the meeting would alter the shape of the Mafia, both in Sicily and in North America.

As the four men gathered around the table, a Montreal Police listening device picked up their conversation. Several items of business were discussed, and the resulting transcript gave police their first inside look at the worldwide reach of the Mafia of Siculiana.

Sciarra introduced Carmelo Salemi to Violi as the new representative in Sicily for the Agrigento family. The men discussed in detail the state of the Mafia, and the changes taking place. Salemi gave Violi a letter from Don Giuseppe Settecasi, and he informed Violi of the positions and responsibilities of the new bosses in power in Sicily.

Carmelo Salemi told Violi that Giuseppe Settecasi had been appointed boss for the Agrigento province, and that Leonardo Caruana, Alfonso Caruana's uncle, had been named head of the Siculiana family in Sicily. Leonardo Caruana had, the previous year, been expelled by the Canadian government; that he hadn't informed either Cotroni or Violi—under whom he was a member of the Montreal family—of his plans or activities remained a sore point for Violi. In Siculiana, it was said, Leonardo Caruana was plotting to overthrow his own brother, Giuseppe, as head of the Caruana-Cuntrera. However, he could garner no support in the rest of the Siculiana family, or with the Rizzuto group.[10]

Violi, clearly wondering if this Sicilian organization was becoming too powerful in South America, where the Rizzutos were now based, asked Carmelo Salemi about Leonardo Caruana. "Where is he? In Venezuela?"

"No, he's with us in Siculiana; he's a member of the Siculiana family," Salemi told him.

The men discussed the issue of respect. Violi interrupted: "Respect is the most important thing in life. If it ends, the world goes wrecked."

He went on to say that as things had changed in Italy, so too were they now different in Canada. "Now, in order to operate here, our approval is required. It is no more in like the old days, when an introductory letter sufficed for being accepted. Now five years at least must pass before a *picciotto*—soldier—can enter our organization."

This judgment flew in the face of accepted practice. Tommaso Buscetta later said: "The title of man of honor was accepted with no problem in the U.S.A. If anyone of us moved there it was enough to carry with him a letter by the Representative that mentioned—in a covert and elusive way, of course—his belonging to the Sicilian Mafia, for him to be accepted in La Cosa Nostra in the United States."[11]

Violi's edict was met with much anger by Cuffaro, who was related to Alfonso Caruana by marriage. But Violi was intractable. "No more equivalence," he said.[12]

While Violi hadn't testified at the organized crime commission, several others had. Their testimony, and the playing of taped conversations made by the Montreal Police, portrayed Violi as a loudmouth, a venal and paranoid whiner, a boss who lived in fear and who couldn't control either his family or his turf. The fact that Violi's boss, Vincenzo Cotroni, was in prison—and he himself was on his way, facing contempt charges in Montreal and extortion charges in Toronto—weighed upon Violi's power and weakened him. The constant strife with the absent but increasingly powerful Nicolò Rizzuto eroded his position and his ego. All these circumstances gathered like storm clouds over Montreal. As far away as Palermo, New York, and Toronto, police intelligence officers and underworld figures awaited the final act.

A delegation from Sicily and New York arrived in Montreal to iron out the differences, and Violi was reportedly able to convince them that Rizzuto had to die. Key at that meeting were Don Giuseppe Settecasi, of Agrigento, and Pietro Sciarra, Violi's key adviser and strategist.

Rizzuto, in Venezuela, where he'd linked up with the Cuntrera brothers, learned of the meeting—and his death sentence.

By Valentine's Day, 1976, Rizzuto was ready to move. First to go was Pietro Sciarra, who was shotgunned to death as he left a showing of the movie *The Godfather Part II* at a theater in the north end of Montreal.

In 1977 a sit-down meeting was held in Montreal. Both Nicolò Rizzuto and Paolo Violi were present. The meeting was called to settle the differences between the two men, but they were unable to agree on any issues of substance.

Again Rizzuto struck. Violi's brother, Francesco, was shot dead.

Neither murder brought any reaction from Paolo Violi. His organization was falling apart; any protection he had had begun to evaporate. Though rumors abounded that he was being hunted, he appeared to be unconcerned. But he looked weak. As an old Montreal mafioso said years later: "*Violi era unu chi non sapiva campari, né dassava campari.*"—"Violi didn't know how to live, or how to let others live."[13]

In early January 1978, police learned that hitmen were stalking Violi. They began surveillance on three Sicilians suspected of planning the assassination. The hitmen were watched as they conducted a series of meetings at their Montreal-area homes, at shopping malls, and at Mike's Submarines, a sandwich shop owned by Giovanni Di Mora and Agostino Cuntrera. Other meetings were held at a coffee bar/social club used as a headquarters for Nicolò Rizzuto.

On January 28, 1978, after three weeks of constant surveillance, the police team took a day off. That night Violi was invited to the Reggio bar on Rue Jean-Talon, once the seat of his power, now owned by

Vincenzo Randisi. He passed the time playing cards with a dozen other people, including Randisi and Domenic Manno, Rizzuto's brother-in-law. He was clearly aware, given the enormous pressures brought to bear upon him, that he was sitting in a room full of his arch-rivals.

Police had a wiretap in the Reggio bar, said Michel Amyot, of the Montreal police. A call was made from one of the men in the bar: "The pig is here."

At 7:32 p.m. a gunman came up behind Violi and shot him to death as he played cards.

The wiretap then picked up another call from the bar: "The pig is dead."[15]

Police charged three men in the murder: Nicolò Rizzuto's brother-in-law, Domenico Manno; Giovanni Di Mora; and Agostino Cuntrera, cousin to Alfonso Caruana. Charges were also laid against Vincenzo Randisi but dropped for lack of evidence.

In his book *Blood Brothers*, author Peter Edwards describes Violi's final seconds, lending credence to the theory that Violi knew he was going to die that night: "At 7:32 p.m., his back was to the door as he played cards. . . . Two armed men wearing ski masks walked through the back door. 'Everyone on the floor,' one of them ordered. . . . The dozen or so customers dived for cover under pool tables, all except Paolo Violi. A gunman leveled a sawed-off .12-gauge at the back of Violi's head and squeezed the trigger. . . . Paolo Violi's anguished wait was over."[14]

Paolo Renda, Nicolò Rizzuto's son-in-law, was originally named in the arrest warrant. He flew to Venezuela and, after the three were convicted, the arrest warrant was cancelled, according to a police report.

The arrest of Agostino Cuntrera caused some political upset. *La Presse*, a Montreal daily newspaper, reported that the bookkeeper for Cuntrera's business was Alfonso Gagliano, an influential member of the Liberal Party in Quebec, a highly successful fundraiser and later member of Parliament. When asked about the connection to Cuntrera, Gagliano said he'd met Agostino Cuntrera at church functions and weddings, and at meetings of the Association de Siculiana, a cultural group Gagliano had founded and of which he was also president. Several years later the presidency was given over to Agostino Cuntrera.

Another client of Gagliano's bookkeeping service was Dino Messina, who was later found to be the financial aide of the Rizzuto organization. And years later in June 1985, as police kept surveillance on a controlled delivery of 58 kilograms of heroin shipped from Britain, one of the traffickers, Filippo Vaccarello, and another man were seen entering

Gagliano's office. (When interviewed by the RCMP, Gagliano denied knowing Vaccarello and Messina.) Also Gagliano's telephone number was found in a notebook discovered after Antonio Ezio Salvo was killed by a shotgun blast in Sicily in 1991. And in 1994, Gagliano's name was on a list of four prominent organized crime bosses found in papers discovered in a San Diego hotel room after the guest was reported missing. The guest, a Montreal businessman, also left behind documents relating to $342 million in real estate transactions as well as documents linked to a Vatican bank.[16]

When asked in Parliament in 1994 about Gagliano and the Caruana-Cuntrera, Prime Minister Jean Chrétien said, "This Parliament would be much better off if we had more Gaglianos." Gagliano was cleared of any wrongdoing by the RCMP and the federal ethics commissioner; he was later appointed Minister of Public Works for the Chretien government.

A new controversy involving Alfonso Gagliano and members of the Siciliana family arose in February 2001 as this book was going to print. In Montreal, police arrested Gaetano Amodeo, wanted in Italy for two homicides. One victim was prominent anti-Mafia police investigator Giuliano Guazzelli, who was shot to death in 1992 in Agrigento. The other was Francesco Triassi, a member of the Agrigento mafia, slain in 1991. Salvatore Catania, another target in the Triassi murder, survived his wounds. As well, Amodeo was wanted in Germany for a mafia-related killing in 1981.

Murder warrants were issued by the Palermo Courts in January 1999 in the Guazzelli and Triassi slayings; however, Amodeo had already fled Sicily and was dividing his time between Canada—where he was seen in contact with members of the Rizzuto family—and the United States, as well as the Caribbean.

Amodeo and the Ruzzutos are from Cattolica Eraclea, a Sicilian town not far from Siciliana, where Gagliano was born and the Caruana-Cuntreras were based. While Amadeo was on the run, his wife, Maria Sicurella di Amodeo, with her two children, obtained permanent resident status in Canada under a federal immigrant entrepreneur program. She said she'd separated from her husband, but later reconciled with him and sponsored him as a visitor to Canada.

After Amodeo was arrested, a Montreal newspaper, La Presse, reported that Alfonso Gagliano had personally intervened in the case on Mrs. di Amodeo's behalf. Under attack in the House of Commons, Gagliano vigorously denied any knowledge in the Amodeo case. Rather, he said, a routine administrative fax enquiring about the case had been sent to Citizenship and Immigration Canada by his riding office. He demanded and received a correction from La Presse. Prime Minister Jean Chrétien, defended Gagliano in the House of Commons, saying an Opposition Member of Parliament was dragging Gagliano "in the mud" because he was an immigrant: "It is disgusting to me."

Gagliano himself said his Italian heritage was part of the reason for the allegations: "I didn't say that it's racist, (but) every time something happens that has to do with an Italian, and as the Member of Parliament is Italian, we make headlines."

After the Paolo Violi slaying, Paolo Renda fled to Venezuela, where he linked up with the Rizzutos. The accused who went to trial, including Agostino Cuntrera, were described by a judge as "model immigrants who performed the most modest tasks in an effort to earn a living and slowly and laboriously build themselves a trade." They were found guilty of planning the killing, but not of having carried it out. They received sentences of less than seven years, sparking public and political outrage in Quebec.

By way of cleanup—Mafiosi always keep an eye to possible future revenge—Paolo Violi's brother, Rocco, was later assassinated by a sniper as he sat in his home with his family.

The elderly Don Giuseppe Settecasi, who had been present with Pietro Sciarra at the meeting that resulted in the decision to kill Nicolò Rizzuto, was murdered in March 1981 in Agrigento.

International lines of drug transit were now up for grabs, and several Mafiosi were murdered as a wave of bloody violence wracked Agrigento and western Sicily.

With the Violi problem solved, the Sicilian faction—now recognized as the Siculiana family—slowly made its way back to Montreal. The Caruana brothers—Alfonso, Pasquale, and Gerlando—regrouped, forming their first trading company, Les Importations Carvel Inc. Each brother applied for and was granted a loan of $10,000 from a branch of the City & District Savings Bank on Dollard des Ormeaux, Quebec.[17] They lived in modest apartments and had difficulty making installment payments on the bank loans.

Throughout the early 1980s the brothers set up several companies in Montreal, all, apparently, to facilitate the movement of drugs and drug profits: Santa Rita Export Inc.; Video Select Inc.; Financement Video Select Corp.; Les Administrations Alger Inc.; Les Importations Carvel Inc.; Canada Inc., Les Exportations et Importations-Thermo. This technique of opening businesses was to become a trait of the Caruana-Cuntrera modus operandi for the next twenty years.

Nicolò Rizzuto quietly returned to Montreal after the Violi murder, along with his son, Vito, and several other members of the new organization. In deference to Vincenzo Cotroni—who would die of natural causes a few years later—Rizzuto quietly paid his respects and kept a low profile as he rebuilt alliances and rekindled old friendships. Rizzuto was well positioned, although he knew it might have gone the other way had it not been for the necessity of having Sicilians in place to conduct the Sicily-U.S. heroin business.

Outwardly hard-working immigrants, the Caruanas, the Cuntreras, and the Rizzutos were perfectly set up to play a key role in what were to become the world's largest drug importation schemes.

The Drug Trade

Like nature, the drug underworld abhors a vacuum.

Until the early 1970s, the international trade in heroin and opiates was controlled to a large degree by Corsican and French organizations. When the famed French Connection case led to the breakup of a Mafia-European heroin pipeline and the dismantling of heroin refineries in Marseilles, France, in 1972, the Sicilian Mafia rushed to fill the void, first setting up laboratories in Sicily, and later in Asia, near the source of the poppies.

According to U.S. Drug Enforcement Administration intelligence sources, "The Agrigento area of Sicily was one of the most important points of landing for morphine base that was shipped, on a monthly basis, from ports in Turkey, Syria and Greece . . ."[18]

With the Caruana-Cuntrera well connected in Agrigento, and with control of the vital transshipment city of Montreal, they were in a perfect position to feed heroin into the largest drug market in the world: the United States.

The years the Caruanas and Cuntreras had spent in exile weathering the increasingly aggressive behavior of Paolo Violi weren't wasted. They used the time to forge alliances in Sicily, the United States, the United Kingdom, several other European countries, and South America. The aim of the alliances was to create a global heroin network that would dwarf any known setup. As early as February 1973, Alfonso Caruana had been seen meeting in Rome with money-laundering wizard Giuseppe Cuffaro and other Sicilian Mafia bosses.

In Brazil and Caracas, where several fugitive Mafiosi were re-establishing their business connections, the Siculiana families were solving the complications presented by the spreading Mafia war in Sicily and remapping the drug routes into North America and Europe. Sicilian Mafia boss Francesco Di Carlo was sent by the Corleone family to England in 1980 to run the heroin network controlled by Liborio Cuntrera and the Caruana families.

At the time, the squabbling between the Cotroni-Violi faction and the Sicilian wing appeared to be nothing more than a local turf war: the newcomers replacing the old, a manifestation of a new reality. But seen in the wider context of the international activities of the Sicilian Mafia—in particular the Siciliana family during the 1970s and 1980s—it's clear that there was more at stake than control of a single city, state, or province. Enormous changes were underway elsewhere in the under-world, but it took a historical perspective—formed much later, after several invisible strands came to light in Canada, the United States, Caracas, and Sicily—to fully understand the true motives behind the decade-long Sicilian Mafia–Cotroni/Violi tensions.

What was happening was that an international alliance, in which the Caruanas and Cuntreras and the rest of the Siciliana family were key players, if not overseers, was being created.

New York City

New York is a power center: it is to America's La Cosa Nostra what Palermo is to the Sicilian Mafia. In the 1970s, the bosses and the senior members of the New York Five Families were almost exclusively of Sicilian heritage. Within the families, some of the "crews" or "wings" might have rejected drug trafficking but made fortunes from gambling and extortion; other families were full-blown narcotics organizations, often with international connections. And every family, in spite of the old belief that La Cosa Nostra had for years banned the drug trade, had a separate, often arm's length component involved in drugs.

By 1980, the Violi murder and the return of Siciliana family members from Caracas had re-established Montreal as the Mafia's heroin gate-way into the United States. Remnants of the Cotroni organization were still in operation, but they were now clearly under the influence of the Caruana-Cuntrera-Rizzuto organization.

In New York City, during the second half of the 1970s, the Sicilian Mafia had been preparing to receive unheard of quantities of heroin from Europe and Asia. Using both Montreal and Niagara Falls as entry points, thousands of *picciotti*—Mafia soldiers—had been "imported" into the United States, many through the facilities of the Cotroni organization in Quebec and the southern Ontario wing of the Buffalo Magaddino La Cosa Nostra family.

Mafia turncoat Luigi Ronsisvalle, a Sicilian heroin trafficker who was active in New York City in the 1970s during the buildup of the heroin network, remembers carrying documents into Canada to distribute to incoming Sicilians. "We have some connections to bring passports from Canada and give them to Sicilian people coming to the United States," he testified before the President's Commission on Organized Crime in 1985, adding that Niagara Falls was often used as a conduit.

Many of the Sicilians who entered the United States by these routes went to work in a growing network of pizza restaurants across the country. There they lived quietly and waited until the Montreal drug pipeline could be declared secure by the Siculiana family.

Two key men acted as obstacles to the new Mafia order in New York: Peter Licata, the boss of the Bonanno family's businesses on Knickerbocker Avenue in Brooklyn, and Bonanno family boss Carmine Galante, who had been the family's man in Montreal before being deported and sentenced to a lengthy prison term on heroin charges.

Licata, an old-time neighborhood boss, had massive power on his turf, but, like Paolo Violi, he strongly resented the emerging Sicilian Mafiosi and resisted the drug trade, believing it would be the downfall of the American families. He was content to be an American man of honor, earning relatively clean money through gambling, loan-sharking, extortion, and bootlegging.

Testifying about Licata, Luigi Ronsisvalle described his power on Knickerbocker Avenue—and he might have been describing Paolo Violi's power on Rue Jean Talon, as well—as "Anything moving in there, even a tree, they got to say to him, I want to move the tree. Nobody moves nothing."

Licata's brother, who was like-minded about the emerging trends, was murdered in a Sicilian-run café in early 1976. Seven months later the

Mafia killed Peter Licata. Almost immediately a Sicilian shopkeeper, Salvatore Catalano, took over Knickerbocker Avenue, and observers noted that an entirely new crew, all of them Sicilians and all of them swaggering with newfound power, had taken over the street. There was no retaliation from the Bonanno family.

The elimination of Carmine Galante would be a bit more complicated.

Montreal, Quebec

In the 1950s, Carmine Galante was the Bonanno family's key man in Canada, operating out of Montreal. A lifelong murderer and prolific drug trafficker, Galante was sent to Montreal from New York by Joseph Bonanno. His purpose was two-fold. First, a U.S. Senate committee—the Kefauver Committee—was gathering steam as it examined organized crime in America. Several American bookmakers had fled across the border to avoid subpoenas and to stay out of the spotlight. The Bonanno family made good money off the bookmakers, and family boss Joe Bonanno wanted to keep control of them and their earnings. But Galante's second mission was more important: to take some measure of control over the city's drug trade, paticularly the routes into the United States.

Montreal's underworld was very loosely organized, and one of the mid-level players was Vincenzo Cotroni, who was operating out of the Faison Dore nightclub. Through Galante's underboss, Louis Greco, Cotroni was brought into the Bonanno sphere of influence.

Federal investigations led to Galante's deportation to the United States in 1955; in his place Joe Bonanno installed another American, Salvatore Giglio. But Giglio too came under investigation and was extradited to the United States. In his place, Bonanno appointed Vincenzo Cotroni.

Galante's pedigree was excellent: he had rubbed shoulders with the cream of the underworld in the United States and Sicily. He had attended meetings between the American La Cosa Nostra and the Sicilian Mafia in Palermo. He had shot it out with police on the streets of New York, and was suspected of carrying out the political assassination of anti-fascist journalist Carlo Tresca. He had met with Lucky Luciano during crucial meetings to help form the *Cupola* in Sicily, set up to arbitrate disputes and organize the operations of the diverse families there. And he had served a lot of prison time, including one stretch for heroin trafficking that netted him a twenty-year sentence.

By 1974, Galante had served most of his time. The Sicilian families were by then entrenched in New York and several other American cities, as well as in Montreal and Toronto. The Sicilians were also setting up shop in dozens, if not hundreds, of small cities and large towns across North America. Small teams—as small as two or three members—were planted, concentrated primarily in the U.S. northeast and southern Ontario.

It had been Galante's idea, during a meeting in Sicily in 1957, to bring young Sicilian "soldiers" into the United States to form crews who would work under him. He liked their no-nonsense style and felt they hadn't been corrupted by soft lives in North America. When he came out of prison he quickly moved the Bonanno family into a key position in the heroin trade as the "collector of rent" being paid by the Sicilian families for the American trafficking franchise. While collecting the "rent," however, he refused to pass on the money to the other New York families, reasoning that if they didn't want to share the risk, they wouldn't share in the profits.

That decision perhaps precipitated his downfall. The new Sicilian faction no longer had much need for Galante: the "rent" could easily be paid through other avenues to the families controlling New York City and the eastern seaboard.

Arrogant and defensive, Galante surrounded himself with Sicilian-born bodyguards. Nevertheless, on July 12, 1979, as he lunched at an Italian restaurant in Brooklyn, three masked gunmen burst into the restaurant and shot him dead. His bodyguards, too, apparently opened fire on him.

Around the world a photograph of the dead Galante appeared on front pages. Much was made of the cigar still stuck in his mouth, but in the underworld it's widely accepted that the cigar was blown out of his mouth by the frenzy of shooting, and one of his bodyguards picked it up and stuffed it back in.

Now the Sicilian Mafia had taken control of the heroin-trafficking wing of the Bonanno crime family. They had removed the aggressive and greedy Carmine Galante and the intractable, old-style Peter Licata in New York. They had likely been behind the elimination of the Cotroni-Violi organization in Montreal, giving them something of a monopoly in North America's key centers. The path was clear for a new order in the underworld, with heroin as the prime commodity of the trade routes.

There was, as always, cleanup work to be done, and there another Caruana-Cuntrera-Rizzuto link emerged. When, in May 1981, other dissident members of the traditional Bonanno crew still hadn't accepted the new reality of Giuseppe Bono, Salvatore Catalano, and the Sicilian faction, they had to be eliminated. Three of them—Philip Giaccone, Domenic Trinchera, and Alfonso Indelicato—all of the Bonanno family, were brought together and murdered. Coincidentally, that very day police surveillance picked up Nicolò Rizzuto's son, Vito, and associate Gerlando Sciascia leaving a motel in the area and returning to Canada.

Key to the future of the Caruana-Cuntrera's heroin pipeline, Galante's position was now taken by Gerlando Sciascia. FBI intelligence reports describe Sciascia as "a renowned narcotics trafficker and financier" and a central figure in the Bonanno Sicilian wing in New York City. Maintaining underworld contacts in the Bonanno and Gambino La Cosa Nostra families, as well as the DeCavalcante family of New Jersey, Sciascia was the preferred replacement to fill Galante's shoes. "Sciascia serves as liaison to Montreal," the FBI intelligence report notes. "He appears to be the main figure in (Salvatore) Catalano's group."[19]

And, most importantly, Sciascia was tight with Nicolò Rizzuto and the Siculiana family.

New York City

The United States government called the Pizza Connection investigation the largest heroin-Mafia probe in history. The time frame of the Pizza conspiracy—including its formation and pre-preparation—stretches from the late 1970s to 1984 and clearly encompasses the years of strife in Montreal and the rise of the Caruana-Cuntrera criminal organization. It ended, finally, with jury verdicts against almost two dozen Sicilians and Sicilian Americans in March 1987.

At the beginning of the investigation, the heart of the heroin conspiracy was thought to be in the Bonanno family's enclave of Knickerbocker Avenue in Brooklyn, New York, now under Sicilian Mafia control. Within the crews that made up the Bonanno family was a group of

Sicilians—called "zips" because of their rapid method of speaking Sicilian dialect—headed by Salvatore Catalano. To all appearances, the Catalano faction was under the control of the Bonanno family, and its members were said to have been brought to America by Carmine Galante to deal heroin and act as his soldiers. In reality, Catalano's crew was a separate and distinct Mafia group, answering solely to Sicily. It was one of many, perhaps dozens, of similar groups set up across North America. And Catalano's direct superior wasn't a Bonanno family member at all: it was Giuseppe Bono, the notorious Sicilian Mafia boss of the Palermo-based Nuvoletta family, one of the premier heroin families and the architect of what was later to be known as "the Pizza pipeline." He was the chief suspect in the 1979 assassination of a deputy police chief in Milan during the crucial setup years of the Pizza Case.[20]

U.S. Justice Department files were blunt in their assessment of Giuseppe Bono, describing him as "one of the most knowledgeable men operating abroad in international drug trafficking . . . the new organizer of drug exportation from Italy to the United States." The report adds: "Giuseppe Bono is involved in an extensive money-laundering operation which also includes . . . the Caruana and Cuntrera organized crime Families." And: "Bono is heavily involved in the trafficking of multi-kilos of heroin between Italy and the United States through Canada."[21]

Such was Bono's position that his brother Alfredo was heard in intercepted telephone calls calling him "Godfather."

Under Catalano, with assistance from Carmine Galante and members of the Gambino family, members of the Sicilian Mafia were spirited into Canada and the United States, where they opened dozens of pizza shops and franchises that were to be used as a pipeline for moving heroin within the United States and as a money-laundering conduit to get the profits out. Many of the illegal immigrants were unknown in the United Sates. Several weren't even documented by Italian authorities. By the time of Galante's murder, the intercontinental heroin pipeline from Europe to the United States had effectively been hijacked by the Sicilian Mafia; the "licence fee" for operating on American soil was still being paid to the New York families, but for all practical purposes the Sicilian Mafia had wrested control of the market, becoming the providers of the product, while the American families were either the buyers or were sidelined as investors.

It was estimated that during the length of the Pizza conspiracy the Sicilian Mafia brought more than one and one-half tons of heroin into North America, with a street value of US$1.3 billion. Much of that money was laundered or otherwise moved out of the United States. When the case was brought down, with the naming of dozens of conspirators, it was rightly hailed as the epitome of cooperation between American and Italian authorities, working together as never before in combating the Sicilian Mafia's international drug activities.

While the case had an international component, it didn't actually address the full scope of the new Sicilian Mafia. Very few seizures were made, of either drugs or money, and the case targeted primarily eastern seaboard criminal groups such as the so-called "Catalano wing of the Bonanno Family." Other cells of the network, operating across the United States, were virtually undisturbed, and none of the Canadian cells of the Sicilian Mafia was affected in any meaningful way. The source of all the heroin and the exit strategy used to repatriate profits was never fully determined, although some was traced to Switzerland and other offshore havens.

What was startling about the Pizza Connection case wasn't the number of arrests, the confiscation of money, or the drug seizures: it was the intelligence value, the revelation that the network was made up almost exclusively of Sicilian Mafiosi who took orders directly from Sicily. And the knowledge that the drugs—from the acquiring of raw materials to refining, packaging, shipping, and sales, and, of course, the laundering of profits—were entirely controlled by the families of the Sicilian Mafia.

And moving through and above the rapidly expanding heroin trade were members of the Siciliana family.

The ties between the Pizza Connection suspects and Canadian Mafia members involved with the Caruana-Cuntrera had been forged in 1969 when Giuseppe Bono met Sicilian Mafia boss Tommaso Buscetta in Montreal, while Buscetta was staying with the Caruana-Cuntrera. The men had discussed the current method of bringing heroin into Montreal by sea, then shipping it across the border down to New York City, where it was sold to La Cosa Nostra families for US$50,000 a kilogram.

At that time, the war between the Caruana-Cuntrera-Rizzuto faction and the Violi-Cotroni family had been heating up. Using the Europe-Montreal-New York pipeline, the Sicilians were running huge heroin shipments through Montreal, without bothering to involve or pay tribute to Paolo Violi. For more than ten years, up until and well past the Violi murder, the Bono-Caruana-Cuntrera-Rizzuto drug network had flourished. With the steady flow of heroin, and the creation of the Pizza Connection on the American eastern seaboard, Sicilians on both sides of the Atlantic were making incredible profits.

In August 1980, when heroin trafficker Antonino Salamone in Brazil needed 60 kilograms of heroin in New York City, he turned to Buscetta, whom he knew to have close ties with Salvatore Inzerillo in Sicily. Inzerillo was then the head of one of Sicily's top Mafia families.

"The operation was completed and Salamone offered me a share of the merchandise, which I refused," Buscetta said. "Salamone told me that his partner was Pasquale Cuntrera, who had arranged for the sea shipment of the goods."[22]

The 60 kilograms of heroin was delivered to Giuseppe Ganci, who was in the pizza business with several members of the Catalano faction in New York City.

As the heroin was funneled into the Pizza drug network, a different kind of connection was made between the victorious Montreal Sicilians and the New York City Sicilian faction. In November 1980, Nicolò Rizzuto, his son Vito, and other members of the Montreal Sicilian clans were invited to a wedding in New York City. The groom was Giuseppe Bono, who had moved to the United States in the face of increasing pressure from Italian authorities, who were preparing a massive indictment against him for Mafia association and drug charges. Several of his business interests had been relocated to Venezuela. Now he lived luxuriously in the United States, having bought a $250,000 house in the upscale southern Westchester community of Pelham, and he had become engaged to the daughter of a prominent pizzeria operator.

The early days of the Pizza Case were underway, and a blizzard of drug profits were flying into the coffers of leading Sicilian Mafiosi. The Bono wedding, held at St. Patrick's Cathedral, was followed by a $64,000 reception at the grand Pierre Hotel. More than three hundred guests were invited, including several from Montreal, Toronto, and Caracas.

With the Caruanas and Cuntreras again exercising their newfound powers, the Rizzuto family was raking in profits as they never had before, operating low-profile drug importation schemes and taking over many of the late Paolo Violi's operations. With the Caruana-Cuntrera's links to Sicily's most powerful Mafia families and outposts of loyal Siciliana family members in South America, the United States, and Europe, the family was ready to stake out its turf.

And although Vincenzo Cotroni was alive—he wouldn't die until 1984—the Rizzutos, along with several Siciliana family members, were clearly running Montreal and had formed their own links to the Sicilian Mafia in Italy and in America.

Rome, Italy

In Rome the missing connection in the Pizza Case came to light during a seemingly innocuous telephone call monitored by Alessandro Pansa, chief of the financial crime section of the Italian State Police.

In 1982 Pansa was probing the Italian side of what was to become the Pizza Case, focusing on Giuseppe Bono, the lynchpin between the Sicilian Mafia and the Sicilian-born traffickers in the United States.

Reviewing a tape of the call made to the Ostia home of Pasquale Cuntrera, Pansa was startled to hear Bono, a man who seldom did more than grunt or give short comments while on the telephone, speak respectfully and quietly with a woman, commiserating on the death of her husband. The woman turned out to be Giuseppa Di Mora, the widow of Liborio Cuntrera, who had recently passed away.

Bono's deference, Pansa realized, illustrated the power and influence of the Caruana Cuntrera in the Pizza Case.

Most of the profits from the transnational heroin trade, Pansa learned, passed at one point or another through the bank accounts of the Caruana-Cuntrera, making the organization almost indispensable to the Sicilian Mafia families world-wide.

The years after the successful takeovers in Canada and the United States brought profits—and danger.

The Caruana-Cuntrera connection was generating massive earnings, all of it in cash. And cash was becoming a problem. In the early days, when the profits were in the upper hundred-thousands and low millions, the money could, if necessary, be hand-carried out of North America and taken to overseas banks.

On November 27, 1978, Alfonso Caruana and his financial mentor, Giuseppe Cuffaro, arrived in Zurich aboard a Swissair flight from Mirabel, Quebec. A search by customs officers turned up $600,000 in American currency in the false bottoms of their luggage. They told officials that the money was profit from the sale of a boat. The men paid a fine and were allowed to leave with the money.

Alfonso Caruana and his brother, Pasquale, shuttled back and forth from North and South America to Europe, maintaining residences in Canada, Venezuela, and Switzerland. They opened several bank accounts through which they funneled their heroin profits. An analysis done on several accounts controlled by Alfonso Caruana showed a flow-through over the years of tens of millions of dollars.

Other money was invested in legitimate businesses. In 1981, Alfonso Caruana opened several firms in Milan in partnerships with the upper echelon of the Mafia, including Giuseppe Bono.

In 1983, seeking new sources of product, Alfonso Caruana and Giuseppe Cuffaro traveled to Bangkok, Thailand, where they spent a month forming liaisons with Asia's top heroin suppliers.

But the late 1970s and early 1980s weren't all easy times for the clan. The war for the heroin trade was underway with a vengeance across Sicily as the powerful Mafia clans from Corleone—known as the Corleonesi—eliminated the old order and murdered hundreds of enemies and friends alike as they grasped at power and the profits of the drug trade.

In 1981, Salvatore Inzerillo, the Sicilian boss who supplied much of the heroin flooding the United States and Canada, was found shot to death in Palermo, with American currency stuffed into his mouth.

The Inzerillo murder was seen as the most significant killing in the Corleonesi wave of terror. Inzerillo had been widely recognized as the man with his hand on the spigot that poured heroin. It was later determined that his murder resulted from his failure to share his drug profits with other powerful clans in Sicily, particularly the Corleonesi. Without Inzerillo's heroin link, the Caruanas and Cuntreras went looking for another, and soon hooked up with Leonardo Greco, the boss of the Bagheria family, who controlled the refineries outside Palermo.

Salvatore Contorno, a key Mafia turncoat whose evidence later tied the Pizza Case traffickers to the Sicilian Mafia, told investigators of the Caruana-Cuntrera link: "I worked for Leonardo Greco, helping him to pack the heroin he treated in his laboratory in Palermo. More than once I heard Greco complaining about the enormous sums he kept receiving from Alfonso Caruana, which he had a difficult time exchanging in Palermo banks."[23]

Another turncoat spoke of the huge amounts of heroin the Caruana-Cuntrera were bringing to North America. Gaspare Mutolo told Italian prosecutors that Pasquale Cuntrera and his brothers had taken delivery of 400 kilograms of heroin in 1988 from Greco's refinery alone. He said he organized the shipment on behalf of all the major Sicilian Mafia familes.

"Among the Caruanas, who were more numerous than the Cuntreras, in particular I remember Alfonso," he said. Mutolo recalls also that he was approached by Gaetano Fidanzati, asking if he could find some more Thai heroin.[24] Fidanzati said, "If so, we'll send it to Canada. To Cuntrera and Caruana. Everything you want, either 100 or 200 kilos, every amount you can send them in Canada, because they control everything over there."[25]

In the grand scheme of things, 400 kilograms wasn't a lot of heroin, and, according to an FBI document, was only a minor portion of the narcotics moved by the Caruana-Cuntrera: "In April 1990 it was estimated by law-enforcement authorities that by 1982 the organization was moving 3 tons of heroin per year into the United States, believed to be about half of the United States' annual consumption."[26]

And on the money side of the operation, the report noted: "According to bank documents, court and police records, from 1978 to 1984 the organization used banks in Montreal, Canada, to launder close to US$33 million in illicit drug profits."[27]

For Alfonso Caruana—not yet the head of the Caruana-Cuntrera—the warfare and politicking of the 1970s made the 1980s a time of huge profits and a previously unimaginable international expansion for the family from rural Agrigento province. Members of the clan were spread around the world: in Germany, France, South America, Canada, Asia, and the United States.

And, during the 1980s, a new market was being developed, one that would bring even more profit and power for the Siculiana family—and even more violence. The expansion into the United Kingdom was about to propel Alfonso Caruana to the head of his family, even as the blood-thirsty Corleonesi clan ordered his assassination.

3

After the harsh times in Sicily in the 1960s, the world was a safer, but not necessarily more profitable, place for the Cuntrera brothers. Following a brief stay in Montreal—a city under the rigid control of the Cotroni-Violi cell of the New York Bonanno family—the brothers went to Caracas, Venezuela. They took up minor traditional rackets among the Italian population there—gambling and some loan-sharking, a little extortion. For a family that had enjoyed massive power in western Sicily, the Caracas operations were quite a comedown.

In the late 1960s or early 1970s, Pasquale Cuntrera met the legendary American underworld financier Meyer Lansky.[1] According to a story Pasquale Cuntrera told a fellow Mafioso, it was a fortuitous meeting that was soon to change the destiny of the Cuntreras and the Caruanas.

Lansky, who for years had laundered and invested organized crime profits for La Cosa Nostra, was widely regarded as the financial wizard who'd brought American gangsters into the modern age, putting them into legitimate businesses, unions, and politics.

Lansky told Pasquale Cuntrera to abandon any plans of returning to Sicily. Instead, he explained how business could be conducted at arm's length, from elsewhere in Italy. Lansky suggested he move to the Lazio region in central Italy where his old American mafia friend, Frank "Three Fingers Brown" Coppola, was living.

As it happened, in the early 1970s the Agrigento Court of Appeal lifted the decree that had forced the Cuntreras to leave Sicily. In their decision, the judges relied on documents that portrayed Pasquale Cuntrera as "a delightful person." Pasquale Cuntrera moved back to Italy and promptly met with Frank Coppola, bringing him greetings from Lansky.

"We're a great family," Cuntrera told the grand old godfather at his Ostia home. "We can attempt what has never been attempted before: laundering heroin money on a massive scale."[2]

Coppola took little convincing. He was impressed with the reputation of the Caruana-Cuntrera and was aware of their expanding influence in the international underworld. He explained to Pasquale Cuntrera the techniques used by Lansky to clean the American La Cosa Nostra's profits. The most successful was the "loan-back scheme," in which illegal profits could be smuggled offshore and loaned back to the original depositor. Others included the use of money orders, traveler's checks, cashier's checks, and bearer bonds. Bulk currency could, if necessary, be body-carried out of the United States and deposited into Swiss banks, or in an *Anstalt*, a share company with a single secret shareholder, in Liechtenstein. Loans could be acquired through the offshore entities, and the borrower, who owned the money in the first place, would pay himself interest on the one hand, while declaring the loan a business expense.

The areas of Ostia and Frosinone were already showing promise as new outposts for the Caruana-Cuntrera. In 1971, Alfonso Caruana and his brother Gerlando had residences there. The Cuntrera brothers bought a Frosinone-based limited company, Cantieri Edili Perelli, and in spite of the fact that it had almost zero assets and no record of success, managed to get contracts for several public works projects in the area. Salvatore Vella, Alfonso's uncle and Pasquale Cuntrera's brother-in-law, soon joined the company. His role was to represent the Caruana interests in the firm's finances and operation.

As they had in Sicily, the Caruana-Cuntrera (although more accurately called the Cuntrera-Caruana at that time) soon influenced local politicians and decision-makers. When tenders were called, it was the Cantieri Edili Perelli that most often got the work. In one case investigated by local police, ten firms were asked to bid on a project worth billions of lire, but only one firm actually filed a tender: Cantieri Edili Perelli. The Caruana-Cuntrera bid for, and won, contracts to build the public slaughterhouse, the teachers' school in Frosinone, the civic hospital in Ceccano, and the Fiuggi water-distribution network.

An empire quickly emerged: by obtaining loans from cooperative bankers, the Cuntreras bought poorly run and failing companies, which suddenly received cash infusions that turned them around and made them viable. The Caruanas later moved to nearby Frascati where they began dealing in cars, buying a local Ford dealership.

In those prosperous years, the Siculiana family managed to establish friendly relations with influential local politicians, according to Italian police documents. Among them were Frosinone mayor and former Christian-Democrat regional councilman Dante Spaziani; the deputy mayor, Giulio D'Agostino, who was also in charge of public works; and Michele Santopadre, who ran the public board responsible for construction of low-income housing in the province. A great asset to the Cuntreras and Caruanas was their connection with Luigi Zicari, a member of the provincial council in Agrigento.

"The Cuntreras had no difficulty in obtaining leases and loans from the banks, quickly expanding their activities and absorbing other companies active in the construction field," a report prepared by Italian police in Rome found. "These companies, bought in very bad financial shape, in a short time recovered, in a suspicious way, their economic solidity."[3]

With a network of complex business relationships—and, of course, overflowing bank accounts—the Caruana-Cuntrera were ready to offer money-laundering services to the Sicilian Mafia families who were drowning in heroin profits.

It was a network of contacts and services that, over the next thirty years, would lift the wandering and widespread Siculiana family far above the cut-and-thrust of the trafficking business carried on by the families that stayed mired in the product side of the heroin trade.

Corleone, Sicily

In 1970, Alfonso Caruana moved back to Italy, at least temporarily. He and his brothers, Pasquale and Gerlando, kept moving around. Alfonso appeared in Siculiana, stayed about a year tending to family business, then moved to Frosinone, where the Cuntreras were already making inroads in politics and industry, positioning themselves to become the money men of the Sicilian Mafia.

The government pressure that followed the 1963 bombing that killed seven *Carabinieri*—what came to be known as the Ciaculli Massacre—

was easing. In retrospect, it would forever be said that had the government shown strength of will and kept up the pressure, the modern Cosa Nostra might have been defeated, within some parts of Sicily at least. But by 1971 the government did ease off, and the bosses in Sicily reconstituted the *Cupola*.

A new era of cooperation was expected, a time when, with strong and fair leadership, the families of the Cosa Nostra could capitalize on the international drug trade, fighting to dominate the marketplace instead of each other. The new *Cupola* was to herald a time of profits, not blood.

Around the world—in Brazil, Venezuela, Canada, mainland Italy—the expatriate Mafiosi among the Caruanas and Cuntreras looked forward to a kind of international free market where the various components of the Mafia would work in harmony. This free market would be fuelled by heroin. The last members of the old French Connection, working with Corsican traffickers, were dying off, imprisoned or killed by police and each other. The absence of competition left a vacuum that the Sicilian Mafia rushed to fill.

The makeup of the new *Cupola* should have guaranteed prosperity and harmony. Gaetano Badalamenti was an old-school Mafioso, a dour and grunting man who headed the Cinisi family. He was respected as an elder statesman who ruled absolutely an area west of Palermo. In fact, when U.S. authorities later asked the Italian police about him, they were told: "His power is such that he can call upon almost all the male population of Cinisi to serve him." Essentially a peasant boss, he was, effectively, the head of the *Cupola*.

Also on the *Cupola* was Stefano Bontate, a more urbane Mafioso who enjoyed the cosmopolitan pleasures of Palermo. His connections to leaders in the financial sector, senior police officials, and politicians were strong and wide. Although opposites in almost every other way, both Badalamenti and Bontate were considered conservatives, men who kept an eye on the past but who also looked forward and planned for the future.

The third man on the leadership of the *Cupola* was Salvatore "Toto" Riina, the acting leader of the Corleonesi clan, a mysterious and secretive family based in a hilltop village south of Palermo. He was standing in for his boss, the homicidal Luciano Liggio, who was serving one of his many prison sentences.

For decades the insular Corleonesi had maintained a distrustful independence from other Mafia families. They refused to divulge the number or identity of their members; they operated without consultation with other families; and they seemed to have no use for the restructured Mafia that emerged in the 1960s and 1970s. They were suspicious of the success of others and derided their failures. At every opportunity they excelled at making mischief among the other families, planting informants and agents within their ranks, sowing distrust, and undermining their decisions with a deadly capriciousness.

In his younger days, Riina was called "Shorty" or "the short one." By the time he had risen to full power in the Mafia—leaving hundreds of bodies in his wake—he was known only as "The Beast," for the murderous campaigns he waged. Through and through, Riina was a peasant, who made no pretentions. He had almost no command of Italian, preferring to speak in dialect, and had barely mastered writing. Having completed only two or three years of primary school himself, Riina married an elementary school teacher.

The name of the town he came from, Corleone, was to become famous as the name of the Mafia family in Mario Puzo's book *The Godfather*. It was said that the very bricks and boards of the buildings in Corleone were Mafia; the dogs roaming the streets and even the sun shining on rooftops were Mafia. The place was thoroughly corrupted, its economy a Mafia economy and its authorities permitted to operate only because of the largesse of the Corleonesi.

Trouble struck the new *Cupola* very quickly, and it didn't come from Riina. Italian authorities got warrants for the arrest of Badalamenti and Bontate, who were then taken to Ucciardone prison, a sprawling facility in Palermo. Using this windfall to their advantage, the Corleonesi immediately violated the rules of the *Cupola* and began kidnapping industrialists and other wealthy people, taking their victims right out of Badalamenti's protected territory. Then they cast their eyes upon the Sicilian banks stuffed with tens of millions of dollars of funds misappropriated by the Mafia, money sent from Rome to undertake massive construction projects on the island. The more modern Mafia families effectively owned the money, but the Corleonesi saw it as investment capital for the heroin market now up for grabs.

While Badalamenti and Bontate were in prison, the Corleonesi waged a campaign of espionage, infiltrating their families, planting spies, and preparing to seize control of the *Cupola*. When the two bosses were freed from prison in 1975, they resumed their positions, unaware that the *Cupola* had effectively come under the control of the Corleonesi. Riina led a campaign to discredit and belittle the Cinisi boss: at meetings Badalamenti's poor vocabulary and speaking skills were mocked; murders were committed on his turf; more kidnappings were blamed on him.

For three years Badalamenti was undermined and ridiculed. He endured the confusing and unpredictable attacks, complaining ineffectually that the Corleonesi were ignoring the rules and power of the *Cupola*. In 1978, he was expelled from the commission and stripped of his position. Under penalty of death, no one in the Mafia was to associate with him, either personally or in the course of their business. He left Sicily altogether, either banished or on the run. His replacement in the leadership was his cousin and enemy Antonino Badalamenti. Michele Greco took the Corleonesi seat and assumed Gaetano Badalamenti's position as head. Stefano Bontate kept his position, but was ineffective and outnumbered two to one.

The following year the Corleonesi went on a murderous rampage, killing anyone—criminals or authorities—who they perceived to be dangerous or disloyal.

In Palermo, police detective Boris Giuliano, who was assisting American drug agents in investigating the Mafia's drug trade, was publicly executed. Judge Cesare Terranova, who had launched a campaign against the Mafia, and the Corleonesi in particular, was murdered. Journalists, more judges, more police officials, politicians—all fell before the Corleonesi.

When Stefano Bontate's outrage over these political killings became too much, he confided in fellow Mafia boss Tommaso Buscetta that he was going to move against Riina and shoot him to death. While Buscetta later said he was able to convince Bontate not to carry out his plan, both the Buscetta and Bontate families had become penetrated with Riina's informants. Buscetta, not unaware that even the private discussion of such a plan would reach the Corleonesi, fled to Brazil.

Stefano Bontate's end came as he waited in traffic for a red light to change. He was torn apart by rounds from a Kalishnikov assault rifle.

His colleague, Salvatore Inzerillo, knew he was on Riina's list, but because he owed "The Beast" payment for 50 kilos of heroin, he believed he was worth more alive than dead. Just how wrong he was became evident two weeks later when he, too, was gunned down.

With the immediate threats to his power nullified, Riina got down to business. Anyone he knew who had ever worked or cooperated with the murdered bosses—dubbed "The Losers" in the Italian media—was hunted down and killed. Bodies were strewn from the streets of Palermo to the sidewalks of New York. One victim, Salvatore Inzerillo's sixteen-year-old son, was a typical victim of Riina's terror campaign: according to several pentiti he was kidnapped and tortured. As he was held down on a table, a Corleonesi member sawed off an arm, waving it around and telling him, "With this arm you can no longer kill Totò Riina." After a few minutes of gloating, the Corleonesi shot the boy dead. Other victims were dissolved in acid, dropped into deep wells, or found slumped on street corners.

With his past, present, and future enemies vanquished, Riina went after his allies, his theory being: "If they're such excellent killers, how long will it be before they kill me?" Another campaign of murder began. The killers who'd killed so efficiently for Riina became, in turn, his victims. Some bodies were found, some weren't, the victims of "lupara bianca"—"white shotgun"—meaning that the body would never have been found.

In spite of his murderous disposition, Riina was to some a very sociable man who loved to cook and enjoyed a joke. He was a gracious host, often throwing massive banquets. One meal he prepared was well received by his guests; after they finished, he told them it was a stew he'd made of foxes. But other surprises often awaited: several stories were told of Riina strangling a guest as he sat at the dinner table.

One of the bodies to fall in Riina's savage blitz belonged to Alfonso Caruana's uncle, Leonardo, slain as he attended his son's wedding in Palermo on September 2, 1981. A former member of the Agrigento provincial commission, Leonardo Caruana had made the mistake of buying drug shipments from Salvatore Inzerillo.

Pasquale Cuntrera, living in Venezuela with his brothers, took over the Siciliana family. Carmelo Colletti, the boss of the town of Ribera, was put in charge of the family's business in Siciliana; two years later he was assassinated by the Corleonesi.

Leonardo Caruana's murder began a killing spree by the Corleonesi that was to claim forty-eight lives and the bosses of three families.

By 1982, their work almost done—although Riina's work, it was said, was never done—the Corleone family was now dominant within Sicily, and in fact had *become* the Mafia. They had power over banks and industries awash in drug money. Their control of huge blocks of votes in Sicily gave them access to many Italian politicians, right up to and including, it was said, the seven-time prime minister of Italy, Giulio Andreotti. They had eliminated any conceivable threat to their control of the heroin trade, and no one rivaled their power.

Except, perhaps, the ever-growing Caruana-Cuntrera.

London, England

When Francesco Di Carlo married in 1967, the wedding was attended by the wealthy of Palermo society. Di Carlo's best man was Prince Alessandro Vanni Calvello di San Vincenzo, a nobleman who was equally at ease with Mafiosi as with royalty. When Queen Elizabeth II visited Sicily in 1980, the prince hosted a gala reception attended by the island's élite, a party held in the dazzling halls of Palazzo Ganci Valguarnera, where in 1962 film director Luchino Visconti had shot the final ballroom scene for his film *The Leopard*. Certainly Queen Elizabeth was unaware that the painstakingly detailed restoration of the palace had been supervised by Francesco Di Carlo, a suspected serial killer who would one day achieve notoriety as the Sicilian Mafia's ambassador to London. Di Carlo spoke proudly of his brush with British royalty: "I attended the reception for the Queen," he said. "My chef of a nightclub I owned at that time prepared the lunch for her."[4]

While suspected of involvement in as many as eighty homicides, Di Carlo—known as "The Strangler"—denies the allegations: "I never killed anyone in my life," he told Italian magistrates.

Born in Altofonte in 1941, Di Carlo entered into Cosa Nostra in 1967. Within five years he became an underboss, and in 1975 he became *capo*. He was one of the first Mafia bosses to recognize the need to modernize Cosa Nostra by turning its criminal profits into clean money. His method was simply to place the funds into a legitimate financial sector and allow them to be put to work. His contacts and range of acquaintances allowed him to deal easily with bankers, investors, and financiers. And his prowess in financial matters impressed Toto Riina, the head of the Corleonesi. "I deposited and invested the money of Riina in Switzerland," Di Carlo said. "He used me always, for my language skills and my brain."

The lifelong ties between Di Carlo, the Mafia boss, and Prince Alessandro, the nobleman, ran deep. Both had attended the Istituto Gonzaga, Palermo's prestigious Jesuit-run high school. Both had been partners in the Il Castello nightclub in San Nicola L'Arena, along the highway from Palermo, where first-class stars such as Amanda Lear and Ray Charles performed for a sophisticated audience. The men attended social engagements together; eventually, Di Carlo said, he brought the Prince into the Mafia. (Prince Vanni Calvello di San Vincenzo was later named in a warrant for Mafia-association charges; he was convicted and sentenced to six years in prison.)

Within Cosa Nostra and in the broader, fine society of Palermo, Di Carlo, it seemed, could do no wrong. His father, a Mafia don, was owed a debt of gratitude for services rendered on behalf of "The Beast" during the Corleone wars of the 1950s; that debt of gratitude was passed down to Francesco. Di Carlo was respected by the members of the ruling *Cupola*—he was of the Corleonesi faction—and he was well situated, having survived one of the most turbulent periods in the Italian underworld.

In 1980, Di Carlo left Sicily and settled in England, a vast and untapped market where the Mafia had few interests, and there he focused mostly on casinos, along with some low-level extortion and illegal gambling in London's Italian community. To outsiders, Di Carlo's move to the United Kingdom appeared to be a step out into the broader world; he appeared to be the Corleonesi's ambassador to Britain, their point man to spearhead a coming campaign to expand the market for heroin. In truth, however, part of the motive for the move was to send Di Carlo into exile.

"Some months earlier [before going to London] he had been given supervision of the arrival of a large lot of heroin belonging to Cosa Nostra," wrote Italian authors Leo Sisti and Peter Gomez. "During the [shipment], however, a part of the load disappeared mysteriously;

Francesco Di Carlo maintained that it had been seized by the police. A pitiful excuse, which could have cost him his life."[5]

If not for Toto Riina's debt to Di Carlo's father, he would have been killed. As it was, he was *posato*: a disciplinary sanction that removed him from the Cosa Nostra, while he remained forever at its disposal. Details of this story were independently confirmed by Giuseppe Marchese, a lifelong Mafioso who ended up cooperating with Italian anti-Mafia magistrates.

Other sources and analysts believe that Di Carlo was sent to London either to infiltrate the Caruana-Cuntrera on behalf of the Corleonesi, or to represent their interests and make sure they got their share of profits from the clan's drug organization, then being run by Alfonso Caruana's cousin, Liborio.

In any case, Di Carlo began working in London as an antiques dealer, operating B&S Antiques, which specialized in furniture. His company kept a main office in London and opened a branch in Liverpool. Shortly afterwards the company acquired a hotel, pub, wine bar, and travel agency. He steadily grew wealthier, and soon he was driving his new Ferrari into the country, buying a home in the exclusive Woking area, and spending his nights at the city's casinos.

Di Carlo's neighbors in Woking, Surrey, were Alfonso and Pasquale Caruana, who also lived in palatial estates. "[Di Carlo] visited the Caruanas once every two weeks," observed Matthew Robertson, Alfonso Caruana's gardener at the Woking estate. "Among those I saw visiting Alfonso, Di Carlo was the dearest friend."[6]

In 1980, just as Di Carlo was embarking on his career, Judge Paolo Borsellino issued warrants for his arrest and those of his brothers, Andrea and Giulio, on drug trafficking charges. Di Carlo's brothers were picked up by police in Italy and were later convicted of mafia association.

The press got hold of the story and the London *Sunday Times* ran an exposé entitled "Mafia Man in London," dubbing Di Carlo "a Mafia godfather." But the media coverage had little effect on Di Carlo's activities and lifestyle; there seemed to be no enthusiasm among British authorities to investigate him, never mind extradite him to Italy.

Di Carlo wasn't the first Sicilian Mafioso to set up operations in

London. Liborio Cuntrera had been there since 1975, living the life of a successful businessman with his mansion and fleet of luxury automobiles. He had quickly set about creating a drug-trafficking network, flooding the United Kingdom with heroin and cocaine. He also set up a parallel money-laundering system, using dozens of dummy companies to move drug profits out of England, and often back again, for reinvestment.

The network in London followed a typical Caruana-Cuntrera template: move in a few people, set up a base, arrange some outlets for narcotics, create an import system for drugs and an export system for money. As the network flourished, Alfonso and Pasquale Caruana regularly traveled from Montreal to facilitate the movement of profits to Switzerland.

As the Caruana-Cuntrera grew more powerful, their success was noticed and envied back in Sicily. Having essentially moved their entire organization off the island, the Caruanas and Cuntreras had become too independent for the Corleonesi. They brought members into their organization without consulting their counterparts in Sicily; they operated around the world; and they would very soon become irreplaceable as sources and facilitators for all the large trafficking groups.

Their greatest sin was success. And what most motivated Riina and the Corleonesi in their efforts to bring down the Caruana-Cuntrera was envy.

Companies associated with the Caruana-Cuntrera—either directly or through other criminal ties—were:

- Elongate Ltd., an import-export company used by the Caruana-Cuntrera to facilitate drug-trafficking activities; operators of the firm were Francesco Siracusa and Antonio Zambito. Their telephone number, according to court documents filed, was Pasquale Caruana's home number.
- Ital Provisions Ltd., operated by Filippo Monteleone and Antonino Luciani. The small food-importing company was actually engaged in importing furniture from Thailand. The furniture concealed hashish and heroin.
- Fauci Continental Import Ltd., an importing firm whose managing director was Girolamo Fauci, a close associate of Francesco Di Carlo's. One of the vans leased by Fauci was later found to contain 348 kilos of cannabis.

When Liborio Cuntrera died suddenly of cirrhosis of the liver in 1982, Alfonso Caruana moved to London to take his place. He was joined a short time later by his brother Pasquale.

Now the brothers were in the thick of the family business. While creating a drug pipeline to North America, Alfonso Caruana traveled across Europe, opening businesses and bank accounts.

From their outposts throughout the world, the Caruana-Cuntrera were aware of the murderous inclinations of the Corleonesi. They were constantly on guard: the homes they lived in were heavily fortified with high fences and thick walls, and armed guards were always nearby. They knew that the unpredictable Corleonesi could strike at any time with no warning. The Caruana-Cuntrera were careful about who got close to them: Riina's corruption techniques were well known.

In 1982, Francesco Di Carlo was ordered by the Corleonesi to assassinate Alfonso Caruana and his uncle, Pasquale Cuntrera. The murders would give the Corleonesi a hold on Di Carlo and thus a strong position in the drug trade routes between Europe and the lucrative American markets. It is assumed that the promised prize for Di Carlo was that he would be allowed to run the network.

"They asked me to have Pasquale Cuntrera and Alfonso Caruana come to Sicily so they could be killed," Di Carlo told Italian prosecutors. "They were way too rich and arrogant." Several warnings had been given to the Caruana-Cuntrera: most of their main Sicilian contacts in the heroin trade had been wiped out by Riina.

But Di Carlo resisted the order. He was continuing to grow wealthy, and he'd become close to the Caruanas and Cuntreras. "I considered Alfonso Caruana my brother," he later said. Besides, the Caruanas and Cuntreras were playing out their game in the world's capitals; they were urbane people, and not peasants like the Corleonesi. And, as most of the Mafia learned in the wake of Riina's bloody cleanups, one who turned his coat in favor of the Corleonesi would never be trusted, would always present a risk of turning the coat back again.

His refusal didn't sit well with the Corleonesi dons. And this, coming on the heels of his involvement in the missing drug shipment, placed Di Carlo in a dangerous position.

Redemption came from an unlikely source. Pippo Calò, the treasurer for the most powerful of the Sicilian families, including Riina's Corleonesi, had a problem that Di Carlo could solve: Roberto Calvi.

In life, Roberto Calvi was of little use to Francesco Di Carlo, but his death offered redemption and a chance to erase "The Strangler's" past mistakes. Di Carlo took the murder contract on Calvi without hesitation.

Calvi came to a very public end on June 18, 1982, hanging from a length of orange rope securely woven into a lover's knot around his neck, and tied at the other end to scaffolding, under the iron and stone Blackfriar's Bridge spanning the River Thames in London. Found that morning, the neat, well-kept, and well-connected banker to two of the most powerful forces in the world—the Mafia and the Vatican—had been dead for most of the night. The cold water of the river was washing over his ankles. The pockets of his grey suit were loaded down with twelve pounds of rocks and chunks of brick, and $15,000 in the currency of various countries.

In life, Calvi had been many things: the head of Banco Ambrosiano, one of the most powerful private banks in Europe; a member of the "P2"—*Propaganda Due*—a secret group of corrupt bankers, businessmen, politicians, and Mafiosi within the Masonic Lodge; an international man of finance, traveling worldwide with a coterie of bodyguards. His wealth was, by all accounts, massive: a fleet of Mercedes, two luxurious apartments in Milan, a sprawling sixteenth-century villa in the Italian lakes district, a residence in the Caribbean, an apartment in Rome.

Known as "God's Banker" because of his ties to the Vatican, he was a man of secrets, of secret connections and links, the subject of whispered rumors so fantastic that many believe them to be true.

In his book *God's Name*, David Yallop suggests that Calvi was one of a small group of men who conspired to murder John Paul I, who had succeeded Pope Paul VI, under whom Calvi and others had free access to the Vatican's fortunes. John Paul I died mysteriously in 1978, only thirty-three days after his election to the Chair of St. Peter.

Rumors of Calvi's secret ties to the Sicilian Mafia's treasurer Pippo Calò had a lot more substance.

Banco Ambrosiano, established in 1896, was the creation of the Catholic bourgeoisie of northern Italy, and it had long been intertwined with the finances of the Roman Catholic Church. In fact, like many "Catholic banks," Banco Ambrosiano was founded with the help of the Church.

When Calvi joined Banco Ambrosiano in 1946, the conservative bank still counted on prayer to keep the finances at peak performance. To get a position with the bank, an applicant had to produce a letter from a priest, attesting to his character and religious inclination. Even shareholders had to provide a baptismal certificate and a statement of good character from a parish priest.

Calvi's rise through the bank was startling. It didn't hurt that he was a diligent financier whose facility in German and French made him one of the few members of the bank who could interact on both financial and social levels with the wealthiest of Swiss bankers. Nor did it hurt that, in the decade after he joined the bank, Italy experienced a rapid economic growth that provided impetus and profit for the financial sector, particularly in Milan, the country's business capital.

As he rose through the bank, it was widely recognized that Calvi had a patron, and as the patron rose through the bank's higher levels, so did Calvi, until he was well positioned to become involved in international finance. He managed to bring Banco Ambrosiano increased profits during the 1960 stock market boom, fueled by the booming economy. He launched Interitalia, Italy's first mutual fund, through which small investors could participate in the stock market. And he was on hand when Banco Ambrosiano bought a controlling interest in Banca del Gottardo, which later became one of the largest foreign-owned Swiss banks.

By the late 1960s, Calvi had achieved every measure of success. Worldly and at ease in any social or business situation, he was among the top six executives at Banco Ambrosiano. But his chances of rising further were blocked by a glass ceiling that was curiously Italian: to rise to the highest levels of finance, anyone, no matter how successful he might be within his own house, had to have a hook, a patron who operated in the gray world of politics—a patron who knew an entirely different set of ropes and rules, and who himself bridged the worlds of politics and finance.

Calvi's good fortune in meeting such a man, Michele Sindona, would ultimately lead to his demise.

Michele Sindona had also enjoyed a meteoric rise to the top: born in Patti, near Messina, Sicily, he was the same age as Calvi. A stunningly intelligent and charismatic man, Sindona studied law at the University of Messina in the 1930s; he later avoided military service by using connections in both the Mafia and the Church, citing the importance of his job producing lemons, crucial for their ability to prevent scurvy. His success was facilitated by both a bishop and by Vito Genovese, an international drug trafficker and boss of a New York City La Cosa Nostra family. Between them, the bishop and the Mafioso were able to ease Sindona through the tough times of World War II.

At war's end, Sindona ran a law practise. He quickly became disenchanted with the confined atmosphere of Sicily and in 1948 moved to Milan. A letter to the Vatican from his patron in the Church, the Catholic bishop, smoothed the way for the ambitious Sindona. In spite of being from the south—prejudice against anyone south of Rome was rampant in Italy's north—he flourished, primarily because of his links to the Church. Using his contacts at the Vatican, Sindona began grooming those who held the pursestrings, and he worked constantly to make the highest connections possible.

In 1960, Sindona bought a small bank, Banca Privata, and soon his efforts to cultivate contacts within the Vatican paid off: the Church began making deposits into Banca Privata. Sindona's empire grew as he used the success of Banca Privata to purchase, in turn, other banks. By the mid-1960s, Sindona was an international businessman with a reputation as a profit-maker. Banks in several countries—including Britain, the United States, and France—bought shares in Sindona's business ventures. Among his friends were Richard Nixon, before he became president, and David Kennedy, who would become Secretary of the U.S. Treasury.

Sindona was named as one of the Vatican's top financial advisers. Sindona bought and resold Vatican-controlled firms, made it a partner in his network of banks, and was ultimately known to be so close to the seat of Catholic power that in many business dealings the other participants didn't always know with whom they were actually dealing.

Through his currency brokerage firm, Moneyrex, he had more than eight hundred client banks worldwide. Moneyrex did US$200 billion in business, and it was used by the upper echelons of government, industry, and the military to ship their profits—legal and illegal—offshore. As insurance against any rainy day that might come along, it was said that Sindona kept "The List of 500," a ledger of transactions by the rich and powerful, to be used for blackmail if need be.

In any case, by the 1970s, "Gruppo Sindona" had six banks in four countries, an international hotel chain, food companies, and approximately five hundred corporations. It was said that the financial wizard in effect controlled the stock market, and that as much as 40 percent of shares traded were under his control or subject to his arm's-length influence. Former Italian prime minister Giulio Andreotti once referred to him as "the savior of the lira."

As his power and influence grew, his ties to politicians became stronger, and he became known as a man who could reach out to the right politician or the right party and trade favor for favor.

But in Italy, Church and politics aren't the only power bases. There are two others, both of them shrouded in secrecy: the Mafia and the Freemasons.

Although Sindona had left Sicily in the 1940s, to the Mafia he was an investment, a man who would always be beholden to them. It had long been believed that his banking network was used to launder the Mafia's profits, particularly the increasing flow of money from the narcotics trade. This tie to the underworld was never denied by Sindona, who perceived that the rumors and whispers were enhancing his power base and the depths of his secret relationships. Although Interpol identified him in 1976 as a money-launderer and corruption specialist for the Mafia families in Sicily—working through Pippo Calò, the Mafia's treasurer—he was also tightly tied to the John Gambino crime family operating both in Italy and on the U.S. eastern seaboard, and to several men involved in creating the soon to emerge Pizza Connection.

Sindona was also a member of the Italian Masons, a secretive society of the country's power élite. He belonged to *Propaganda Due* (P 2), a "covered" lodge whose membership was secret. Under Licio Gelli (who would later become significant in a shameful chapter of Italian justice), P 2 used connections with financial, political, military, and national security agencies to infiltrate itself into the highest offices of the country.

When Michele Sindona met Roberto Calvi, he decided to take him under the wings of his power, to provide to him the entree that would elevate him above his senior, but still relatively powerful, role in the Banco Ambrosiano. With the help of his patron, Calvi became chairman of Banco Ambrosiano in late 1975.

But, pressured by his own secrets, Calvi had become paranoid and obsessive over his security. He had sophisticated protection devices installed, surrounded himself with bodyguards, and put bulletproof glass in his offices, apartments, and country farmhouse. Anti-eavesdropping measures were taken, cutting-edge technology that cost a fortune. He obsessively carried a briefcase containing all his sensitive documents and correspondence, and seldom went anywhere without it.

Like a man who had traded his soul to the devil—or in this case, to Michele Sindona—Roberto Calvi was finding that pact an immense burden.

The perfect life of a perfect banker began to crumble around Roberto Calvi in 1974 when Sindona—tipped off by P2 powerhouse Lucio Gelli—fled Italy in anticipation of criminal warrants being served on him. At the heart of the warrants was the looting of both his Banca Privata and the American bank, Franklin National. Settling in New York and protected by the John Gambino family, Sindona reached out to Lucio Gelli for assistance. Gelli began a campaign to have the allegations dropped, collecting affidavits from prominent Italians and Americans testifying that Sindona was of good character, and he started a whispering campaign suggesting that Sindona was the target of a Communist plot.

But when Sindona reached out for help from one of Italy's most powerful men—his apprentice, Roberto Calvi—Calvi either wouldn't or couldn't assist him. In any case, he didn't.

Angered, Sindona began a vendetta against Calvi. Newspaper articles began to expose Calvi's banking deals and practices. A smear campaign occurred—literally—when buildings near Banco Ambrosiano's offices were covered with posters alleging Calvi's financial irregularities. Lists of his bank accounts, where he had reportedly hidden tens of millions of dollars, were plastered around Milan. But the incident that led directly to an official investigation came when a Sindona supporter sent a letter to the governor of the Bank of Italy, carefully detailing Calvi's financial misdeeds.

Under a back-breaking amount of pressure from several sources—and mindful of Sindona's connection to not only the Sicilian Mafia but other organized crime groups as well—Calvi increased his security.

Over the next few years, investigations—including one into the activities of the P2 lodge—repeatedly led magistrates to Roberto Calvi. His name appeared in a file seized in a raid on Lucio Gelli's home. In 1981, eleven financiers were indicted on charges of illegally exporting us$20 million from Italy through a complex series of share transactions. On the list, essentially unprotected, was Roberto Calvi. He was arrested in May 1981; out of custody, he disappeared in June 1982. One month later, he was found dead under Blackfriar's Bridge. Two months after his body was found, Banco Ambrosiano collapsed.

Calvi's death was ruled a suicide. Citing an earlier suicide attempt, the bizarre method of death, the $15,000 in currency in Calvi's pockets, the two expensive watches found on the body, and the strenuous pressures "God's Banker" was under, an inquest made its finding in a majority decision. The decision pleased no one. An Italian magistrate reacted to the verdict in disgust, referring to the death as "that car accident." Calvi's family filed an appeal, and Britain's attorney general granted the request. Few believed the inquest had received all the information it required about Calvi's connections to the Vatican, to corrupt businessmen and politicians, and to the Sicilian Mafia. A second inquest the following year came back with a verdict that did not exclude the possibility of a murder.

But what was already a mysterious circumstance would lead to even deeper mysteries in the coming years.

In 1991, Francesco Marino Mannoia, a Mafia member who became a government witness, told his interrogators that he had been at a farm in western Sicily with Corleonesi member Ignazio Pullarà on the day Calvi died, and he recalled what happened when the speculation that it might have been a suicide hit the news. Pullarà, Mannoia said, burst out: "What bloody nonsense—he was strangled by Francesco Di Carlo." In a later conversation Mannoia had with a fellow prisoner in jail in Trapani, he was told: "Di Carlo had been expelled from the Commission [*Cupola*] because of a snub [his refusal to kill Alfonso Caruana]. That's why he put himself at Cosa Nostra's disposal and strangled Calvi." The prisoner told Mannoia that Calvi had stolen millions from Pippo Calò, the treasurer of Cosa Nostra, and from the P2 Worshipful Master Lucio Gelli.

Italian authorities, acting on the revelations, filed Notices of Investigation in connection with Calvi's death. Di Carlo was interrogated and admitted that he'd been asked by Pippo Calò, through a third party, to murder Calvi.

"When I received this order I called Bernardo Brusca, who was the *capo mandamento* of my family," Di Carlo said. "And I asked if I had to do it. Brusca said to put myself at the disposal of Pippo Calò."

In interviews with magistrates Giovanni Salvi and Andrea Vardaro in September 1996, Di Carlo said he was on a trip in Italy when Calvi was killed. "Nunzio Barbarossa, a Camorra member with links to the Sicilian Mafia, told me that Pippo Calò didn't need me any more because he had used two Camorristi to do the murder," Di Carlo said.[7]

In addition, he said, had he killed Calvi, the murder would have been carried out in a far different fashion. "It was a sloppy job. If I had done it, I would never have left Calvi under a bridge." He would have preferred, he said, to use *lupara bianca*.[8]

He admitted, however, that he had no alibi for the time of the murder. His trip to Italy had been spent evading police.

Di Carlo's testimony was found to be credible, and the investigating magistrates turned their sights on Pippo Calò and Flavio Carboni, a Sardinian millionaire property developer, naming them as masterminds of the Calvi death. The actual strangulation, many believed, was done by Camorra member Vincenzo Casillo.

Casillo as the killer is a theory that gained credence, according to research the authors did for this book. In an interview in the fall of 1999, Camorra boss Oreste Pagano confirmed Casillo's role. Pagano, who met Casillo in Italy in 1982, said he discussed the Calvi murder with him: "He told me he did it, that he killed Roberto Calvi with two other Camorra members," Pagano said.[9]

Casillo was to die in a car explosion in 1983.

An inquiry into Calvi's death was later held in Milan; it too concluded that murder could not be ruled out. Another inquiry in a Milan civil court came back with a conclusive finding of murder.

In 1997, fifteen years after Calvi's death, prosecutors in Rome named four people Pagano alleged were involved in the death: Flavio Carboni, the Sardinian businessman; Pippo Calò, the Sicilian Mafia's financial wizard; Vincenzo Casillo, of the Camorra; and Francesco Di Carlo. The judge ordered Italian police to exhume the body. Calvi's son, Carlo, a banker

The Calvi case continues to spark investigations, rumors, and inquiries. In December 2000, reports circulated that three court-appointed scientists would deliver a report in Rome that would conclude Calvi was murdered. And the allegations of ties to the Vatican became even more solidified when Czech bishop, Pavel Hnilica, admitted he used the Vatican Bank's money to buy documents belonging to the late Calvi. (The documents later vanished.)

living in Montreal, attended the exhumation. Carlo Calvi said new evidence from Mafia informants had convinced him that his father did not commit suicide, but that he had been murdered because he had dangerous information about the financial activities of both the Vatican and the Mafia.

The finding of the Rome inquiry again did not rule out any possibility. Italian magistrates are continuing their probe.

The collapse of the Caruana-Cuntrera network in England began on December 2, 1984 when a British Customs drug dog "went positive" while sniffing a shipping container of furniture shipped from India to England.

Customs agents found 250 kilograms of high-grade Kashmir hashish cleverly concealed inside the furniture. The furniture was destined for Elongate Ltd., a firm used by the Caruana-Cuntrera and owned by Filippo Monteleone and Antonino Luciani. Customs agents repacked the hashish into the furniture and allowed it to proceed to Elongate's warehouse in London.

Surveillance was set up around the warehouse and cameras were installed inside. Police watched as Francesco Siracusa and Alberto Gualtieri—a resident of Montreal—used paint to black out the Indian markings on the crates of furniture and replace them with British ones.

When Siracusa and Gualtieri drove from the warehouse, police pulled their car over and arrested them. An envelope found in the car showed that Alfonso Caruana had paid the car's service bill.

A search of Siracusa's home found shipping documents falsely indicating that the furniture was of British origin and was to be transshipped to a Caruana front company in Quebec, Santa Rita Imports. The Royal Canadian Mounted Police were notified, and they responded that Santa Rita was a firm with confirmed Sicilian Mafia connections.

Backtracking the activities of Francesco Siracusa and his partner in Elongate Ltd., British authorities learned that the men, along with

Filippo Monteleone and Antonino Luciani, owners of Ital Provisions Ltd., had been bringing in drug shipments since at least late 1982, when Siracusa went to India to arrange a shipment of furniture from a firm in Kashmir, Shalimar Enterprises Ltd. The furniture shipment was transshipped successfully through the United Kingdom in May 1983 and cleared Canadian customs a month later. It was received by Santa Rita, in Montreal.

In October 1983, records showed that Siracusa again traveled to India. A second shipment was successfully made; it arrived in England in February 1984 and was subsequently received by Santa Rita in Montreal.

In April 1984, Siracusa again arranged a shipment of furniture; like the previous two loads, it too was transshipped through the United Kingdom to Santa Rita in Montreal.

Coincident with these shipments, banking records showed that several financial transactions were undertaken. The first shipment was paid for when Siracusa arranged to have Shalimar Enterprises' account at the National Punjab Bank, in Srinagar, India, credited with US$20,000; the second was paid for through a deposit of $25,000 into Elongate's Lloyds Bank account and a letter of credit for Shalimar. The third was paid for with a deposit to a bank in Bangkok, Thailand, this shipment having come from the Chiangmai Treasure Company in Thailand. And the fourth—the one seized after the British Customs' dog detected it—was paid for in a similar fashion. Authorities believe that some shipments were feelers to test the viability of the Asia-Indo network; others contained either heroin from Asia or hashish from India.

Profits from the drug sales flowed into Caruana bank accounts. In a single day, Alfonso and his brother Pasquale deposited a quarter of a million dollars.

By now, in addition to Elongate, police had uncovered the Sicilian Mafia's links to Ital Provisions, and shipments destined for that company were scrutinized. A test run was done by the Caruana-Cuntrera: a legitimate shipment of furniture containing no drugs was ordered from Chiangmai Treasure. It was inspected, found to be clean, and allowed to enter Britain, where Ital Provisions left it sitting unclaimed on the docks for months, until it was delivered to the residences of Alfonso Caruana and Francesco Di Carlo.

Another Ital Provisions shipment from Chiangmai Treasure was undertaken, this one with 36 kilograms of heroin hidden inside. When it arrived at Southampton on May 26, 1985, police set up a controlled delivery that would allow the drugs to reach Canada, where both ends of the network could be taken down. Working with intelligence from British Customs, the RCMP set up surveillance on a warehouse on Halpern Street leased by Thermo Import and Export Inc., a Montreal firm owned by Filippo Vaccarello. Suspected conspirators were kept under watch and their telephone calls were monitored.

When the shipment arrived in Montreal, it was cleared for entry into Canada. Wiretaps recorded Pasquale and Gerlando Caruana discussing the arrival of the shipment.

On June 21, 1985, police arrested Gerlando Caruana, Filippo Vaccarello, Luciano Zambito, and Lucio Beddia on heroin importation charges.

In London, police swooped down on Leo's Wine Bar and arrested Di Carlo, Monteleone, and two other members of the organization. All the suspects in Canada and Britain were convicted, except for Lucio Beddia, who was acquitted.

Di Carlo, sentenced to twenty-five years by a British court, and wanted on warrants in Italy, was interviewed in prison by Palermo deputy-police chief Antonino Cassarà. Three days after returning to Sicily, Cassarà himself became a victim of Toto Riina's Corleonesi clan.

The Caruanas had already felt the heat of the ongoing investigation and had made plans to leave the United Kingdom. Two days after the arrests in the British drug ring, Alfonso Caruana had transferred his bank accounts to financial institutions in Canada and the United States.

With his narcotics network exposed after almost ten years in operation, with his brother Gerhand and Francesco Di Carlo in custody and Scotland Yard and British Customs hunting him, Alfonso Caruana and his brother Pasquale moved their families to Montreal.

4

The Italian Connection: Giuseppe Bono + 151

In 1983, Giovanni Falcone, Leonardo Guarnotta, and Giuseppe Di Lello, the investigating magistrates of the Tribunal of Palermo, authorized the arrest of a staggering list of suspects, accusing them of Mafia association. A portion of the Palermo indictment dealt extensively with Alfonso Caruana and the key players of the Siculiana family, including his brothers, Gerlando and Pasquale. A five-page, closely written list read like a Who's Who of the Sicilian Mafia. The suspects in several international drug and other criminal organizations were listed, including those who would later be arrested in the Caruana-Cuntrera U.K. trafficking ring and those in the U.S. Pizza Connection.

The magistrates said the accused were also involved in crimes ranging from cigarette, weapons, and currency smuggling to drug trafficking.

The vast indictment laid out the activities of the Siculiana family; it took every previous investigation, listed every criminal activity, and named every family member to come to police attention.

"Giuseppe Bono + 151" was a formidable document: it was an indictment of the major Sicilian Mafia families, their worldwide drug and money-laundering network, and their increasing collaboration with the Neapolitan Camorra.

The indictment reads, "The investigation shows a huge and well-connected organization of major influence involved in many activities, particularly in the international narcotics trade in Europe and in North and South America."

Further investigations revealed the finances of the Siculiana family: millions of dollars of bank transfers into and out of accounts owned or controlled by the Caruana-Cuntrera.

One transfer showed Alfonso Caruana's account with the Discount Bank Overseas, of Lugano, Switzerland, transferring US$200,000 to a bank account in Cyprus that belonged to Emanuele Corito, "one of the largest traffickers in the Mediterranean and owner of the ship *Fidelio*, aboard which about 6.5 tonnes of hashish was recovered and sequestered in March 1986."[1]

Corito was also the business partner of Yasar Musullulu, the head of the Grey Wolves, a Turkish terrorist organization that in the 1980s attempted to assassinate Pope John Paul II.

An examination of two accounts controlled by Alfonso Caruana and Pasquale Cuntrera at the Swiss bank showed that more than US$10 million had been deposited and then moved from the account between October 2, 1979, and March 23, 1982. Many of the notations attached to the deposits showed that "Canadian Bank Checks" were used.

Project Pilgrim

For Sgt. Mark Bourque, "Project Pilgrim" was aptly named: like one seeking enlightenment, Bourque knew the path in front of him was long and might, ultimately, lead nowhere. While police forces—the FBI and DEA in the United States, law-enforcement officials from the United Kingdom, the RCMP drug squad, and anti-Mafia magistrates in Italy—were attempting to build drug cases against Alfonso Caruana and the Siculiana family, Bourque was taking a different approach.

Bourque, a veteran RCMP investigator, was based in Montreal, attached to the anti-drug profiteering section (ADP). The ADP's mandate was to track criminal money. In the early 1980s, a shift in law enforcement had begun to take shape: as well as following the narcotics trail, police began following the money trail. Assets that could be proven to have been purchased with criminal profits were liable for seizure by the government. After reviewing police and intelligence reports gathered from Italian, American, British, and Canadian law enforcement files, Bourque realized that the Siculiana family had made untold millions. He suspected that banks in Montreal were being used to launder the profits the Caruana-Cuntrera were earning through international drug operations.

"The anti-drug profiteering investigation began after RCMP drug officers seized fifty-three kilos of heroin in June 1985," Bourque recalled. "We'd arrested some of the Caruana-Cuntreras in Montreal, including Alfonso Caruana's brother, Gerlando."[2]

After the four men were arrested, ADP officers raided the suspects' homes, as well as the homes of Giuseppe Cuffaro and other Montreal-area residents with close ties to the Caruana-Cuntrera.

When Bourque arrived at Gerlando Caruana's home in Longueuil, a suburb of Montreal, he was amazed at the sheer luxury in which the trafficker lived, with expensive cars, jewelry, and furnishings. "It was," he recalls, "a million-dollar lifestyle."

But it was the documentation that showed him the true wealth behind the players in the heroin network. "Gerlando Caruana's personal papers revealed activity through a dozen of accounts in four different Montreal banks. And it was while tracing the accounts that we came across Alfonso Caruana."

Working from the paperwork for the investigation on Gerlando Caruana, the RCMP visited the banks. With René Gagnière of Revenue Canada, and armed with a taxation warrant, similar to a criminal code search warrant, Bourque began unraveling the trail of the Siciliana family's finances.

"At one branch of the City & District Savings Bank, a teller mentioned there was similar activity in the account of Gerlando Caruana's brother, Alfonso. The account showed several millions of dollars in U.S. currency being deposited, then sent on to Swiss bank accounts. These deposits occurred on a regular basis, often three or five times in a single week."

And, surprisingly, the bank records showed that the Caruana-Cuntrera organization had "tested" the bank for its viability as a laundering vehicle as early as 1978—the year Paolo Violi was assassinated and the Caruana-Cuntrera family's heroin pipeline was running at full capacity. By 1981, as the American Pizza Connection case was producing millions of dollars in heroin profits, the records at City & District Savings Bank indicated that US$15 million had been laundered through the bank branch.

For the bank, it was easy money. The Caruana-Cuntrera would deposit U.S. cash into their Canadian fund accounts, then request the purchase of U.S. bank drafts, and the bank would convert it back to U.S. funds. The bank made a percentage on each transaction: a two percent fee for converting the money from U.S. to Canadian funds, and a two percent fee for converting it from Canadian to U.S. bank drafts. On occasions when counterfeit American bills were discovered in deposits made by Alfonso Caruana, a debit would be deducted from Giuseppe Cuffaro's account, not Caruana's.

"We suspect the City & District Savings Bank of clearing up to a half-million dollars in fees for helping the Mafia launder this money," Bourque said, calling the bank's activities "willful blindness."

That the Montreal banks were so easy manipulated could be attributed to Giuseppe Cuffaro, who seemed to be a master at co-opting people. Besides, at that time in Canada it was harder to import cheese under government regulations than it was to bring a suitcase of cash into the country.

The Caruana-Cuntrera's contact at the bank was manager Aldo Tucci, who, according to police files, had been "contaminated in 1978" by Giuseppe Cuffaro. This was one of the recurring themes that arose during the Project Pilgrim investigation: each contaminated bank employee was of Sicilian or Italian origin. They were "tested" for their discretion and efficiency to the organization, and once they were approved, their bank branches were used to launder an escalating amount of money, usually for less than a year, until senior management became uncomfortable with the situation.

Bourque estimated that between 1978 and 1981 Tucci assisted the Caruana-Cuntrera in the laundering of us$15 million. "Tucci would even threaten employees if any one would hint at or reveal [who made] the incredible deposits," Bourque said, adding that certain tellers would be told to arrive early for work to count the money as it was delivered.

In addition to the suspicious nature of the deposits and the labor-intensive job of counting them, something else about the money sparked complaints from bank staff. Said cashier Denise Maille, "The thing that intrigued me was the smell," which she described as "musty."[3]

Men who had become familiar to the staff arrived regularly and would always proceed directly to Aldo Tucci's office. For security reasons, the money was counted in the bank's kitchen. When the count was completed—it took several hours because almost all the bills were of denominations less than $20—an armored truck would be summoned to pick up the deposit.

The increasing flood of cash into Caruana accounts caused suspicion at the bank. Management ordered an internal audit, and a security officer met with Alfonso Caruana and Giuseppe Cuffaro. The money, Caruana explained, came from casinos and oil refineries managed by another company of their group, based in Caracas. "These are normal transfers, taking place weekly," he said.

The company was Aceros Prensados s a. Investigators found out little about the company's operations, but they did determine that it was managed by Paolo Cuntrera.

Later, Bourque discovered that Venezuela didn't permit casinos and that oil companies were owned by the government.

To Bourque, this made it all the more obvious that the banks were simply turning a blind eye: "It was so obvious: why would some business operating in South America not transfer their money directly to Switzerland? Why go to all the trouble and divert it to Canada first? An overview of the laundering process observed in Montreal clearly indicates that all deposits made by this organization were the 'in-and-out' type. When large and bulky cash amounts, always in U.S. currency, would be deposited and either immediately or shortly thereafter withdrawn in draft form—which is less conspicuous and much more manageable—the willful blindness by the Canadian banks is crystal clear."

Meanwhile, the situation at the bank was so blatant that Alfonso Caruana was arriving in a pickup truck filled with bags of cash and dragging them into the bank. One day the cash deposit was more than $1 million. A special account—"Alfonso Caruana International Department"—was set up.

In the fall of 1981, the stench of the dealings at Tucci's branch got to be too much. The president of the City & District Savings Bank, Raymond Garneau, a former Quebec minister of finance, notified the branch that it was forbidden to do business with the clients who were making the huge, suspicious transactions. The accounts of the Siculiana members were closed and Tucci was relocated to another branch. By then, his ties to the Caruana-Cuntrera were many: he'd opened six companies for them, was socializing with them, and might have appeared, to any reasonable observer, to be a business partner in the organization.

At the new branch Tucci continued to deal with the Siciliana family on a regular basis. He was asked in 1984 to resign. Tucci sold his $100,000 home and built himself one worth $250,000; he then bought a new Corvette.

The breakdown of the final tally of money laundered by the Caruana-Cuntrera organization through City & District Savings Bank between October 1978 and December 1983 showed an ongoing criminal syndicate operating at full power: Alfonso Caruana had made sixty separate drafts totaling US$9,019,440 in a six-month period in 1981; and Paolo, Liborio, Gaspare, and Giuseppe Cuntrera had made five drafts totaling almost $2 million. The remainder were smaller deposits ranging from $10,000 to $885,000.

So much drug money, in U.S. currency, had flowed into the bank that it became part of the banking process itself. "The deposits of U.S. cash were so significant that they allowed the Dollard-des-Ormeaux branch of the City & District Savings Bank to replace the Bank of Canada in satisfying the needs for U.S. currency of all other eighty-five branches of the same bank in the Montreal areas," Bourque said, estimating the banking requirement for the branches at $1 million a week.

With the Montreal end of the money trail well under investigation, Bourque traveled to Rome, where he met with senior Italian organized crime investigators. Here, Bourque was in for a surprise. The Italians had uncovered two other Canadian banks—the National Bank and the Hellenic Canadian Trust—through which drug money had flowed.

The RCMP's anti-drug profiteering section found that US$3.5 million went through the Hellenic Canadian Trust branch on Park Avenue in Montreal in the second half of 1981; at the National Bank branch on St. Michel Boulevard in Montreal the RCMP discovered that between November 1981, when the bank was "tested" with small deposits, and October 1982 US$14 million had been laundered. In one case, $3.2 million had gone through in one five-week period.

At the Hellenic Canadian Trust, where Giuseppe Cuffaro maintained a U.S. dollar account, he wasn't plagued by the two-percent-in and two-percent-out conversion fee paid by Alfonso Caruana. Instead, the bank profited through the daily interest rate on the funds until the issued draft was presented to a Swiss bank. This could often take up to a month, allowing the bank to make an interest rate of 6 to 7 percent. Between May and November 1981, Giuseppe Cuffaro laundered US$3.4 million through the branch.

At the National Bank branch, Bourque found that Giuseppe Cuffaro's campaign of "contaminating" bank staff had begun in 1979. Using a "tame" manager, Cuffaro would deposit bags of cash into the accounts, often bringing Pasquale Caruana along to do the heavy lifting. Bank staff told Bourque that when tellers asked Cuffaro where the endless bundles of U.S. currency came from, he would stare at them through his sunglasses and smile. And when complaints were made that the counting of the money was too time-consuming, Cuffaro cheerfully agreed to bring it in already counted out in $5,000 bundles. At the National Bank, Bourque found forty-six wire transfers worth US$12,990,106 had been purchased by Cuffaro.

At yet another financial institution, Forexco Exchange House Ltd., on St. Jacques Street in Montreal, ADP investigators found a deposit of US$1.2 million, believed to be the proceeds from a hashish shipment.

"We estimated that between 1978 and 1982, plus a five-week period in 1984, the Caruana-Cuntrera organization laundered in excess of US$34 million. We don't know exactly what was laundered in 1983," Bourque said.

Beneficiaries of the deposits included Alfonso Caruana—whose Swiss account received a total of US$6,167,200 from the National Bank alone—Pasquale Cuntrera, Giuseppe Cuffaro, and Gerlando Caruana. In addition to several banks in Switzerland, they had accounts in Venezuela, Aruba, and the United Kingdom that swelled with drug profits. According to Bourque, the Caruana-Cuntrera, between 1978 and 1985, trafficked 700 kilograms of heroin, and between 1984 and 1987, 70 tons of hashish.

Giuseppe Cuffaro had long been of particular importance within the Caruana-Cuntrera organization, especially in its formative years in Montreal in the late 1960s and 1970s. Born in 1932 in Montallegro, in Agrigento, western Sicily, Cuffaro came to Canada on August 10, 1953, and was well established during the years the Bonanno family was gaining its foothold in Quebec.

Throughout the history of the Siculiana family, Cuffaro's presence is felt every step of the way. When the earliest members of the Caruana-Cuntrera arrived in Canada, Cuffaro was already active in the narcotics business as part of the increasingly rebellious Sicilian faction led by Nicolò Rizzuto that was struggling to break away from the suffocating hold of Vincenzo Cotroni and Paolo Violi. When Sicilian Mafia boss Tommaso Buscetta came to Montreal in the late 1960s, he met regularly with Cuffaro. Other high-profile heroin traffickers were often seen in meetings with Cuffaro, including Giuseppe Bono, who later organized the Pizza Connection. Cuffaro was present in Rome on February 23, 1973, when Alfonso Caruana met with Giuseppe Settecasi, the boss of Agrigento, at which time the Paolo Violi problem was discussed and plans were made to ship tons of heroin to the United States through Canada.

In Canada, a taxation review of Cuffaro's activities between 1980 and 1985 revealed the money-laundering circuit—and Cuffaro's facility as an international criminal—through the recorded use of his American Express Card.

A sample from the review:

> January 20–23, 1981: Montreal-Zurich-Caracas-Miami-Aruba-Caracas-Montreal;
> April 13, 1981: Montreal-Zurich-Caracas-Miami-Montreal-Aruba-Caracas;
> April 18–20, 1981: Montreal-Zurich-Lugano-Caracas; and Montreal-Zurich-Caracas-Zurich-Montreal; and Rome-Bologna-Rome-Palermo-Rome;
> September 22, 1981: Montreal-Nassau-Montreal;

December 2, 1981: Montreal-Zurich;
April 6–8, 1982: Montreal-Miami-Caracas-Miami-Montreal;
April 1982: Montreal-Rome-Bologna-Rome-Montreal, and Montreal-Zurich-London-Nassau-Miami-Montreal;
October 1–November 21, 1982: Montreal-Hollywood, Florida-New Delhi, India;
November 25, 1982: Nassau;
December 1, 1982: New York.

In 1983, Cuffaro and Alfonso Caruana spent the month of October in Thailand where Caruana was exploring alternate sources of heroin and connecting with Somchai Liangsiriprasert, one of the country's most prolific heroin traffickers, based in Thailand's heroin capital, Chiang Mai. After returning to Canada, Cuffaro made the rounds in Nassau, Atlanta, Montreal, London, Barbados, and Toronto. In the same year, Cuffaro continued to travel the circuit through Switzerland, Italy, New York, and the Caribbean.

The following year was also a high-miler for Cuffaro, with twelve trips on his money-laundering circuit, to Rio de Janeiro, Milan, Bologna, Geneva, Singapore, and Bangkok. Investigators were able to round out much of the scope of the Caruana-Cuntrera's activities simply by following the dates and travels of Giuseppe Cuffaro.

That Cuffaro's wealth equaled that of any of the Caruana-Cuntrera is apparent in an FBI report showing him with homes in Montreal, Switzerland, London, and Caracas. In 1974, after his wife passed away, Cuffaro spent $75,000 on her mausoleum.

And when Mark Bourque followed the Caruana-Cuntrera's paper trail through the Montreal banking system, he found that more money had been laundered directly by Cuffaro than by any of the other Siciliana family members—almost double the nearly US$10 million deposited by Alfonso Caruana.

According to the Bundeskriminalamt (BKA), Germany's federal criminal police, Giuseppe Cuffaro belonged to "a group that had organized, in the past few years, the shipment of 800 kilos of heroin and 75 tons of hashish from India and Thailand to Canada, going through Sicily, Switzerland, and Great Britain." Also, according to the BKA, Cuffaro, along with Alfonso Caruana and his brother Pasquale, "intended to settle in Germany in order to manage drug traffic coming from Southeast Asia and subsequently to launder the revenues invested in legal economic activities."[4]

The Caruanas and Cuntreras could avail themselves in Germany of a solid network of accomplices, formed by Italian store owners. Most of them were Siculiana-born men of honor, with reputations as honest businessmen and owners of pizzerias. German documents showed that Cuffaro stayed in the country from September 1987 to November 1988: he left only to make visits to Canada, Thailand, and Venezuela. Cuffaro stayed at the best hotels in Baden-Baden, Frankfurt, and Wiesbaden. Using rental cars, he traveled more than 33,000 kilometers in 145 days; when he wasn't traveling he was ensconced in a hotel room, making hundreds of phone calls around the world.

In retrospect, considering the timing, authorities believe that he and Pasquale Caruana were creating a European version of the Pizza Connection.

Montreal, Quebec

Back in Montreal, with his London home in the hands of a realtor, Alfonso Caruana bought a house in Laval, Quebec, and opened Toscana Pizzeria on Rue Jean Talon in St. Leonard. He was often seen tossing pizzas while his wife, Giuseppina, worked the cash register. Even with his brother, Gerlando, in custody and his U.K. operation in tatters, he seemed to have no fear of being arrested himself.

In May 1986, RCMP Sergeant Mark Bourque discovered that most of the targets of his ongoing probe were now banking at the Caisse Populaire St-Damase branch on Villeray Street in Montreal. Through the financial institution's security department, Bourque was told that an Alfonso Caruana, accompanied by his uncle, Salvatore Vella, had presented and tried to cash a personal check drawn on a London branch of the Lloyd's Bank for US$827,962.83, the proceeds from the sale of his mansion in London, England. The bank's clearing protocol gave police a two-week window of opportunity to apply to seize it against unpaid taxes on the millions passing through Caruana's bank accounts.

When the check cleared and became redeemable, Bourque and Revenue Canada investigator René Gagnière showed up at the Caisse Populaire with a Revenue Canada jeopardy assessment in hand. The doors opened at 10:00 a.m., and Bourque and Gagnière were waiting.

"We presented ourselves to the branch manager, Charlie Piazza," Bourque recalls. "We gave him the jeopardy assessment and requested payment of the check in the name of Alfonso Caruana."

Piazza, Bourque said, laughed and said that Alfonso Caruana's account contained only $2,000.

"Really?" Bourque asked. Then he proceeded to explain in fine detail the check's travels back to the bank. Bourque recalled that Piazza became angry and demanded to know how he had gained access to restricted information. Bourque seized the check, adding: "Oh, and we'll take that two thousand, too."

On June 13, 1986, Alfonso Caruana appeared before the Commissioner of Oaths for the City and District of Montreal and swore and signed an affidavit under oath. The government was after taxes it maintained he owed, based on the tens of millions of dollars that had made its way through his bank accounts in Montreal and then left almost immediately for destinations offshore. In the affidavit, Alfonso Caruana swore:

> In 1973 I became involved in a business venture in Venezuela, which required me to reside in Venezuela for approximately six (6) months of every year from 1973 to 1980;
>
> On November 12, 1980, I was granted the status of resident of Venezuela. By that time I was spending most of my time in Venezuela;
>
> My wife and children remained in Canada until January-February 1982, at which time they became residents of England, after spending a few months in Switzerland;

In 1982 my wife acquired a mansion in England where my children and wife have resided until late 1985;

Between 1980 and late 1985 I was residing in Venezuela where I spent approximately eight (8) months of every year;

In October 1985, I decided to come back, with my wife and children, and establish, in Montreal, my principal residence and domicile;

For this purpose, a business enterprise was acquired by my wife in Montreal in April 1986;

In May 1986, my wife acquired, in Laval, a house to serve as the family residence;

The mansion owned by my spouse in England was sold on April 30, 1986 for 420,000 pounds sterling;

A banker's draft representing the sale price of the said property was deposited in early May 1986 in the Caisse Populaire de St-Damase;

It is only on or about May 20, 1986 that the bank's' draft was honored, and that funds were deposited in my account at the Caisse Populaire St-Damase;

On May 20, 1986, the Minister of National Revenue seized, in the hands of the Caisse Populaire St-Damase, an amount of $827,962.83 on the basis of an assessment dated May 20, 1986, in regards to my 1981 taxation year.

The RCMP countered that Alfonso Caruana had indeed lived in Montreal in 1981 and had laundered more than US$9 million during that same year. They noted that he was wanted by Italian authorities on drug-trafficking charges.

When Caruana was invited to a meeting to discuss the situation, he withdrew his appeal and told Revenue Canada to keep the money. He sold his properties and moved his family to Caracas, along with Salvatore Vella, Alfonso Caruana's uncle.

It is hardly a coincidence that after Mark Bourque took Alfonso Caruana's check from the Caisse Populaire, Revenue Canada began investigating Giuseppe Cuffaro for unpaid taxes.

By the time Revenue Canada affidavits were filed in court in 1988,

Cuffaro's entire life had changed. He and Pasquale Cuntrera, while traveling in Germany, were kept under tight police surveillance, notably when they checked into the Frankfurter Intercontinental Hotel and met with several Siculiana family members, as well as international arms dealers. On September 9, 1988, when the two men attempted to cross the Germany-Switzerland border at Weil Am Rhein, German authorities arrested them on warrants from the Italian government.

In October 1988, while in custody in Italy, Giuseppe Cuffaro was assessed for $6.2 million in unpaid taxes. Revenue Canada was able to prove that he had received $8.27 million between January 1, 1979, and December 31, 1985. The government seized several of his Quebec properties. Mark Bourque's well-documented reports detailed Cuffaro's activities in the Caruana-Cuntrera organization, and added four volumes of financial and real estate documentation to the already huge Caruana-Cuntrera file.

Somehow, Cuffaro was "accidentally" released from custody. He remained in Germany until his arrest in Baden-Baden two months later. Both Cuffaro and Pasquale Caruana were extradited to Italy. On May 31, 1991, they were sentenced by the Palermo Tribunal on Mafia-association and drug-trafficking offenses. Pasquale Caruana got fifteen years; Cuffaro was sentenced to nineteen and a half years. On appeal, the judge recognized only the drug-trafficking allegations and reduced their sentences to eleven years for Caruana and eleven years, eight months, for Cuffaro. Each was fined $100,000.

Windsor, Ontario

As Mark Bourque was attempting to move a major investigation on the Caruana-Cuntrera, Alfonso Caruana was continuing to bring heroin shipments into Canada. The reason for the trips to Thailand by Caruana and Giuseppe Cuffaro in 1983 and 1984 became apparent in 1988 when a crew of the Siculiana family's drug-trafficking network was dismantled in Windsor, Ontario, a city located across the U.S. border from Detroit.

In the 1980s, the Montreal–New York connection—and the Caruana-Cuntrera players running it—fell under increased scrutiny. The seizure in June 1985 of 58 kilograms of hashish, and another seizure a month later of 11 kilograms of cocaine, was putting pressure on the group to find other border points to breach.

Toronto, a ninety-minute drive from Niagara Falls and the bridge to the United States, was already being utilized by several crime groups, some of them Sicilians being directly supplied with heroin by the Caruana-Cuntrera out of Montreal. In fact, members of the Nicola Genua crime cell, part of a complex network of Sicilian crime groups in Toronto, were being investigated for heroin trafficking by the RCMP. Links between that early case and the eventual downfall of Alfonso Caruana would later emerge.

Other pipelines were operated by members of Toronto's powerful and secretive Calabrian Mafia cells. Southbound heroin out of Toronto was delivered to members of the Buffalo La Cosa Nostra family, or transited to New York City for the Five Families there.

Low-profile on the map of international drug trafficking, Windsor is nevertheless a city with a long history of organized crime activity dating back to Prohibition days, when alcohol was smuggled to the early Detroit mafia. Aside from location—just minutes from Detroit—the border route into the United States is choked with traffic as tens of thousands of vehicles cross each day. It was ideal for the Caruana-Cuntrera.

There was a strong criminal infrastructure in Windsor, made up of branches of the Detroit La Cosa Nostra families. The Calabrian Mafia had a presence in the city—notably from the Commisso crime family of Toronto—but their power, as in most Canadian cities with "twin" American La Cosa Nostra families just minutes away, was minimal. As a secret police report confirmed, "The Detroit La Cosa Nostra activities in Ontario is largely restricted to the Windsor area."[5]

Further, a review by intelligence analysts in Canada and the United States determined that the Sicilian Mafia faction operating in Windsor—consisting of perhaps fewer than six individuals—was part of a larger, international network run by Gaetano Badalamenti, the former Mafia boss of Cinisi who was jailed in the Pizza Connection investigation. Badalamenti had strong connections with Detroit and Windsor Sicilians, having once operated a pizzeria on the American side.

It wasn't just the Sicilian Mafia who were interested in Windsor's strategic location. In March 1982, several strategy meetings were held at Liberty Township, Ohio, between U.S. La Cosa Nostra members and members of the Cotroni family of Montreal to arrange heroin shipments out of Canada through Windsor.[6]

And it wasn't just as an outlet for heroin that Windsor drew the attention of Canadian federal authorities. A secret RCMP document—file #88–1428, dated November 25, 1988—clearly outlined the strategic geographical position that Windsor held as a link between Canada and the United States, noting that Windsor-Detroit was "the perfect area to join hands with American agencies in combating the vast illegal use, by both Americans and Canadians, of the Canadian financial system to launder and secret illegal funds."

The document—one of several in a file marked "Project Mercury" that passed that year among the RCMP London subdivision, the RCMP Windsor detachment, RCMP "O" division in Toronto, headquarters in Ottawa, and the provincial attorney general's office—called for a joint investigation with U.S. law enforcement into money laundering.

"Previous major cases have already shown that Windsor is the main Canada/U.S. border point through which much of the drugs entering, and leaving, Canada are funneled," the report said. "This is also felt to be the case for money laundering and other major criminal activity."

It added: "Based on present facts and intelligence solely within Windsor and Detroit, we are aware of tens of millions of dollars in illegal funds secreted in or moving through Canadian banks in Windsor."

Several currency exchanges are named in the file as being used by "major subject files" on both sides of the border to launder criminal profits. Money used in a multi-million-dollar stock fraud, involving victims in both the United States and Canada, was laundered through Windsor-Detroit. "There are numerous other investigations where millions of U.S. dollars, which were the proceeds of crime, have been and still are being laundered through Windsor alone."

In the Windsor heroin case—dubbed "Jade Rock"—the "sleeper" trend of the Sicilian Mafia was apparent. As with the Pizza Connection, the suspects had been in place for some time but hadn't attracted police attention.

"The Windsor subjects were unknown to the law enforcement communities before their arrests," a secret RCMP briefing document, prepared after the Jade Rock case, noted. "[But] enquiries conducted after the arrests showed direct family blood relationships to several members of the Montreal Sicilian (Siculiana/Caruana-Cuntrera) Mafia . . . particularly Giuseppe Cuffaro."

When the Jade Rock case began breaking in May 1988, the Caruana-Cuntrera's Thailand-Montreal-Windsor-Detroit heroin conspiracy had already been operating for at least two years. As much as US$300 million in heroin had passed through the pipeline, most of it dumped into the United States for distribution in Michigan, the Midwest, and along the eastern seaboard. The recipients were Sicilian Mafia members, many of them part of the Pizza Connection case in New York and New Jersey. Although the main players of the Pizza Connection were before the courts, they, and several dozen unindicted co-conspirators, were maintaining their criminal operations, barely slowed down by the FBI's relentless assault.

Jade Rock began innocently enough in 1988 when Canada Customs officials tried to track down a shipper who'd failed to pay excise on two shipments of jade rocks that had been sent to Canada from Thailand the previous summer. An investigation was sparked when details of the case were found to fit a profile used by customs agents to detect narcotics shipments: the shipping documents had a false name and address on them; the shipment came from a major heroin-producing region, it hadn't been insured, and shipping charges were prepaid. A notation said that a person named "Beniamino," in Montreal, was to be notified when the jade rocks arrived there. The telephone number belonged to an east Montreal espresso bar, the Bar Sportif de Montreal. Two previous shipments in 1987, customs documents showed, had also been sent to the espresso bar.

The information on the shipment was loaded into the Canada Customs database—one accessible by U.S. Customs authorities—and when another shipment of jade rocks arrived in Seattle in May 1988 en route to Vancouver, British Columbia, American officials notified Canada Customs. The cargo of five crates was opened and the jade rocks were X-rayed, revealing the heroin inside, wrapped in paper. Each rock had been cut apart and then glued back together by the traffickers. In total, 20.5 kilograms of heroin was found.

A controlled delivery was set up. Most of the heroin was replaced with a white powder, the rocks were repacked, a listening device was installed in one crate, and the shipment was allowed to continue on to Montreal by cargo plane. RCMP teams set up surveillance at a Dorval customs warehouse for three weeks, watching the shipment.

Police wiretaps on the Bar Sportif—then owned by Emanuele Guaragna, a business partner of Giuseppe Cuffaro's, and father of Joseph Guaragna, a key player in the jade rock operation who was later arrested—recorded an incoming telephone call saying that "Mr. Beniamino's shipment has arrived." The caller was told that the message would be passed on.

Police surveillance teams followed as Thai national Suchart Areephan picked up the cargo and delivered it to two men, Antonino Zambito and Joseph Guaragna, at a motel. Zambito and Guaragna transferred the jade rocks into a van and began a 900-kilometer trip out of Quebec and across southern Ontario.

The shipment was taken to a small farm near Windsor, where it was stored in a garage. On June 6, when the hidden listening picked up the sounds of crates being ripped open, police drove a cruiser through the garage's aluminum door and, armed with shotguns, arrested Joseph Guaragna, Antonino Zambito, both Montreal residents, and the farm's owner, John Laudicina.

In July, Suchart Areephan, who had fled back to Thailand, arrived at Los Angeles to arrange another drug shipment. He was then arrested and extradited to Canada.

In November, the RCMP arrested Joseph Dennis Cuffaro, Giuseppe Cuffaro's son, outside a Montreal shop. Police described him as the "mastermind" of the drug conspiracy.

That a major heroin smuggling organization had been operating in Windsor—one tied to the Caruana-Cuntrera—was now evident. The accused had links to the Siculiana family: Joseph Dennis Cuffaro via Giuseppe Cuffaro; Joseph Guaragna via his father, Emanuele; John Laudicina was Giuseppe Cuffaro's brother-in-law; Zambito was wanted by Italian authorities on Mafia-association charges; and Suchart Areephan was a member of the Thailand-based Somchai narcotics organization.

A Chevrolet Caprice seized at the farm had been modified with hollow bumpers, and police suspected that it had been used to carry massive loads of heroin into the United States. A backhoe was brought in, and more than two dozen buried broken jade rocks were found, indicating previous successful drug shipments. Forensic examination on the broken rocks and the Chevrolet's bumpers revealed traces of heroin. A search of license plates documented by U.S. Customs on cars entering the United States showed that the Chevrolet had crossed into Detroit seven times in the second half of 1987.

In November 1990, after abruptly changing their "not guilty" pleas, Joseph Guaragna, Antonio Zambito, and John Laudicina were sentenced to eighteen years in prison; Suchart Areephan received fifteen years; and Joseph Dennis Cuffaro was freed after a series of wiretaps were ruled inadmissible.

5

Putting the Windsor–Detroit pipeline out of business was a serious, but not fatal, blow to the plans of the agile-minded Alfonso Caruana.

Earlier, the Pizza Connection had been successfully severed by the F B I and Italian law enforcement, but the demand for heroin for the Sicilian Mafia families on the U.S. eastern seaboard and in the Midwest continued unabated.

The United Kingdom–Montreal pipeline had been dismantled, but there, too, the appetite for cocaine and heroin was stable, and the market in the rest of Europe was increasing.

With a single-mindedness, Alfonso Caruana continued to find new routes, develop new markets, and activate "sleeper" Sicilian Mafia cells. Money continued to flow into the coffers of the Siculiana family's accounts in Switzerland and offshore havens.

Having always hovered near the top of the Caruana-Cuntrera power structure, Alfonso Caruana appeared to have reached the pinnacle at last. The Canadian investigations, so far, hadn't effectively touched him. He'd lost more than US$800,000 to Revenue Canada as a consequence of Mark Bourque's extensive—perhaps even obsessive—dossier, but in a world where literally tons of heroin was being traded, $800,000 was written off as the cost of doing business, a cheap re-soling of an expensive pair of boots.

At the end of the 1990s, however, there was a new spirit of cooperation among law-enforcement agencies, often overpowering the traditional rivalries and distrust that had allowed the Caruana-Cuntrera to develop into an unparalleled international criminal organization. The Italian government was going after the Siculiana family with a renewed vengeance, collecting evidence from cases in the United States, Canada, South America, and Europe.

In Canada, as a direct result of the transparent activities of banks and Mafiosi in Montreal, increasingly effective measures were being taken to deal with the proceeds of crime and with money laundering. Even the banks were trying to present a clean face: one Quebec financial institution fired two officials for an outrageous case of money laundering in which a gas station manager had brought briefcases and hockey bags stuffed with cash to the branch and had it quietly and quickly laundered.

The major Siculiana family players of the 1970s and 1980s were disappearing from the scene. In 1990, Giuseppe Cuffaro and Pasquale Caruana were in Italian police custody, on their way to Palermo's Ucciardone prison, by then stuffed with Sicilian Mafiosi awaiting trial, many of them for drug and Mafia-association offenses related to the Caruana-Cuntrera network.

Gerlando Caruana, once the most powerful of the three Caruana brothers, was in a Quebec prison serving a sentence of twenty years for heroin importation.

In December 1990, a month after some of the main players in the Jade Rock case had been given lengthy prison terms, Italian investigating magistrate Gioacchino Natoli arrived in Canada from Palermo. Natoli held three days of hearings. The financial activities of four key members of Caruana's family were of specific interest to him: Giuseppe Cuffaro and Pasquale Caruana, and Gerlando Caruana and Luciano Zambito.

Aldo Tucci appeared before Natoli to explain his activities in the dirty 1980s, when Alfonso Caruana was appearing at his bank branches with bags stuffed full of small-denomination American currency. Claiming he was just following orders, Tucci testified that officials at his bank encouraged him to keep the business of the mysterious Sicilians who were flooding the bank's vaults with U.S. money: "They [the bank] were making a fortune." The chief executive officer of the bank, Raymond Garneau, Tucci said, had authorized the continued acceptance of the transactions. But, he admitted, he had misplaced the letter of authorization that he claimed Garneau gave him.

Tucci's strategy was to blame the bank—a posture not very different from the findings of Mark Bourque in two detailed reports he'd sent his superiors, or the comments of a police investigator who asked not to be named: "I don't know how to define Mr. Garneau's conduct in those circumstances," he said. "The money of the Mafia came in handy for the banks, and everybody closed their eyes. Even in front of the evidence."

Tucci said he once received a telephone call from the bank's foreign-exchange section, which was lacking in U.S. currency. They asked him if he could provide enough to cover the shortage. And when he was transferred to another branch, his Siciliana family accounts went with him because his superiors at the bank, he said, "wanted it that way."

Bank staff appeared at the hearings and named the money men as Pasquale Caruana, Gerlando Caruana, Giuseppe Cuffaro, and, they said, on at least one occasion, Joseph Dennis Cuffaro. A bank employee identified another man as Luciano Zambito.

An assistant accountant at the bank, Danielle Lavigne, described the financial activities going on as "shady." "We didn't feel right about this," she said.

Natoli found that US$40 million in criminal profits had been laundered through the Montreal banks between 1978 and 1983. Much of the money had then ended up in Swiss accounts, which were closed to Italian investigators.

Raymond Garneau was interviewed by the authors in February 2001. He said his recollection of the money laundering was hazy, but recalled he had received a legal opinion from the bank's lawyers advising him he could be sued if he refused service to the Caruanas and Cuntreras. "There was no [money laundering] law at the time," he said. "I couldn't even ask them where the money came from. Today, with the legislation in place, it would have been handled differently." Garneau said he "either tripled or quadrupled" the service charges on the suspicious deposits, and that finally drove the Caruanas and Cuntreras from the bank. He said Aldo Tucci was let go from the bank, not for his financial dealings, but because of unrelated information uncovered by private investigators hired by City & District Savings Bank. Tucci was never charged.

For Mark Bourque, there was satisfaction in seeing his meticulous intelligence report put to good use, even if it was in Italy and not at home, where the primary suspects came and went as they liked.

For all his efforts to build a solid case around Alfonso Caruana and the other key players of the Siciliana family, Bourque's investigation came to nought in Canada. The case, he was told, was too complex; no jury would be able to follow the money trails, the numerous characters, and the constant traveling of the conspirators. The complexities of international drug trafficking and money laundering, too, would be lost on a jury. And the cost would be huge: millions of dollars just to bring witnesses together at the same place and time—Bourque had traveled to nine countries and interviewed three hundred witnesses. His massive report ran to 3,600 pages, and he knew there was still more to find out.

Behind the scenes, the Canadian banking system wasn't happy with Bourque and the government didn't back his efforts. After the Pilgrim operation, he was effectively sidelined, assigned to the RCMP protection services for visiting dignitaries.

Alfonso Caruana would continue to pile up tens of millions of dollars in profits, using Venezuela as his base of operations and flooding North America and Europe with tons of cocaine.

Raymond Garneau, the former chief executive officer of the Montreal City & District Savings Bank, entered federal politics as a member of Parliament. He was later appointed to the board of directors of the Bank of Canada.

But in Italy it was a different story. Having worked for the first time with American authorities during the Pizza Connection case, Italian magistrates welcomed the depth of intelligence and evidence Mark Bourque had to offer. Bourque's work would lay the foundation for one of Italy's most powerful strikes against the Sicilian Mafia.

Venezuela

Venezuela is not only a beautiful and expansive country with a wealth of natural resources, it is also a place tailor-made for criminals on the run.

Though far from Europe, Venezuela possesses a cosmopolitan character that rivals Rome, Palermo, and even, to some, the most worldly of cities, Buenos Aires. In the 1970s, Venezuela was home to a large Italian population, making anonymity easy; financial controls were nonexistent, permitting the easy laundering of criminal profits through investment in a booming economy flush with natural resources; and citizenships and new identities could be easily purchased. As naturalized citizens, the fugitive Mafiosi couldn't be extradited. Some shed everything when they arrived—their names, their family histories, and in some cases even their faces, undergoing expensive plastic surgery.

Venezuela was also a thoroughly corrupt country, where public management was traditionally entrusted to mediocre and greedy politicians. Former dictator Marcos Perez Jimenez, who would be remembered "as a curse from God," had been deposed in 1958 by a military coup. And President Carlos Andres Perez, who was first elected in 1973, would later be deposed as well, allegedly for pocketing US$17 million in secret funds.

Venezuela also has what modern realtors refer to as "location": hundreds of miles of unpatrollable coastline on the Caribbean; the financial haven of Aruba nearby; and easy access to the cocaine capital of the world, Colombia. For criminal organizations seeking a hub for the cocaine trade between South America and both the North American and European markets, Venezuela was ideal.

The Cuntrera side of the Siculiana family, led by brothers Pasquale, Paolo, and Gaspare, had been in Venezuela since 1963, having first touched down in Brazil. They quickly became central figures in the Sicilian Mafia's "gateway from the South" as they set about forming legal and illegal enterprises, opening dozens of companies, and corrupting powerful figures in both government and industry.

In the late 1960s, Pasquale Cuntrera was traveling back and forth between Caracas and Montreal, where the early alliances of the Siculiana family had been formed and a war for the city was being fought. By 1974, the Siculiana family had a solid financial base of both legal and illegal operations fully underway in Venezuela. With the Caruana brothers, and his own brothers, Paolo and Gaspare, Pasquale Cuntrera set up a wickerwork of companies that facilitated money-laundering services for both their own criminal operations and other expatriate Sicilian groups. The Siculiana family concentrated their legitimate

According to the U.S. Justice Department, "the Cuntrera brothers, Pasquale, Paolo, Gaspare and Liborio, moved from Montreal to Caracas. . . .

"The most active members on the Cuntrera side are three brothers, Pasquale, Gaspare and Paolo, as well as Paolo's son-in-law Antonino Mongiovì."

Antonino Mongiovì was rated as the leading drug trafficker in Miami, Florida, according to the U.S. Drug Enforcement Administration.

investments in "real estate, construction, cattle raising, meat packing, agro-industry, furniture, interior decorating, travel agencies, oil, casinos, water, gas, car concessions, a shirt factory, a bedspread factory, and a sizeable fleet of ships," according to an American intelligence review.

Intelligence officials believe several dozen companies were privately controlled by the Caruana-Cuntrera in Venezuela. Among those that were identified are:

- Multicolor Venezolana, a decorating company purchased in 1979; Paolo Cuntrera and Angelo Mongiovì were listed on the board of directors. Capital—8 million bolivares (bol.)
- Grupo 8 Seleciones, a real estate firm that purchased and sold buildings. Bought in 1978; Angelo Mongiovì and Giuseppa Cuntrera (wife of Pasquale Cuntrera) were listed on the board of directors. Capital—2 million bol.
- Naviera Turistica de Oriente SA, a travel agency purchased in 1974 by Angelo Mongiovì and Paolo, Gaspare and Pasquale Cuntrera. Tourism among Venezuela ports and sea-and river-going trade. Capital—1.6 million bol.
- Commercial Brasil, a real estate company established in 1974 and founded by Gaspare Cuntrera and others. Alfonso Caruana was listed in the board of directors. Capital—4 million bol.
- Corporacion del Mueble Riz-Mari CA, general trading. Owners included Gaspare and Paolo Cuntrera. Capital—3 million bol.
- Chochinera San Jorge, a meat packing firm; directors included Pasquale and Paolo Cuntrera. Capital—3 million bol.
- Ganaderia Rio Zappa, a cattle company; directors include Angelo and Francesco Mongiovì, Nicolò Rizzuto, Salvatore Greco, John Gambino and Gaspare Cuntrera. Capital—1 million bol.
- Agropecuaria Amanacu: a breeding farm. Founders were Giuseppina and Antonina Caruana. Director was Gaspare Cuntrera. Capital—1 million bol.
- Inmobiliaria Tropical, real estate company. Directors were Paolo, Pasquale and Gaspare Cuntrera, Angelo Mongiovì, Giuseppina Vella, Giuseppina Cuntrera and Antonina Caruana. Capital—8 million bol.
- Agropecuaria Gas Michelan, a food trade company. Directors included Gaspare Cuntrera, and Michel Phelan.
- Fabrica de Cubre-Camas Americanas, a bedspread company. Directors included Angelo Mongiovì and Giuseppa Cuntrera.
- Cosmos Record: production, distribution, marketing, importing of records and cassettes. Directors included Luciano Zambito and Paolo Cuntrera. Capital—716,000 bol.
- Inversora Ganipa CA: mediator in real estate. President was Paolo Cuntrera. Capital—1 million bol.
- Inversora Cuntrera, real estate trading and development and general import-export. Directors were Antonina and Giuseppina Caruana, Giuseppina Vella, President Paolo Cuntrera. Capital—2 million bol.
- Commercial Hotelera: management of hotel, restaurant, bar. Directors included Paolo Cuntrera. Capital—50,000 bol.

- Cilindros Tanques SA: distribution and general trading. Established in 1964. Director was Paolo Cuntrera. Capital—500,000 bol.
- Aceros Prensados SA: the group's holding company in Caracas.
- Promotora de cilindros Procilinca CA, contractor for two companies: Tanques Para Gas, Bomobas Venezolanas. Established in 1976. Capital—900,000 bol.
- Swecoven CA, metal fabrication of pressure tanks. Capital—5 million bol.
- Inversiones Otuzirma CA, established in 1976. Director was Paolo Cuntrera.
- Inversora Paogas, established in 1978, hotel management and general trading. Directors included Antonina and Giuseppina Cuntrera. Capital—2 million bol.
- Inversioned Odeon, established in 1972. Real estate brokering, construction. Founders and shareholders were Antonina Caruana, Giuseppina Vella, Giuseppina Cuntrera. Paolo Cuntrera was President. Capital—23,7 million bol.
- Vera Pizza CA, management of stores, bars, restaurants and discos. Director was Paolo Cuntrera. Capital—20,000 bol. Established in 1980.
- Inversora Nigapa CA, real estate mediations. Established in 1980. Capital—20,000 bol.
- Gruppo Financero Commercial Siculo Srl. Established in 1979, services, and accounting. Directors were Paolo Cuntrera and Giuseppina Cuntrera. Capital—20,000 bol.
- Boulevard de Paris CA, established in 1981, management of restaurant and banquet hall. President was Paolo Cuntrera. Capital—50,000 bol.
- Four hotels: Odeon (8 million bol), Eden (3,6 million bol.), Ariston (4.2 million bol), terminus (4.3 million bol.), one villa: Quinta Dalila (2.6 million bol.), two buildings: Iviaca I and II (30 million bol.), two condominiums: Altamira and El Marques. In the 1970s and 1980s the Caruana-Cuntrera obtained mortgages from several banks for 23.8 million bolivares.

In addition, the Caruana-Cuntrera created a massive building trades complex, MAPLISA, in the northern Valencia region of Venezuela, where they built four hotels on prime commercial real estate.[1]

The necessary seed capital came from traditional underworld industries, according to the U.S. Justice Department: "Their financial empire included gambling, loansharking, extortion, prostitution and drug money–laundering enterprises."[2] All the most notorious names of the underworld—many, but not all, on the run from Italian and U.S. investigators and the Corleonesi—were safely ensconced in the country's political and business milieu, and had been since the early 1960s.

The first and most prominent Sicilian Mafioso to emerge in Venezuela was Salvatore "Little Bird" Greco, who fled Sicily after the 1963 Ciaculli bomb massacre. Italian authorities believed he'd met with "lupara bianca," but in reality he'd made his way to South America, where he took on an entire new identity as Renato Martino Caruso. For the next decade and a half he ran an almost-invisible international drug cartel that

The other primary Sicilian Mafia players operating jointly with the Cuntreras in Venezuela were all of international stature in the narcotics underworld. Documentation filed with the Venezuelan government named several key players:
• Antonino Napoli, identified as early as 1974 by the Italian National Police as an international heroin trafficker;
• Nicolò Rizzuto, the Caruana-Cuntrera's main Canadian contact and senior Sicilian Mafia member;
• Angelo Mongiovì, a transplanted member of the Agrigento Mafia of Don Giuseppe Settecasi;
• Luciano Zambito, who would later be charged by the Royal Canadian Mounted Police with heroin trafficking;
• John Gambino, the Sicilian Mafia's U.S. representative for heroin trafficking.[3]

funneled billions of dollars of heroin and cocaine into North America and Europe. The fit between his operations and the growing Caruana-Cuntreras was a natural.

In the 1970s and 1980s, as the Caruana side of the Siciliana family fought for control in Canada and opened outposts in the United Kingdom and across Europe, setting up heroin trade routes in Asia, the Cuntrera side of the family concentrated their efforts in South America. Their underworld power increased when Alfonso Caruana's uncle, Giuseppe Caruana, ceded leadership of the organization to Pasquale Cuntrera in 1978 and retired to Brazil.[4]

The business press took note of the success of the Cuntreras' companies, although for years no one bothered to look closely at the finances or acquisitions. While creating a gigantic framework of legitimate businesses, the Cuntreras, with overseas support from Canada and Sicily, built the criminal side of the organization, making it a powerhouse responsible for arranging shipment of 3 metric tonnes of heroin into the United States.[5] And as the global need for narcotics swung heavily towards cocaine, the Cuntrera brothers and the Caruanas took control of 80 percent of the Colombian cocaine being shipped through Venezuela.

As in other countries and jurisdictions, the Caruana-Cuntrera family spent a good deal of time and effort seeding corruption within the power structure, from the cop on the beat to heads of state. According to a U.S. Justice Department criminal intelligence profile on the Siciliana family: "The Caruana/Cuntrera Organization has historically used police to facilitate their operations. . . . Pasquale Cuntrera was found not guilty after a trial for bribery in the 1970s (no further details are known regarding this trial). However, the connections with many local political leaders were more than certain." The report adds: "[T]he Caruana/Cuntrera organization received government support from Venezuela when they arrived with $30–$40 million to invest in Venezuela."

The Caruana-Cuntrera would target key authorities necessary to their enterprise. An FBI source in Los Angeles reported in February 1987 that his job for the Siciliana family was to establish contacts with customs agents in Venezuela, who would undervalue imports and allow shipments to enter the country without being inspected. One scheme involved the importation of unassembled lamps from Italy. "Once the shipment arrived in Venezuela, the source met with the customs agent and arranged for the necessary paperwork and transportation to Valencia, Venezuela. . . . Sources advised that, based on statements made by the Siciliana [Family members] operating the company, drugs were being smuggled into Venezuela in the shipments of unassembled lamps. . . . The lamps were assembled at the CMC factory in Valencia, Venezuela and then shipped through the world, specifically, Canada and the United States."[6]

It was broadly reported and widely believed that the marriage of Paolo Cuntrera's daughter, Maria, to drug trafficker Antonino Mongiovì, in the 1980s, was attended by Luis Herrera Campins, at that time the president of Venezuela. The ceremony was televised, and although Campins has repeatedly denied his attendance, several people in Caracas swore to having seen him in television footage.

Also targeted for corruption were powerful figures who could be brought into the sphere of the Siciliana family. The head of the DISIP, the Venezuelan intelligence police, was a close friend of members of the family, intelligence sources told the FBI. "A security officer's wife was hired by Paolo Cuntrera to work in one of his companies. . . . The officer provided the Cuntreras and Zambito with gun licenses and honorary membership in police organizations."[7]

Security was paramount in the family; hundreds of thousands of dollars were spent annually on protection. Paolo Cuntrera himself monitored the activity in one of his offices through state-of-the-art closed-circuit televisions and microphones. Only those "of the blood" were able to get close to him. "The Caruana-Cuntrera organization utilized only Sicilians in the upper management positions of the companies and factories," an FBI report stated.

The Caruana-Cuntrera mansions and compounds were protected by the most modern security technology and armed guards. In Venezuela, they lived much of the time in seclusion, maintaining two main residences—"Mary" and "Dalila"—on the Calle Terepaima, in the upscale El Marques neighborhood, guarded by fifteen-foot-high concrete walls, security systems, and bodyguards.

One Cuntrera property, a ranch named "Ganaderia Rio Zappa," was owned jointly by the Caruana-Cuntrera and the "Torretta Mafia Faction" and was strategically situated near the Colombian border. Its two paved airstrips were reportedly kept secure by local police officers, hired when flights from Colombia were arriving, presumably containing shipments of cocaine.

During a ten-year period, the Cuntrera clan, and to a lesser extent the Caruanas, built a financial empire worth an estimated $1 billion. While some observers initially believed this to be a grossly inflated figure, it was actually the conclusion of an accurate analysis conducted by the Venezuelan intelligence service.

Publicly, the Venezuelan government and law enforcement denied the existence of the Cuntreras. Though the family was prepared to undermine

Torretta Faction. A modest village on a hilltop near the Palermo-Trapani highway, Torretta was truly the town that heroin built. When police raided Torretta during a Mafia investigation in 1986, they discovered that behind the modest facade of the houses were signs of fabulous wealth, ranging from luxury furnishings to gold-plated detailings in the bathrooms. From Torretta came a steady stream of traffickers, most famously the women who wore girdles created for the smuggling of heroin into the U.S. Typically, the woman, usually middle-aged and a pillar of her community, secreted four to six pounds of heroin in the girdles, was driven to Palermo's airport, and sent to America. Heavy perfumes were poured on the drug stash to hide the smell of the drugs. Village men were also used to "mule" heroin: during the raids police found pants with stashes sewn into the legs. Since the 1970s Torretta was the Sicilian base for the aged Mafia boss Rosario Di Maggio who died during a police raid on his home. Believing the Corleonesi were coming to kill him, he dropped dead of a heart attack.

The importance of the Torretta Faction linkage is difficult to overstate when examining the Caruana-Cuntrera organization. Di Maggio's organization was part of a broad federation of families whose make-up rivals the complexities of the Siciliana family. This federation consisted—as it does today—mainly of four Sicilian families, the Gambinos (separate from the American crime family of Carlo Gambino), the Inzerillos, the Spatolas, and the Di Maggios. Through intermarriages the clans came to number hundreds of members with outposts throughout the world. Di Maggio maintained a strong relationship with the Siciliana family in Venezuela through the Cuntrera brothers.

authorities, a U.S. government report notes that they seldom had to resort to that: "Members of the Caruana/Cuntrera organization have never been prosecuted in Venezuela," states a 1992 U.S. Justice Department report, written with assistance from the Criminal Intelligence Service Canada. "In 1984, while Siculiana family members were moving narcotics by the ton across four continents, a report by the Venezuela national intelligence service (Direccion de Los Servicios de Inteligencia y Prevencion) concluded that 'the Mafia as such does not exist in Venezuela; a few Mafiosi just come here for rest and recreation.'"

That same year, Venezuelan judge Rafael Avila-Vivas ordered all cash and assets of both Paolo and Pasquale Cuntrera frozen pending a review for drug trafficking, but no assets were ever forfeited to the government.

The Siculiana family was encouraged by President Carlos Andres Perez, who had announced in 1974: "The State will own some key sectors, such as oil, iron, aluminum, electricity, mines and high technology for military uses. Consumer goods, light industry, construction, transports, banks and small- and medium-sized enterprises will be run in a mixed-property way—with the State as a partner of entrepreneurs and workers."[8] Everything was up for sale—a populist program ideally suited to the aims of the Caruana-Cuntrera.

Investigators from both Canada and the United States discovered that, by the early 1990s, family members owned or had control of sixty bona fide companies in Venezuela and Lesser Antilles (and there were probably several dozen that hadn't been discovered), branching out through a host of legitimate sector industries.

"Satellite families"—after all, the Cuntreras were to all outward appearances executives of major companies and above the day-to-day operation of traditional criminal activities—handled gambling, low-level drug trafficking, and loan-sharking. There was a steady influx of Sicilian criminals who, for one reason or another, had to lie low; they provided the underpinning of the Caruana-Cuntrera organization, the "day workers" of the underworld.

The huge, interlocked Caruana-Cuntrera organization—growing and expanding through both business and family ties with other expatriate Sicilian Mafia clans—had by the 1980s built a powerful network worth billions of dollars, one strategically situated to control the flow of narcotics out of Colombia. It was, to quote top Italian investigator Alessandro Pansa, "the structure and hierarchy of the Mafia . . . entirely reproduced in Venezuela." He said the clan had direct links with the ruling *Cupola* of the Sicilian Mafia and was acknowledged by the American La Cosa Nostra.[9]

The fantastic financial power of the Caruana-Cuntrera also impressed Salvatore Contorno, a Sicilian boss who had become a turncoat. "They operated in Caracas, they lived there, they centered their activity there. They had begun with a smallish house. Now they have more millions than they care to count."[10]

For Alfonso Caruana, going to Venezuela was like going home.

That the Caruana-Cuntrera were behind massive shipments of heroin and cocaine into the United States wasn't lost on the Drug Enforcement Administration (DEA), which was aware of their involvement in the Pizza Connection. A U.S. Justice Department report titled *La Cosa Nostra in Canada*, produced in 1985, made the connection between the Canada-based Siculiana family and major American traffickers.

The document also noted the attendance of Nicolò Rizzuto at Giuseppe Bono's wedding at the beginning of the Pizza Connection case; it described him meeting with Bono in Milan; it documented meetings between Rizzuto family members and members of Sal Catalano's Sicilian crew within the Bonanno family.[11]

Alfonso Caruana is the only clan member mentioned in the report; he is listed as "a major narcotics trafficker" with a home in Melide (Canton Ticino) Switzerland. The Cuntrera family isn't named at all. But, on balance, the exclusion of the Cuntreras is understandable: that side of the family was considered Venezuelan rather than Canadian.

Their notoriety was such that the U.S. government set out to trap them in a project called "Wiseguy." DEA Agent John Costanzo, posing as Don Vincenzo, the *capo* of a New York crime family, spent eighteen months working his way close to Pasquale Cuntrera. The initial introduction was made through Italian-born Raffaele Bellizzi, a businessman living in Miami who operated in Venezuela. Bellizzi, who owned a shipping company, used his ships to carry drugs and cash from Caracas to

Europe, and had been a sponsor of the Cuntreras in Venezuela.

On October 27, 1989, a meeting was arranged at Bellizzi's home in San Antonio de Los Altos, on the Colombian border. "There was myself, [undercover DEA agent] David Lorino, Cuntrera, Bellizzi and an Ignazio Fiannaca, who worked in a hotel owned by the Caruana-Cuntrera," Costanzo said. "Lorino and I were introduced as people dealing money laundering, trading of chemicals used in making drugs, and trading of drugs."

Fiannaca told Lorino he'd worked with the Cuntreras for twenty-five years, following them from Italy to Brazil, Canada, France, and Venezuela.[12]

With a vanity that's a trademark of the Caruanas and Cuntreras of a certain age, Pasquale Cuntrera had blackened his graying hair. Costanzo recalls: "He looked like my grandfather."

The men had long discussions about worldly matters: economics, politics, and, of course, drug trafficking. Cuntrera mentioned "favors" the men could do for each other.

When his daughter got married, Cuntrera invited Costanzo to the wedding. "Of course, I didn't go, for safety reasons," Costanzo said. "But I sent a gift through Bellizzi, an envelope containing five thousand dollars."

Pasquale Cuntrera was impressed with Costanzo, whom he firmly believed to be Don Vincenzo, a New York City Mafia boss. He offered to sell him 6,000 kilograms of Lebanese hashish that was to be routed through Sicily and Canada. "We didn't close the deal, however," Costanzo said. "He wanted me to deposit two hundred thousand dollars."

Costanzo later told Bellizzi that his money was tied up in a large shipment of heroin. The DEA knew it would be difficult, if not impossible, to catch Cuntrera in Caracas. But a reverse sting—selling the drugs to the traffickers—might work. "I told Bellizzi, 'When you go back to Caracas and see Cuntrera, ask him whether he's interested.'"

Cuntrera went for it, agreeing to pay US$90,000 per kilo for 20 kilograms of 97-percent-pure heroin. However, when Costanzo demanded 25 percent up front, Cuntrera scoffed, saying that in his circle heroin was always paid for one week after delivery. Costanzo agreed. Arrangements were made to complete the deal in New York.

In mid-April 1990, a plainclothes police officer parked his car, as instructed, near the Road West Berry Country Club on Long Island. Cuntrera's men—Ignazio Fiannaca, Canadian Pietro Martello, and Antonio Lo Giudice—were arrested after taking delivery of the shipment. All were convicted. Bellizzi was sentenced to thirty years.

An arrest warrant was issued for Pasquale Cuntrera, but the veteran Mafioso was too cagey to expose himself. He remained in Venezuela, protected by wealth and surrounded by corrupt officials.

The greatest strength of the Caruana-Cuntrera was also their greatest weakness: their willingness to form strategic alliances. On the plus side, alliances formed globally would lead to a wider market in which to profit, a more diversified workforce able to operate in various cultural spheres, and a more broad-based infrastructure that, as it developed, would move the Caruana-Cuntrera ever further from the frontline risk of their business.

The downside was the lack of familial loyalty on the part of non-Sicilians brought into the Caruana-Cuntrera criminal structure. In a criminal culture where Sicilian Mafiosi born just a few kilometers up the same dusty road were treated with a measure of distrust—even when they belonged to the same "family" or cell of the same organization—the importance of family loyalty was a touchy subject.

But the Caruana-Cuntrera found it productive and profitable, if ultimately dangerous, to entrust the outer circle of their business affairs to outsiders, whether they were Thai heroin producers and Colombian cartels at the front end of their schemes, or the Neapolitan Camorra and Calabrian 'ndrangheta members below them. More than any other group, the Sicilian Mafia limited their exposure to detection by operating on a need-to-know basis, a key precept of the espionage business. And the Caruana-Cuntrera, as they built their international networks, were aware of what every Sicilian Mafioso knew: outside of immediate blood family, everybody was a potential traitor.

The relationship between the Colombian cocaine producers and the Sicilian Mafia was symbiotic: Colombians, while sophisticated within their culture in South America, were ignorant when they left their own borders. When, for example, they needed to repatriate money from cocaine sales in Europe, they dealt with a ruthless cast of characters who took advantage of their awkwardness, often charging as much as 30 percent for their laundering services.

"Outside Colombia, and maybe Peru and Bolivia, they're afraid," a mid-level trafficker said. "They can't function in a society that requires documentation and where you can't just pull out a wad of bills and pay your way. They don't know how to open a bank account, sign a lease, exchange money. In the 1980s they were hiring front men to just do day-to-day commerce: buy cars, find houses. They can't speak the language and they don't understand the customs."[13]

These nouveau riche underworld players were totally out of their league in the European countries. But with the market for cocaine being created in Germany, Italy, the United Kingdom, and France by the Sicilian Mafia, the profits from this rich new consumer base needed to be funneled back to Colombia. So, in addition to the mechanics of actually getting their product to market, the Colombians were faced with a new set of problems: repatriating cash.

What Alfonso Caruana offered was the best of both worlds: he'd get the Colombian product to European markets, and, with his growing financial infrastructure, he'd repatriate the cartels' profits back to Colombia, or any other designated safe haven.

Curaçao, Dutch West Indies

Antonio Scambia had spent most of his life in the Calabrian underworld, comprised of the many 'ndrangheta cells controlling crime in the toe of the boot of Italy. Born in Motta S. Giovanni, Calabria, the sixty-four-year-old had been a prolific and successful smuggler of cigarettes and other products throughout southern Europe in the 1950s and early 1960s. One of his prime customers was the Mazzaferro family, who were from Marina di Gioiosa. In the early 1980s, Scambia and Vincenzo Mazzaferro, head of the clan, were charged with murder. Scambia fled to the United States but was captured and extradited to Italy. Both men were ultimately found not guilty. When Scambia was released from custody, he contacted Mazzaferro, who was in the early stages of setting up a drug importation scheme.

Mazzaferro was aware that in the turbulent world of Calabria—where each cell of the *'ndrangheta* ruled its own kingdom, as did the Sicilian Mafia on their island—a sudden infusion of drugs, and the profits they generated, could lead to anarchy. Much of the history of *'ndrangheta* is marked by feuds and murder sprees. Uncontrolled shipments of cocaine would generate wealth, and wealth would generate envy; the envy would translate into gunfire and grudges that could continue for decades.

Mazzaferro's ambitious plan was to develop a cocaine cartel involving the leading *'ndrangheta* clans in Calabria: Barbaro, of Platì; Ierinò, of Gioiosa Ionica; Morabito, of Africo Nuovo; Pesce, of Rosarno. Members of this carefully selected syndicate would be permitted to purchase a specific quantity of each cocaine shipment for US$16,000 a kilo—generating a $9,000 profit, less his in-Italy expenses, for Mazzaferro. With the drugs appearing for sale in controlled quantities and at specific times, the market would maintain a degree of stability.

It was decided that Scambia would be the point man for bringing cocaine directly to Italy from South America. To make the connection, Mazzaferro sent Scambia and one of his soldiers, Giuseppe Agostino, to Curaçao to link up with the man who would provide the shipments.

At a hotel in Curaçao, Scambia and Agostino met with Alfonso Caruana and his companion, identified only as "Riccardo." Introductions were made and negotiations were begun.

Emphasizing, quite unnecessarily, his family ties to the Cuntreras, Caruana said that his representative, a Sicilian cousin named Vito Genco, would contact Scambia in Italy and work out the details of transportation and payment.

Vito Genco's name and position in the Caruana-Cuntrera organization were well known in law enforcement circles. Born at Partanna, in Trapani on the west coast of Sicily, Genco was a lifelong drug trafficker. The examination of financial and real estate records showed that Genco was also strongly tied to the Cuntrera side of the organization. As Caruana moved throughout the Caribbean—particularly Aruba during the early 1990s—and South America, Vito Genco was never far away.

At the conclusion of the meeting Scambia and Agostino made the deal on Mazzaferro's behalf: Caruana agreed to supply cocaine to the

Siculiana, the village in Agrigento province where the
Caruana-Cuntrera family came from.

Sanctuary of the Church of the Holy
Crucifixion in Siculiana. The names of
Mafia families are engraved on brass
plates on the pews of the church.

The tomb of Carmelo Caruana
(b. August 13, 1915; d. January 27,
1965), Alfonso's father, in Siculiana.

Police surveillance photos of Alfonso Caruana at his daughter's wedding held at the Sutton Place Hotel, Toronto in April 1995.

Francesco "The Strangler" Di Carlo, the Caruana-Cuntrera's U K connection.

Pasquale Cuntrera, chief of the Cuntrera side of the Siculiana family, following his removal from Venezuela.

COURTESY: LA PRESSE

Gaspare Cuntrera, Alfonso's cousin, who operated Siculiana family businesses in Venezuela and Aruba.

Agostino Cuntrera, the most prominent member of the Siciliana family in Quebec.

The passport of Alberto Minelli, money-runner for Oreste Pagano's organization.

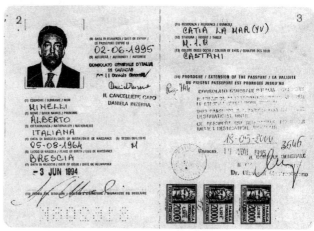

Interpol photo of Alfonso Caruana dated 1993.

Nick Rizzuto, in a photo taken in 1996, Montreal Mafia boss and head of the Sicilian Canadian Mafia.

Nunzio LaRosa, part of the Montreal connection, who arranged for the shipment of drugs and money into the United States.

Antonio LaRosa, Nunzio's son, who was arrested for conspiracy.

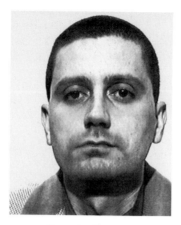

Ignazio Genua.

Richard Court (*top*) and John Hill, drug-runners, who
were arrested in Texas in May 1998 with 200 kilograms
of cocaine barely hidden in the back of their pickup truck.

(left) Bags of cocaine confiscated by Texas police when Hill and Court were arrested.

(below) Bulk currency from Canadian cocaine sales sent to the United States in payment for the drugs. Most of the money went down a pipeline between Montreal and Miami.

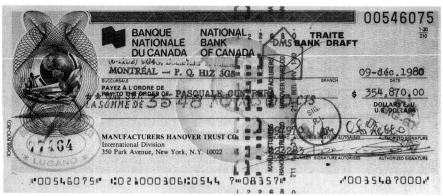

Examples of the checks run through Alfonso Caruana's family members' accounts in Montreal that moved drug profits to family members or family businesses. These checks alone represent more than US$1 million, a fraction of the money laundered by the Caruana-Cuntrera.

'ndrangheta families, but only in limited quantities, because it was difficult to get large enough shipments to make it worthwhile. The men agreed on a price of US$5,000 per kilo. A 130-kilogram cocaine deal was structured in typical Caruana fashion: each load would be divided into three—one third for Caruana's group in Europe; one third for Mazzaferro's 'ndrangheta family; and the final third for the Colombian suppliers.

After returning to Italy, Scambia arranged to take delivery of the shipment. When Vito Genco visited him at his home and told him the load was ready, Scambia, too, was prepared.

The scheme to get the cocaine into Italy was arranged by Giuseppe Scibilia and another man. Using the false names Renato Vasino and Dr. Rinaldi, and operating through a lawyer in Lugano, Switzerland, the men set up a company called Generalunternehmungs A.G. The firm purchased candies and coffee from South America; the goods were to be shipped in crates with false bottoms where the cocaine would be stashed. Scambia found a warehouse in Alba, near Turin in northern Italy, and had Scibilia rent it; he also brought in a heavily armed security team belonging to the Saverio Saffioti crime family of Turin to guard it and to provide secure transport as it was delivered.

The ship, *Pelagos*, left Sao Paulo, Brazil, on December 16, 1990, and arrived at Genoa on January 6, 1991. The drugs were removed from the containers and loaded into a Fiat and taken to the Alba warehouse.

Vito Genco collected 320-million lire from the 'ndrangheta, which he sent to Alfonso Caruana in South America. Caruana's first direct shipment to the Calabrian 'ndrangheta cartel was an unqualified success.

Venezuela

With the pipeline established and now proven, three more cocaine shipments, of 150 kilograms each, were sent. They were hidden in containers of coffee, candies, and "shoes, skirts, bathing suits, and pants," according to ships' manifests.

The Italian end of the pipeline was expanded. In addition to Generalunternehmungs A.G., two other Swiss companies were set up to cover the importation of various products, including more candies, coffee, shoes, shirts, bathing suits, trousers, hydrogenated asphalt, and mineral oils. The shipments, once moved by passenger car, now required the leasing of tractor-trailers. More than 10,880 kilograms of cocaine were sold to the Calabrian clans through Alfonso Caruana's network. One setback was that a shipment of 3,000 kilograms was seized on a ship before it got to sea.

Vincenzo Mazzaferro's well-planned cartel system brought wealth and power to the clans of Calabria, even after he himself was slain in an ambush in 1993. According to Scambia, Mazzaferro's brother, Giuseppe, immediately took over the lucrative operation and continued to provide a stable and strategic link between the Caruana organization and the cartel members.

As with most modern entrepreneurial criminal enterprises, a financial criminal structure was set up to complement the trafficking side. Initially, Vito Genco would transfer the money to Switzerland, but as the network became increasingly prosperous, banker Angelo Zannetti set up a complex structure to move the profits into Switzerland through several company accounts. The money was changed into U.S. dollars or Swiss francs, then wire-transferred to financial institutions in several countries, including the United States, France, the Netherlands, Brazil, and Venezuela. A financial review later showed that 34 billion lire was moved out of Italy by the organization.

Washington, D.C.

By 1991, the Caruana-Cuntrera were showing up as a strong signal on the radar of U.S. Justice officials. A steady stream of information was being gathered, using RCMP intelligence files, various bits of data in American law-enforcement databases, and media accounts. While an earlier effort—*La Cosa Nostra in Canada*—had barely mentioned Alfonso Caruana and his uncle, Leonardo, a new document entitled *The Caruana-Cuntrera Sicilian Mafia Organization Racketeering Enterprise Investigation Intelligence Profile* laid out in meticulous detail the structure, history, makeup, and financial dealings of the Siculiana family.

Noting the Caruana-Cuntrera is "the only Sicilian Mafia organization that is headquartered outside of Sicily," the report states: "The most active members on the Caruana side are three brothers, Alfonso,

Pasquale and Gerlando, and two of their uncles, Giuseppe and Giovanni. . . . The most active members on the Cuntrera side are three three brothers, Pasquale, Gaspare, and Paolo." Severla Cuntrera family members are named, including Paolo Cuntrera's son-in-law, Antonino Mongiovi.

The Caruana-Cuntrera organization had been active since the 1960s, operating on three continents and controlled a heroin, cocaine, and hashish smuggling network, as well as being "one of the most powerful money laundering organizations involved in drug trafficking today."

The Intelligence Profile tracked the rise of the clans, detailing deaths and murders as it rode to international prominence. Ties to the ruling commission of the Sicilian Mafia are shown through the Caruana brothers' uncle, Leonardo, who sat on Cosa Nostra's "board of directors" until he was assassinated in 1981.

All the players involved in the bloodshed in Montreal of the 1970s— Paolo Violi, Vincenzo Cotroni, the Rizzutos—as well as the rise of the the U.S. Pizza Connection were detailed. Biographies of eleven prominent Caruana-Cuntrera members are included in the report, the leadership (in 1985) shown to center around four men: Alfonso Caruana's uncles Pasquale and Paolo Cuntrera, and Alfonso and his brother, Pasquale Caruana.

Taken in its entirety, the Intelligence Profile brought together all the strands, many long ignored, that made up the interlinked fabric of the Siciliana family, as well as its links to several diverse criminal organizations.

Valencia, Venezuela

In 1991, Alfonso Caruana and his family were living in a massive villa in the city of Valencia, Venezuela, surrounded by bodyguards. Cocaine profits and money invested from his heroin smuggling in the 1980s were fueling a very comfortable lifestyle, rivaling that of the earlier Mafiosi who'd fled to Venezuela from Italy.

Caruana, barely suffering from the loss of the drug networks in the United Kingdom and his pipeline into Canada through Windsor, Ontario, was now focused on a cocaine supply route directly from South America to Europe, to meet an expanding demand for the drug. But, frustrated by the meager shipments, Alfonso Caruana needed a supplier who could provide more than small 135- or 150-kilogram amounts.

The man who was key to Alfonso Caruana's cocaine pipeline out of South America was Oreste Pagano. A longtime member of the Camorra—the Mafia of Naples—Pagano was a criminal from his earliest years. He was well connected to major drug traffickers and had served time with Raffaele Cutolo, the leading player in the rebirth of the Camorra.

Born to a family of modest means in Naples, Italy, in 1938, Oreste Pagano was the third of four children. His father, Enrico, was a hardworking man, a creative sort who was known as a fine musician and artist. His mother was Luisa Liguori, a housekeeper.

By the time war came to Italy, Pagano's family had, like many Italian families south of Rome, fallen upon hard times. The Naples area, a strategic port, was constantly under air bombardment.

"My father couldn't work any more," Pagano remembers. "I spent the first years of my childhood between poverty and hunger and amid bombs, and running night and day to bomb shelters."[14]

Money was increasingly hard to come by. In 1944, when he was six, Oreste Pagano began his schooling, but he was also offered a job running errands for a local bartender. By the time he was nine years old, he had left home and was associating with other street kids, who would one day make up the infrastructure of the Neapolitan Camorra.

At fourteen he was put into a reformatory; at eighteen he was arrested in Rome for what was a great sport of tough young men of that time and place—beating and mugging gay men. He and a friend, Antonio, a minor, he said, were walking through Rome when they were, as Pagano recalls, "approached by a pedophile, a fag, or let's say a homosexual, that tried to—how do you say? He tried to make contact with us. We smacked him to the ground and stole his wallet." In an interview in 1999, another version of Pagano's story cast him in a more heroic light: "[He] tried to make advances to my friend and I hit him, and he took his wallet out and wanted to give me money. . . . I took the wallet and I hit him."

The youths were arrested, charged with robbery, and convicted. Pagano was sentenced to four months and Antonio eleven. It was this early charge that, he said, shaped the judiciary system's harsh reaction to his crimes for the rest of his life: "The judges just saw robbery, they didn't see—what type of robbery it was. They thought it was a bank robbery, they didn't know if it was a bank robbery, armed robbery, they didn't know anything. And because of this charge everything else was made worse, anything I did in my life was aggravated because of that charge."

When he was freed, Pagano moved to the town of Brescia, where he married his first wife, Mirella Romano, and got into local drug trafficking. Over the next several years the street thug ran the gamut of criminal activity that would soon draw the attention of the Camorra. But it was his activities in 1973 and 1974 that put him on the path to international drug trafficking.

"I was arrested in Naples because at that time I worked for a certain Nunzio Guida and his brother Enzo," Pagano said. "I would go to Peru and send luggage with 4 or 5 kilos of coke at a time to Italy."

He had a falling out with Nunzio Guida when someone told the trafficker Pagano had sent a suitcase back to Italy that, instead of going to the Guida brothers, went to a rival trafficker. When he returned to Naples to iron out the problem, police pulled over his car and seized a gun.

"[The police] forced me to say it was mine, and I was sentenced to four years' imprisonment. While I was in jail, I met a certain Raffaele Cutolo."

Meeting Cutolo in jail wasn't a unique experience for tough young street criminals in Naples, and it was often a major career turning point. Dubbed "The Professor" because he'd successfully made his way through elementary school, Cutolo was creating a massive criminal organization—the New Organized Camorra—from within the prison system. His method was simple: when a new prisoner was jailed, Cutolo invited him to his carpeted cell, where he was offered coffee and other jail-house comforts in return for pledging allegiance to Cutolo's organization. Cutolo's members were looked after during their custody—it was estimated that Cutolo spent $20,000 a month on supplying food, clothing, blankets, and drugs to his imprisoned followers—while their families on the outside were given financial assistance and, when possible, positions in the organization.

Dividing his time evenly between prison cells and insane asylums, from which he ran numerous rackets on the outside, the flamboyant

Cutolo was building an organization that was slowly taking over the disorganized criminal activities of the old dying Camorra. The New Organized Camorra introduced a structure of leadership, an oath of allegiance, and a way for criminals to make their way through the pitfalls of the underworld.

For Oreste Pagano, it was leadership he could use. Cutolo's organization would relieve him of the day-to-day stresses and uncertainties of being an outsider, cannon fodder for the criminal groups he associated with.

After Pagano was released, he regularly took packages of food and clothing to Cutolo's sister, Rosetta, who would deliver them to her brother. Rosetta, who had the nickname "Ice Eyes," was herself a formidable person. A highly competent accountant, she managed the organization's business affairs and carried out missions on the outside for her brother. The most notorious was a plan to blow up the Naples police station, a scheme that was foiled mere hours before the explosion was to go off.

Later, when Cutolo escaped from jail, he contacted Pagano, who hid him from authorities at a home he owned in northern Italy.

During the months Pagano hid his boss, he was invited to join the Camorra. Cutolo made a strong case for the protective qualities the organization offered, Pagano remembers.[15] "He made me take an oath, an oath for the Camorra, and I entered to be part of the New Camorra Organization," he recalled.

In 1979, Italian authorities announced that they wanted Pagano for criminal association—his name had been found on financial documents when they finally caught up with Raffaele Cutolo. Pagano was jailed for two years.

Several members of the Camorra who cooperated with the State told investigators that Pagano was the "head of the Camorra" in Brescia. They told of Pagano's current and past activities, including drug trafficking, extortion, and robbery.

When he was released from prison in 1981, Pagano went to Germany, where he met some Calabrian mafiosi. They in turn introduced him to a "gentleman from Brazil," and suddenly Pagano was back in the drug trade.

"These people in Brazil would be able to put vast amounts of drugs on an airplane for me without being inspected, and at the stop in Frankfurt, there was a way of getting out of the airport without being inspected," he said.

This new drug ring came under police scrutiny. When Pagano spotted officers taking his picture from the balcony of a hotel, he clutched himself and called: "Take a picture of my balls."

A short time later he was arrested, convicted, and jailed for importing large shipments of cocaine into Italy. In 1988, after serving seven years in jail, Pagano said he was granted five days out of prison at Christmas, "because I had been good."

But not too good: visiting his children—Massimiliano, Gianluca, and Enrica—and seeing them living poorly "without a lira" made him flee the jurisdiction to make money. He headed to Spain, where he met a Colombian and a Peruvian who were involved in the drug trade. He first bought a half-kilo of cocaine and smuggled it himself back into Italy. "Then little by little, after that, a kilo here, a kilo there, I continued to in order to, ah [sell drugs] for my own betterment and for the betterment of my family."

One of his contacts, citing the high price of US$22,000 a kilo in Spain, suggested that they go to South America where, in Colombia, they would pay only $2,000 a kilo. Pagano and his partner moved to Colombia and began organizing shipments every couple of months. Concealing 3 or 4 kilos at a time in suitcases, the men built up an outbound drug flow and an inbound revenue stream that was the template of a modern trafficking-laundering network.

In the early 1990s Pagano was living in Venezuela as "Cesare Petruzziello." By this time he had had so many identities, he couldn't recall them all.

Pagano was moving cocaine by 100- and 1,000-kilogram loads. Most countries in South America now had strong organized crime groups firmly entrenched: Colombian cartels of varying sizes, several Mafia families transplanted almost in their entirety from Sicily, members of the Camorra and the 'ndrangheta, and Mexican drug networks.

The Colombians and the Sicilian Mafia together, in particular, had vast international networks to move product out and repatriate money home, where it was poured into literally thousands of companies throughout South American business sectors.

With his background in the Camorra and his high-level contacts at the source of cocaine, Pagano made an ideal partner for Alfonso Caruana.

Margarita Island, Venezuela

Oreste Pagano would often visit his old friend Giuseppe "Pippo L'Agrigentino" Friscia, a Sicilian drug trafficker who'd also fled an Italian prison and headed for South America. Having reconnected in Venezuela, the two met daily over drinks or coffee. One day in 1991, Pippo L'Agrigentino invited Pagano to his clothing store on Margarita Island where Alfonso Caruana and his cousin, Vito Genco, waited.

Although it was the first time Pagano and Alfonso Caruana had actually met, Pagano recognized him instantly. Several years before, Caruana's uncle, Pasquale Cuntrera, had come to Pagano to give him a photograph of Alfonso in order to have documents made up.

Caruana said he was looking for a high-level source for cocaine, and had heard about the Camorra member Pagano, who was then living in Venezuela, hiding out from Italian authorities. The men made arrangements to meet for dinner that night.

Privately, Pagano asked Pippo L'Agrigentino about Alfonso Caruana. He was familiar with the Caruana-Cuntrera, but in Venezuela the Cuntrera side of the family was the more well known.

"Pippo told me that they were big—that they were part of a big Italian Mafia family that lived in Venezuela," Pagano said.

Pippo L'Agrigentino said he had been involved with the family before, and one time there'd been a disagreement about whether or not a delivery of drugs had taken place. He believed the drug shipment in question had indeed been completed, but the Caruanas told him it hadn't, and that he'd have to absorb the loss. Pippo L'Agrigentino continually complained to Alfonso Caruana over the shipment, to the point where Caruana gave him a billion lire and told him he never wanted to see him again. Later, when Caruana was being sought by Venezuelan police, he went to Pippo L'Agrigentino's house, and Pippo's wife refused to let him in: "Never to set foot here again. . . . We don't ever want to see you again."

But with the new Caruana-Pagano network being set up, Pippo L'Agrigentino put aside his mistrust of Caruana and told Pagano the reality of dealing with the Caruana-Cuntrera: "Big fish eat little fish."

Pagano checked further into Caruana, asking Umberto Naviglia, another alleged Camorra member, about the families. "He confirmed they were big Mafia men that had always managed the contraband of heroin, the contraband of hashish, and the contraband of cocaine," Pagano said.

In fact, Pagano added, the Caruanas and Cuntreras are seen as a single family. "I always speak of the family. When one refers to the Cuntrera and Caruana family, to me it is one family. And all capital from any sources is always connected to the entire family."

He was impressed with the Caruana-Cuntrera's expertise in business: "They are not people, for example Alfonso—they are not families that commit offenses such as homicide and things. They are people that get others to commit offenses. They belong to a small circle of bosses who decide what needs to be done. They are more or less the men that look after the finances."

So adept were they in the financial world, Pagano said, "they always received the investment funds from other families.

"The hotels and all these other things—all came from money that was invested from the trafficking that they did. And then they received the money [from other families], and instead of sending it [to them], they would invest it and then would send the earnings to these other families."

At the dinner in Margarita, Caruana asked Pagano if he had any contacts with access "to huge parcels of cocaine—at the height of being able to do big drug jobs."

Pagano outlined his South American connection, but like any canny businessman he didn't give too many details, fearing he himself could be cut out of the pipeline. The men struck a deal for 400 kilograms of cocaine. The shipment would be divided up among Alfonso Caruana, Oreste Pagano, Vito Genco, Giuseppe Friscia, Erman Rubio, and Guglielmo Buonomo.

The shipment was, like the many others to come, sent to Genoa, Italy, by ship, where Alfonso Caruana's organization unloaded it and distributed it to the partners. As the drugs sold and the profits piled up,

Caruana's money-laundering specialists either hand-carried it to Venezuela or funneled it through Swiss banks.

A second shipment—500 kilograms—was brought to a building near Caruana's villa, where it was hidden in canisters of steel wool that had been covered with a metallic paper and filled with an asphalt-type liquid to cover the smell and deflect drug-sniffing search dogs. It arrived at Genoa in crates marked "Mineral Oils."

After each shipment was sold, the proceeds would come to Alfonso Caruana, who—having paid 10 percent up front for his portion of each shipment—would keep his share of profits and pass on the rest to Erman Rubio and Oreste Pagano. A woman in a currency exchange office in the town of San Antonio, near the Colombian border, was the financial bridge between Caruana and Pagano on one side and the Colombian suppliers on the other. Adjustments to this system had to be made later when the woman was kidnapped, tortured, and murdered by robbers, who were after the huge sums of money she trafficked.

6

Connections between organized crime and the government of the island of Aruba were revealed in an exposé in the Italian newspaper *Corriere della Sera*. The newspaper detailed the activities of the Caruana and Cuntrera families' campaign of corruption and infiltration of the island's political and financial sectors. Perhaps overstating the case, though not by much, the newspaper declared Aruba "the first state to be bought by the bosses of Cosa Nostra."[1]

Since the early 1980s, the Cuntrera family, led by Alfonso Caruana's uncle Pasquale Cuntrera and his brothers Paolo and Gaspare, had taken advantage of a heated economy on the island sparked by a booming tourist industry. Awash in profits from more than a decade in the heroin business, the brothers, who had in the past regularly used the island's obsessively secretive banking system to launder money, had been regular visitors to Aruba. In the early 1980s, they realized that they had discovered a banking paradise and an investment arena that was almost unparalleled in the Caribbean.

Through a combination of financial muscle and a successful campaign of corruption, the Cuntreras—and increasingly the Caruanas—were able to function as an integral and even crucial factor in the island's economy. And their reach into the highest levels of power guaranteed them a safe haven from any international investigations that might result in warrants for their arrest.

Clearly feeling bulletproof, they lived a fabulously wealthy lifestyle, treating their critics with an habitual indifference. "They were lords of the manor, and the manor was Aruba," a former government minister privately said. "It was frustrating. They could buy you and sell you and there was nothing you could do about it. Corruption in this place was thorough; their power wasn't through force of muscle, it was almost an emanation."[2]

The *Corriere della Sera* report was hardly news to the people of Aruba: almost five years earlier, a government minister, Elio Nicolaas, had raised the specter of organized crime laundering money through the financial system of the Caribbean tax haven. "The contraband in the island is institutionalized," he said.

Nicolaas's statements brought strong denials from the government. Minister of economic affairs Henny Eman called them "speculation without foundation." But later the director of the Aruban Security Service too raised an alarm, writing to the chief of the Dutch security service (Aruba is a semi-dependent island of the Kingdom of the Netherlands) that corruption and organized crime were in danger of severely damaging Aruba's democratic process. An even stronger report from the U.S. Central Intelligence Agency actually put names and faces to those responsible for corrupting the island's political and business sectors—prominent were the Cuntrera brothers. And a feature story in the April 18, 1988, issue of *Business Week* magazine looked into the Caruana-Cuntrera and brought to light their drug trafficking and money-laundering activities in the United Kingdom and Canada.

According to several sources, the Caruana-Cuntrera, using their own criminal profits and the profits of other Sicilian Mafia families, had invested in an estimated 60 percent of the commercial holdings on the island, primarily real estate, casinos and hotel complexes, restaurants, and other small businesses key to the island's tourist industry. They had also purchased the government by loading money into the election campaign of a top politician. In 1987, Henny Eman, then-prime minister, had personally signed a license for Paolo Cuntrera and his son Giuseppe that allowed them to open a nightclub called the Visage. When another government official—Eman's minister of economic affairs Leonard Berlinski—refused to authorize an additional license for the Cuntreras, he was forced to resign, curiously enough, over charges of corruption. (Berlinski was later cleared.) A new request for a license for the Cuntreras was eventually applied for by Maria Albertina Eman, the sister of the prime minister.

Prime Minister Eman's take on the Cuntrera family, at the time he signed the license, was that they were "honorable" people who were not engaged in criminal activity on his island.

An international arrest warrant for Paolo Cuntrera was available on demand either from the Italian government or from Interpol. Press reports in nearby Venezuela regularly detailed the drug-trafficking activities of both the Caruanas and Cuntreras. When Aruban officials accompanied RCMP officers on an investigation on the island, they discovered that a member of the Nicolò Rizzuto crime family had stayed in a room reserved and paid for by Pasquale Cuntrera.

Finally, with pressure against the government building, the Cuntreras were "expelled" from Aruba.

Venezuela

It was with ease that the Cuntreras landed back in Venezuela. The government of Aruba insisted that it had kicked them out, but in truth the Cuntreras had just moved on and re-established themselves, and would quickly earn a reputation as the most powerful Mafia family of South America.

The infrastructure and power base that had begun forming in the late 1970s in Caracas welcomed them. In reality, the Cuntreras and Caruanas were at the center of power, surrounded by all manner of fugitives from investigations in other countries or from Corleonesi clean-up crews. Like Aruba, Caracas by then had become thoroughly corrupted by the Sicilian Mafia, and it was unthinkable that any foreign jurisdiction could touch them there.

The Cuntreras continued to channel their money into commerce and buying political protection. A 1984 review of the cash flow for their hotels, for example, showed that the numbers only balanced if every room had been rented around the clock for seven minutes at a time.

Had the Caruana-Cuntrera been merely drug traffickers, it is likely they would have, at some point, been arrested or deported. But their persistent and seemingly endless infusion of cash into whatever jurisdiction they were in made them economically indispensable.

Giovanni Falcone was one of the earliest anti-Mafia magistrates to recognize the true power of the clans; often he commented: "If we want to bring the drug trade to its knees, we have to catch the Cuntrera-Caruana."[3]

Falcone, a Palermo-born magistrate, had come to symbolize the State's campaign against the Mafia. In the early 1980s he convinced Mafioso Tommaso Buscetta to turn informant. And building upon Buscetta's information, Falcone brought together the first Maxi-Trial in Palermo, which led to hundreds of convictions. But Falcone's greatest success came in proving the existence of the *Cupola*, the powerful ruling commission of the Mafia.

In 1991, Falcone was moved from Palermo to Rome, where he was appointed director of criminal affairs at the ministry of justice. He continued to focus his efforts on the Siculiana family.

In Rome, in May 1992, he spoke with Mendoza Angulo, the Venezuelan minister of justice, to discuss Italy's repeated requests for the extradition of the Cuntrera brothers. But Falcone routinely met with resistance or inertia from the Venezuelan government. An earlier Venezuelan justice minister, Jose Manzo Gonzales, when presented with evidence from Italian authorities to support the extradition of the Cuntrera brothers, had merely shaken his head in disbelief. In Caracas, Luis Pinvera Ordaz, the Venezuelan minister of the interior, flatly told reporters: "In Venezuela there is no Mafia operation center."

Three days after his meeting with Mendoza Angulo, Falcone was assassinated in Sicily. Shortly afterwards, Falcone's colleague and friend Paolo Borsellino and five bodyguards were also slain.

The murders of the magistrates sparked international outrage against the Mafia. Within Italy, authorities reacted with an unprecedented crackdown on organized crime throughout the country, particularly in Sicily. The public created shrines to the magistrates, conducted marches against the Mafia, and attacked politicians who attended the magistrates' funerals, citing them for having allowed the Mafia to become so powerful, and for having failed to protect Falcone and Borsellino.

Several memorials were held; flowers and cards and notes were placed at the scenes of the assassinations.

The Italian government responded with soldiers in the streets and the wholesale roundup of Sicilian "men of honor." Outside the walls of Ucciardone, prison wives and other family members grieved as their husbands were locked up.

The murders also intensified the Italian government's desire to make a bold international strike against the most powerful of the Mafia's clans. They turned their sights on the Caruana-Cuntrera operating freely in Venezuela.

That Pasquale Cuntrera was safely ensconced in Venezuela was also a sore point for the U.S. government. They held a drug-trafficking warrant for him from the "Wiseguy" case, and at every turn they were rebuffed by the Venezuelan government. Now the Venezuelans were told that if they insisted on protecting Pasquale Cuntrera, a Drug Enforcement Administration strike force would go into the country and kidnap him.

The media was after the Cuntreras as well. A German television crew attempting to do a story on the family had its equipment smashed.

In Venezuela, Oreste Pagano said, "They felt completely safe and well-protected by the big important friends that he [Pasquale Cuntrera] had there in Venezuela. . . . They felt as strong as steel."[4]

But on August 31, 1992, President Carlos Andres Perez was deposed under allegations of corruption, and the Siciliana's wide circle of friends suddenly contracted. It was a time of great confusion at the top of the political ladder. Within days of Perez's loss of power, Guillermo Jimenez, chief of the Policia Tecnical Judicial, responsible for the organized crime division, decided to go after the Cuntreras.

As if suddenly awakened by the glaring light of truth, Jimenez told Italian magistrate Nitto Palma: "Investigations carried out in Venezuela have shown that the companies belonging to the Cuntreras were simply a cover for national and international drug trade."

In Rome, the Cuntreras' lawyers appealed the extradition warrant, arguing that their clients were Canadian citizens. Magistrate Nitto Palma countered these arguments with several pieces of documentary evidence, including a report noting that the DEA had, in frustration, threatened a "military action" in Venezuela to get the Cuntreras.

First, police detained Paolo Cuntrera's lawyer, Pedro Arevalo, and held him incommunicado to forestall any appeals or motions to halt their plans. Then they made night raids on the Cuntreras' homes, handcuffed the brothers, and held them under guard until they were tossed aboard a flight to Rome.

At Rome's Fiumicino airport, the exhausted and confused Cuntrera brothers were led off the plane. With their black-tinted hair, solid gold watches, and white shoes, they were turned over to Italian authorities.

After the arrests, Palermo police chief Antonio Manganelli said it took a "change of political climate" to get the Cuntreras into custody.

Documentation seized during the arrests showed a meticulous network of offshore companies and revealed that the Cuntreras and Caruanas had about US$100 million in assets, several dozen companies in Venezuela, and bank accounts in Canada, the United States, Bahamas, Dutch Antilles, Venezuela, Panama, the United Kingdom, France, the Netherlands, Belgium, Switzerland, Thailand, India, Cyprus, and Italy.

The extradition warrant was upheld. In January 1996, Pasquale Cuntrera was sentenced to twenty years in prison; Paolo and Gaspare Cuntrera were sentenced to thirteen years each. At the same trial, Alfonso Caruana was sentenced *in absentia* to twenty years for Mafia association and international drug trafficking. Key evidence came from the recently discovered tapes recorded in 1974 at the Montreal bar belonging to Paolo Violi.

On July 30, 1997, the Palermo Court of Appeal confirmed these sentences. Alfonso Caruana was sentenced to an additional one year and ten months in prison.

Venezuela

The arrest of the Cuntrera brothers left the underworld in Venezuela stunned. Many began making arrangements to get out of the country; others began planning for a renewed campaign of corruption. "There was chaos in Venezuela because Pasquale [Cuntrera] was well protected," Oreste Pagano recalled.[5]

But Alfonso Caruana said he wasn't surprised at the expulsions: he said Cuntrera had been careless and had allowed U.S. DEA undercover officers—John Costanzo and his partner—into his house, and had gone so far as to invite them to attend a family wedding.

The sudden absence of the Cuntreras effectively moved Alfonso Caruana up the ladder in the Siculiana family and, by 1993, he was at the top. His brother Gerlando was serving a twenty-year sentence in Canada for heroin trafficking, and his other brother, Pasquale, was in custody in Italy. But the moment the Cuntreras were bound for Italy, Caruana knew his days of protection, too, were numbered. He had an exit plan in place, but he wasn't ready to put it into effect just yet: the Siculiana family still had contacts at the highest level of government, and he would get a warning if any moves against him were to be made. If the police were to move in to arrest him, he could always return to Canada and take up residence there.

As a precaution, for three months after the midnight deportations of the Cuntreras, Alfonso Caruana went to ground, hidden by Oreste Pagano, who tucked him away in an apartment in Puerto La Cruz.

Caruana told Pagano that he knew he was wanted, and that he was aware of the dangers in Venezuela's new uncertain political situation: "In Caracas I don't know what can happen to me by the Italians. Therefore I prefer to go back to Canada because I feel safe."[6]

But before leaving he wanted to see his daughter, Anna Maria, wed to Carlo Napoli in Valencia. When Caruana invited Pagano to the ceremony, he confided to him that he didn't feel secure. "The police are all around," he acknowledged. "No one will come here to bother us during the wedding, but I have to leave later."[7]

And he wanted to arrange the biggest shipment of cocaine to Italy that he'd ever made. During the wedding reception, Caruana and Pagano held a meeting and hatched a scheme to procure and ship 5,466 kilograms of cocaine to Italy.

That was more cocaine than Erman Rubio could supply, so Pagano purchased the drugs from another Cali cartel supplier. The load was guaranteed by the cartel, Pagano was told. He gave US$6 million in cash to the supplier, and just before Christmas 1993 the cocaine was on its way.

Once the shipment had left for Italy, Alfonso Caruana, carrying a Venezuelan passport, fled to Canada.

When the money from the 5,466-kilo shipment didn't flow back to him in Venezuela, Pagano began to worry. He flew to Canada—bearing a Christmas gift for Caruana, a solid-gold Rolex watch—to find out what was causing the delay. Caruana told him things were fine, but there'd been some obstacles, and the cocaine would soon be picked up in Italy by members of his organization there and distributed.

During the visit of Pagano, Caruana did something to indicate that he had risen in the Siculiana family: he introduced Pagano to other family members, including Gerlando Caruana, who was finally on parole for heroin trafficking, and Luigi Vella, Alfonso Caruana's cousin.

Reassured, Pagano took Caruana's suggestion that he fly down to Bogota, Colombia, and start putting together another shipment. But on his way to Bogota, Pagano picked up a newspaper and got a shock: "While I was on the plane, I learned about the seizure of five thousand and four hundred kilos . . . "[8]

The 5,466 kilograms of cocaine seized by Italian police had been guaranteed by the Cali cartel. Pagano immediately went to Erman Rubio, his Colombian back-end, and demanded his down payment back. Rubio quickly paid the money, while telling Pagano, "If we continued to work, we could make this money back." Pagano took his money.

When he called Alfonso Caruana in Toronto to tell him about the situation, Caruana exploded. "He said it was my fault," Pagano recalled, ". . . that they had assurance of delivery."[9] Caruana didn't want the down payment back: he wanted the profits the cocaine shipment would have generated.

Undeterred, and figuring there was no point in wasting time, Pagano bought 60 kilos of cocaine from Rubio and sent it to Luigi Vella, Alfonso Caruana's cousin from Montreal, who oversaw the shipment in Miami. The drugs went through easily, aided by Cubans working at the Port of Miami, and was forwarded to Canada.

The pipeline to Miami was successful, Pagano told Alfonso. Now enthusiastic, Caruana immediately put together a shipment: 1,600 kilos. Half the load would belong to Caruana, the other half to the Colombian suppliers. It too slid through. When the Cubans had the drugs secured, Pagano called Caruana to let him know it was clear. Luigi Vella was dispatched from Canada to pick up Caruana's 800 kilos. Vella turned the cocaine over to a truck driver, who brought the drugs into Canada. On Alfonso Caruana's instructions, Vella later sent the truck driver to Miami with US$7 million in cash from the drug sales. Several more shipments were made in 1993 and 1994. Pagano regularly traveled to Canada, conducting meetings with members of the Vella family and Gerlando Caruana.

The organization did lose one shipment of 1,100 kilograms of cocaine at the Port of Miami. The Cubans working at the port spotted DEA officers looking over the container and got word to Pagano that the load was hot. Pagano called Rubio to pass on the information. "He did not believe me because he said that he himself had sent the merchandise, and that this time it was actually him personally that had placed the merchandise in the container," Pagano said. "And that the container was addressed to one of his aunts."

Rubio didn't believe anyone could have informed the police.

"Look, containers inspected by the police cannot be picked up," an angry Pagano told Rubio.

But Rubio sent his aunt to sign for the load; she was arrested, convicted, and sentenced to thirty years. What had made the load "hot" was that someone had opened it after Rubio sealed it, and added a 300-kilo shipment of his own.

"After this . . . these disputes, due to issues of mistrust we had had confrontations with Rubio and all ties were broken with him and the work through Miami was cut off," Pagano said. "We remained idle for several months."[10]

Italy

The men who became the heirs of assassinated judges Giovanni Falcone and Paolo Borsellino did not sit idle. With the seizure of 5,466 kilograms of cocaine from the *Cartagena des Indias*, the Anti-Mafia District Head Office in Turin set about tracing the source of the cocaine. Marcello Maddalena, in Turin, and Giancarlo Caselli, in Palermo, Sicily, both led the hunt for Cosa Nostra's most notorious leaders and financial advisers. But it was Maddalena who conducted the investigation that led to the dismantling of Alfonso Caruana's treasured and profitable Calabrian connection.

Following the seizure of cocaine aboard the *Cartagena des Indias*, several suspects were quickly rounded up and some turned informant. One of them was Antonio Scambia, the lifelong smuggler of cigarettes into Italy, and the key man who had been sent by Vincenzo Mazzaferro to meet Alfonso Caruana in Curaçao.

For the investigating magistrates, a better informant than Antonio Scambia would have been hard to imagine. And from Scambia's point of view, cooperating would mean a lighter prison sentence and an end to his financial problems with Alfonso Caruana. Scambia was on the short end of the US$300,000 down payment for the "guaranteed" cocaine shipment that was seized on the *Cartagena des Indias*, but while blood relatives of the Caruana-Cuntrera could always count on lawyers and funds to support their families, "outsiders" like Scambia were usually abandoned.

In meticulous detail, Scambia told the incredulous magistrates that the *Cartagena des Indias* shipment wasn't the only major shipment sent by Caruana—it was the eighth that Scambia himself had been involved in. He gave details of shipments adding up to almost 11,000 kilograms. Of that, about 8,500 kilograms had been seized—the current 5,466 kilos, and a 3,000-kilo load seized at Rio Grande, Brazil. But although far less than half the drugs shipped had made it to market, it was clear that the loss had been written off with indifference by the Caruana-Cuntrera as the cost of doing business.

Scambia said he precisely remembered several meetings he'd had with the men and linked the players throughout the entire conspiracy. He gave up not only the drug routes but the financial and commercial infrastructure of the organization as well.

And, he said, there were other Mafia cocaine groups being supplied aside from the *'ndrangheta* cartel of the Mazzaferro. Two of the ringleaders of the other groups, Arturo "Gianni" Martucci and Luigi "Nino" Rutigliano, provided evidence against Alfonso Caruana and Vito Genco. Rutigliano revealed that part of the profits from cocaine shipments was earmarked to finance the escape of Gaetano

Badalamenti, who was still in prison in the United States as the consequence of his involvement in the 1985 Pizza Connection case. "Some of the money was to be used to corrupt government officials to get him out," Rutigliano said.[11]

The "white collar" man of the Caruana Italian connection was Angelo Zannetti. He'd set up a series of bank accounts and companies to funnel the cocaine profits back to Caruana in Venezuela.

Zannetti, too, turned informer and provided documentation for bank accounts used to launder Caruana's profits. Initially, he said, Vito Genco would transfer the money to Switzerland, but as the network brought increasing profits, Zannetti was directed to set up a complex structure to move the money into Switzerland though several company accounts. The money was changed into U.S. dollars or Swiss francs, then wire-transferred to financial institutions in several countries, including the United States, France, the Netherlands, Brazil, and Venezuela. A financial review later carried out showed that 34-billion lire was moved out of Italy by the organization.

After sifting through thousands of pages of investigative reports, informants' statements, financial paperwork, and documentation from the Raggruppamento Operativo Speciale (ROS), in October 1996 Judge Paola Trovati brought forward a massive indictment naming dozens of suspects involved with the Caruana drug organization. Among them were members of 'ndrangheta and

There are five significant Italian-based organized crime groups: the Sicilian Mafia, the Calabrian 'ndrangheta, the Camorra of Naples, Sacra Corona Unita, and Stidda. Stidda is a purely criminal organization gathering momentum in the Italian underworld. In the wake of government crackdowns on the Sicilian Mafia and the Calabrian 'ndrangheta, Stidda is attempting to replace some of the influence of these criminal groups. Stidda members—many of them disenfranchised or disillusioned Cosa Nostra members—make up a direct-action organization that functions principally as an underworld mutual-aid society in the towns facing the Mediterranean Sea. Since 1989, when Cosa Nostra informer Francesco Marino Mannoia first mentioned the group to Italian magistrates, Stidda has spread throughout Italy and has made some significant global connections. Stidda members are called *stiddari* or *stiddaroli*. Informer Leonardo Messina predicted Stidda would replace a crumbling Cosa Nostra suffering the excesses of the Corleonesi bosses. Many of the murders involving the Agrigento Mafia—including the deaths of some Caruana-Cuntrera family members and supporters—have been blamed on Stidda's expansion. Stidda members undergo an initiation ceremony and exhibit a five-pointed tattoo resembling a spider's web on their right hands.

several who belonged to the Italian crime organization known as *Stidda*. Charges ranged from Mafia association to several homicides committed before and during the years Alfonso Caruana's South America-Italy cocaine conspiracy was underway.

Vito Genco was arrested but was released after the pretrial custody deadline passed. He fled to Venezuela where he kept a low profile, emerging only years later when wiretaps recorded him speaking to Alfonso Caruana on calls from Venezuela. Genco spent his days trying to obtain false identity documents for himself and planning several cocaine shipments to Italy.

The path of the money, though, led Italian investigators to yet another haven for Mafiosi, a place described as "the new Colombia," where corruption was an art and money laundering a craft.

Brazil

Brazil has always been an important touchstone for the Sicilian Mafia in general and the Caruana-Cuntrera in particular. As far back as the 1950s and 1960s, members of Sicily's Mafia clans regularly visited the South American country. A study by the Instituto Brasileiro Giovanni Falcone—named after the murdered magistrate—has documented at least fifty members of Italian criminal organizations in the country, most of them on the run from either each other or from the law.

In the early 1970s, Brazilian police captured several members of the Corsican underworld near Rio de Janeiro. And Tommaso Buscetta was arrested near the border of Uruguay a short time later. At the hands of Brazilian authorities he underwent a horrible bout of torture: his anus was penetrated with a cattle prod, his fingernails were torn from his fingers, and his genitals were badly beaten. Under the intense torture, he confessed to his involvement in the drug trade and revealed the names of other members of the Sicilian Mafia who were also players.

Even though Giuseppe Caruana left Sicily several decades ago, the Italian authorities hadn't forgotten about him. In 1996, he was convicted *in absentia* to five years in prison for Mafia association. Repeated requests for extradition were, and continue to be, ignored by the Brazilian government. Now a Brazilian citizen and the father of a prominent cardiologist, he lives well on two pensions, one for old age, the other for a back injury.

Gaetano Badalamenti, the expelled leader of the *Cupola*, based himself in Brazil, as did the super-boss in the heroin trade, Antonino Salamone.

It wasn't only the Sicilian Mafia that used Brazil as both headquarters and hideout. Antonio Bardellino, a Neapolitan Camorra boss wanted for drug trafficking in Italy, found the country to his liking, particularly the very upscale Copacabana district.

Giuseppe Caruana, Alfonso Caruana's uncle and father-in-law, was the first of the Siculiana family to settle in Rio de Janeiro. Ninety years old, the former leader of the Siculiana family lives there today in a luxurious apartment, often caught on wiretaps speaking to clan members in Canada.

Alfonso Caruana also liked Brazil, but for other reasons. He regularly visited both Rio and São Paulo, the country's financial centers, and maintained strong links to powerful politicians and businessmen. Following his own advice—"If you shoot, you make enemies; if you share you make friends"—he created a network of corruption made up of some of the most powerful and influential "friends," who themselves grew rich from his wealth. Police reports alleged that he used contacts in the Brazilian banking system to launder profits from the cocaine trade, and a spokesman for the Brazilian Securities Exchange Commission would later express fears that Mafia drug profits were being cleaned through the country's stock exchange.

After the seizure of the cocaine shipment near Turin that had been routed through Brazil, Italian authorities found a financial link between Alfonso Caruana and a powerful Brazilian businessman well connected to the government. Almost US$8 million from the cocaine sales in Italy were traced to the bank account of Paulo Cesar Farias. Farias was the election campaign treasurer of President Fernando Collor de Mello.[12] According to a report prepared by Brazilian anti-drug magistrate Walter Fanganiello Maierovitch, Alfonso Caruana, who he said was responsible for 70 percent of the cocaine moving through Brazil, and Farias were "well connected" to each other.[13]

For Alfonso Caruana, contacts like Paulo Cesar Farias were an integral part of the entire money-laundering and corruption network, no matter where in the world he settled. Farias was wealthy and wanted to get wealthier, and as de Mello's campaign treasurer he was close to the seat of power. However, Farias didn't need to rely on a fickle electorate to remain powerful, and he had his own avenues of corruption in the country's financial structure. In addition to dealing with Alfonso Caruana's money he was allegedly laundering drug profits for Domenico Verde, a naturalized Brazilian citizen wanted by Italian authorities for Mafia association.

A master influence-peddler and corruptor, Farias was the target of a four-year investigation by Brazilian authorities that ended with his arrest and conviction, and the impeachment of President Collor de Mello. After serving almost two years of a six-year sentence under house arrest, Farias was released. In 1996 Farias was to appear before a congressional commission to testify about organized crime and his activities during de Mello's term in office, but that June, before he could testify, he and his girlfriend were found shot to death in his heavily guarded home. A pistol was found near the woman's left hand. The inquest quickly ruled the deaths a murder-suicide—a crime of passion—but suspicions about the timing of the event led to a second investigation. Forensic tests showed that the woman hadn't discharged a firearm, that the path of the bullet through her body pointed away from suicide, that she was right-handed, and that Farias's body had been moved after he was killed.

Brazilian authorities reviewed the findings of the second investigation and formally accused Farias's brother, Congressman Augusto Farias, and seven of his employees of both the murder and the engineering of the coverup. The motive for the murders, they said, was to gain control of Paulo Farias's tens of millions of dollars in Mafia money, much of it profits made through the Caruana-Cuntrera. The investigation remains ongoing.

7

When Alfonso Caruana moved back to Canada to avoid capture in Venezuela, he decided to steer clear of Montreal, where the investigations of family members were becoming increasingly persistent and resulting in publicity, even notoriety. Not that he had anything to worry about: as far back as 1986 the Italian government had requested the extradition of Alfonso and his brother, Pasquale. But, the Italians were told, the RCMP was conducting their own active investigation—Mark Bourque's Project Pilgrim—into the brothers.

Eight years later, in 1994, Italian authorities again asked for help in tracking Alfonso, this time through his uncle, Giovanni (1929–01–01), who was living in Montreal. The organized crime section reported to the Italians that Giovanni Caruana was "one of the first generation of Caruana brothers of the Siciliana Family, living at 6349 rue de Beauvais, in St. Leonard (Quebec).

"His son, Giuseppe Caruana (1956–05–21) was arrested 1982–03–02 in Canada for heroin trafficking and sentenced to seven years," RCMP said, noting Giovanni was the uncle of Gerlando Caruana, who had been arrested in 1985 for trafficking heroin.

Married to Maria Cuffaro, Giovanni Caruana had no criminal record in Canada, but he was well-documented in both American and Canadian intelligence databases. As early as 1982 wiretaps had recorded telephones registered in his name in Montreal being used to call a telephone subscribed to by Gaspare Cuntrera, in Venezuela—at a time when Gaspare, Paolo, and Pasquale Cuntrera were under active investigation for heroin trafficking in New York City. A meeting Giovanni Caruana attended with the Cuntrera brothers and several Montreal organized crime figures in Miami, Florida, was noted.[1]

*

Montreal was home to dozens of Siciliana family members, notably the Rizzutos and Cuntreras. Caruana knew his return to Montreal would spark even more police and media attention. His older brother, Gerlando, was on federal parole for heroin trafficking, and his younger brother, Pasquale, was in prison in Italy. With the imprisonment of the Cuntrera brothers and their lengthy detention in Italy, Alfonso Caruana was now the acknowledged head of the Siciliana family.

In January 1995 the Court of Palermo sentenced Giovanni Caruana to four years in prison—*in absentia*—for Mafia association.

Instead he chose Toronto—Canada's largest city, where Sicilian Mafia activities were low-key and overshadowed by investigations into Calabrian and U.S. La Cosa Nostra–related activities. Caruana had already set family members to work buying residences and businesses and making connections with the city's Sicilian Mafiosi, who had long worked from the shadows organizing heroin and cocaine shipments.

Toronto has a lengthy history of Sicilian Mafia–related drug trafficking, but except for relatively minor turf wars within criminal syndicates, it was considered an "open city," where several organized crime groups could operate both together and separately. Toronto was also where fugitive Mafiosi on the run could go to ground.

In November 1994, a police wiretap in Italy led to the arrest of Salvatore Ferraro, who had fled Sicily in the wake of the crackdown following the Falcone-Borsellino assassinations. Just prior to leaving for Canada, Ferraro had been listed by Italian police as the new boss of the Mafia in Caltanissetta's province, the old boss having been arrested in the Falcone-Borsellino aftermath.

Badassare Di Maggio, driver and confidant of Toto Riina, had moved to Toronto to escape his boss's wrath, returning later to Sicily where he became instrumental in Riina's capture.

With its several Italian communities, Toronto is a transit point for Sicilian Mafiosi making their way into the United States. Many of the players involved in the U.S. Pizza Connection case were funneled through Toronto with the assistance of the locally based Calabrian crime families. Some of them stayed in the city, where they opened pizza restaurants and fast-food franchises, or took low-profile construction jobs. Some police authorities believe that Canada had—and still has—its own version of the Pizza Connection, and a full grasp of the network still hasn't been reached.

Repeated waves of violence in Toronto in the 1960s led to police targeting Calabrian crime groups at the expense of investigating Sicilian crime families. Early intelligence showed drug-related contacts between several 'ndrangheta clan leaders and Sicilian heroin traffickers.

Of primary interest among the Calabrian group was Rocco Zito, who was often seen in company with the Sicilian Mafiosi who operated vast drug networks between Italy and the United States. As far back as 1970, RCMP surveillance teams had watched Zito meeting with Giuseppe Indelicato, a prolific, Siculiana-born heroin trafficker who had been deported to Canada from the United States after serving a prison sentence for smuggling a kilo and a half of heroin. Other investigations documented Zito meeting continually with members of the city's Sicilian faction. While the links between the 'ndrangheta and the Sicilian Mafia emerged in several investigations, the focus of police attention remained on the local activities of the 'ndrangheta.

Toto Riina's reign of terror against the Sicilian Mafia and the Italian State came to an end when he was arrested in January 1993. In October 1997, Guido Lo Forte, Palermo's assistant chief prosecutor, warned of a Cosa Nuova—a new Sicilian Mafia—made up of those who disdained Riina's bloody methods. This new Cosa Nuova was guided by Bernardo Provenzano, Lo Forte said: "The era of Riina is over. An extremely refined plan, being hatched by a mind that is particularly intelligent and involving international crime, is establishing a new Mafia order."

The rise to power of the Sicilian Mafia in modern Canada—specifically Toronto and Montreal—coincided with two overseas events: the strategy meeting in Palermo in 1957, when the Sicilian Mafia and the U.S. La Cosa Nostra formed an alliance to gain control of the international heroin trade, and the Ciaculli massacre of 1963.

There were numerous heroin traffickers operating in both Toronto and Montreal, as well as in some smaller centers, but no cohesive organization was ever uncovered.

"We'd make a drug case, arrest the suspects and seize the heroin," former RCMP assistant commissioner Richard Dickins recalls. "Mostly we thought they were just a bunch of bums bringing in small shipments, selling them off, and bringing in more. We had no idea of the significance of what happened in Palermo, or that after the [Ciaculli] massacre we had an imported criminal organization." Dickins, who ran several drug cases involving the Sicilian Mafia, added: "Suddenly, they were just there."[2]

In 1990, the RCMP produced a secret report naming the main players in the Sicilian Mafia. The report concentrated almost solely on the importation and distribution of heroin, and outlined the links between several members of Sicilian Mafia groups, as well as their ties to the *'ndrangheta* and American La Cosa Nostra families.

John Papalia, La Cosa Nostra representative in southern Ontario, traveled to New York City with members of Toronto's Sicilian clans in the late 1950s, the report said. The purpose of the visit was to attend meetings in anticipation of setting up the famed French Connection pipeline. Papalia was later among those convicted in the case.

The report noted the activities in the early 1970s of Benedetto Zizzo, the brother of Salvatore Zizzo, the boss of the Salemi (Sicily) Mafia, in Toronto. Benedetto Zizzo was convicted in Toronto of heroin trafficking.

Police found two factions of the Sicilian Mafia operating in Toronto: the Trapani faction and the Agrigento faction. One of the leaders of the Trapani faction was Nicola Genua, a prolific heroin trafficker known as "the little old cheesemaker." In one case, Genua sold heroin to the RCMP from the family's midtown upscale foodshop, Nicola's Choice Meats. One of the leaders of the Agrigento faction was Giacinto Arcuri, described in police intelligence notes as a close associate of the New York Bonanno family. Arcuri had long been a mystery to police in Italy: after a murder in Sicily in 1955, he was named in a murder warrant, but the warrant was later canceled because police believed he was dead. He turned up in Canada where he operated a paving company, which police surveillance teams believed was used for Mafia meetings. U.S. authorities were well aware of Arcuri, documenting trips he made back Sicily.[3]

Giacinto Arcuri is currently before the courts, charged with killing Enio Mora.

While both groups were involved in heroin trafficking, the Agrigento faction was more prominent. Their links were shown to be to the Bonanno New York family—notably the Sicilians who ran the Pizza Connection—and to the Nicolò Rizzuto crime family of Montreal—both prominent clients of the Caruana-Cuntrera heroin pipeline.

The RCMP's report documents international connections as well: "The Genua faction is aligned with their Mafia counterparts in Trapani, Sicily, possibly the Mafia 'cosca' (family) based in Salemi and Vita (Sicily)."

The realization that there was a strong Sicilian Mafia network in place, one that worked with other Toronto organized crime groups, began to dawn on authorities in the 1970s. The RCMP report points out: "Investigations resulted in heroin importing charges [being laid] against members of the Toronto Sicilian group, the Rocco Zito group and the Bonanno La Cosa Nostra family. The source for this heroin were members of the Rizzuto group."

Under the Rizzuto wing of the Caruana-Cuntrera, heroin from laboratories in Sicily was flooding in to the United States and Canada. Italian police were constantly hunting the laboratories and shutting them down. Several times in 1982, associates of Nicola Genua traveled to Italy and visited the heroin producers, who were receiving their morphine base from Bangkok, Thailand. In March 1982, one multi-kilo shipment of pure heroin had already moved through the pipeline, and police were expecting several more. Profits were being hand-carried back to Italy by Trapani Faction members.

Cargo ships making their way from Palermo to Naples carried drugs—facilitated by a corrupt harbor master—and moved them into North America. In March 1983, Nicola Genua went to Sicily to arrange shipments directly from the laboratories, buying from Salvatore Miceli, a Sicilian trafficker who was the nephew of Salemi Mafia leader Salvatore Zizzo.

The growing power of the Sicilian families in Toronto coincided with the coming of age of the Caruana-Cuntrera in Montreal and South America, and the most profitable years of the Pizza Connection traffickers. Many of the senior members of the Caruana-Cuntrera were supplying heroin to the Toronto Sicilian wing. Unlike Montreal, however, where a lengthy struggle was fought to oust Paolo Violi, in Toronto the Calabrian families accepted offers to partake in the profits from the new

Salvatore Miceli had previously lived in Toronto in the 1960s but had returned to Italy after being charged with drug trafficking in Vancouver in 1971. Toronto police intelligence files show him meeting with Calabrian bosses as he set up fresh drug networks. Miceli died of natural causes in Italy in 1984.[4]

reality of heroin. The influence of the Buffalo La Cosa Nostra was waning, and that organization was falling apart because of internal struggles. With the exception of some "honor" killings and a few struggles for turf and position, Toronto was a calm oasis in the storms gathering around Alfonso Caruana.

What Caruana didn't know was that Toronto would be the place where two policemen, who between them earned as much in annual salary as he spent on wristwatches, would begin to attack his reign as head of the Siculiana family.

Montreal, Quebec / Venezuela

Oreste Pagano made a half dozen trips to Canada after Alfonso Caruana fled Venezuela a few steps ahead of police. The organization needed to make more drug shipments to keep itself going.

Pagano was introduced, member by member, to the Montreal wing of the Caruana-Cuntrera, the Rizzuto family. Caruana told Pagano that "Paolo" and "Pietro" Rizzuto were Mafiosi, and that "Paolo" was the "Mafia leader of the Italian Mafia [that] is in Canada." (He was confused when later discussing the meeting: from his statements he clearly meant Vito Rizzuto, and his father Nicolò Rizzuto, the man who had orchestrated the death of Paolo Violi and the usurping of the Vincenzo Cotroni organization in the late 1970s.)

Life for the Rizzuto family had been uneven for the past decade. Leaving his son Vito—described by some investigators as "the John Gotti of Montreal" because of his fine clothes and grooming—in charge, Nicolò "Zu Cola" Rizzuto, had moved to Venezuela to arrange cocaine exports to North America. He remained close to both the Caruana and the Cuntrera families. Venezuelan police amassed a huge intelligence file on him, likely used by the government to extract increasingly large bribes.

In February 1988, police raided Rizzuto's home in Venezuela and seized 700 grams of cocaine. Four other men were arrested with him, including Gennaro Scaletta and Paolo Cuntrera's son-in-law Antonino Mongiovì.

Rizzuto was sentenced to eight years in prison, and his associates undertook a campaign to convince corrupt Venezuela officials to free him. After five years of negotiations, according to an RCMP affidavit, Montrealer Domenic Tozzi—a money launderer for both the Caruana-Cuntrera and the Rizzuto family—reportedly took US$800,000 to Venezuela to bribe officials.

Rizzuto was greeted by many of his family at the airport in Montreal in May 1993. Repeated requests from the Canadian government to determine the circumstances of his sudden parole went unanswered. Rizzuto, by then an elder statesman of the Mafia, settled again in Montreal, where he spent much of his time attending social functions and advising his son, Vito, on family business.

Then, on November 30, 1987, Vito Rizzuto was arrested in Newfoundland for conspiracy after 16 tons of hashish, worth US$350 million, was seized. (Three years later the charges would be dropped when the Newfoundland Supreme Court ruled that evidence used in the case was illegally obtained.)

So high-profile was the Rizzuto name in Canada that when police arrested fifty-seven people on cocaine and money-laundering charges in 1994, some newspapers led their coverage with the fact that Vito Rizzuto *wasn't* among them. A prosecutor said publicly that Vito Rizzuto was "part of the conspiracy," but noted that they had insufficient evidence to charge him.

The case revolved around a storefront "sting" operation set up by the RCMP to snare drug traffickers. The storefront took in CDN$98.3 million in cocaine and hashish profits over a three-year period. Eight countries were targeted in the trafficking and laundering scheme: Canada, the Netherlands, Aruba, Colombia, Venezuela, Brazil, England, and Panama. Among those

Gennaro Scaletta (born in Italy, February 22, 1938) was an important but largely ignored member of Rizzuto's Sicilian faction in Montreal and in Venezuela. In 1988 he was hit with a Revenue Canada jeopardy assessment for $390,000 after $250,000 was found in a Montreal bank account. In November 1987 he had entertained two women at his Montreal home. The women were relatives of Eduardo Fernandez, who ran against Carlos Andres Perez for the presidency of Venezuela the following year. Fernandez lost the 1988 election after allegations of Mafia association were raised. Information from FBI sources suggests that Scaletta is "known for his successful illegal financial schemes in Caracas. In September 1987 he left Caracas and moved to Montreal to take over the business duties of Alfonso Caruana."[5]

In an internal RCMP document dated April 30, 1993, Sergeant Mark Lavoie wrote an account of a luncheon meeting between Tozzi and an undercover police officer, in which Tozzi told of paying the bribe. Tozzi later denied taking the money to Venezuela.

arrested, or sought on warrants, were Sicilian Mafiosi, La Cosa Nostra members in Montreal, Hells Angels motorcycle club members, lawyers, and businessmen.

Court papers filed in the case did mention Vito Rizzuto and his efforts to liquidate us$3 billion worth of gold stolen by Philippine president Ferdinand Marcos. The gold ingots disappeared after Marcos was overthrown in 1986. The gold was hidden in Hong Kong and Zurich, Switzerland. Police believe that Rizzuto—who was documented traveling to Switzerland, Hong Kong, and Manila—was involved in liquidating the fortune.

In 1994, Nicolò Rizzuto's wife, Libertina, was arrested on money laundering charges in Switzerland after she was caught trying to deposit $3 million at different banks in a single day. She was acquitted for lack of evidence, sparking a controversy in the Canadian House of Commons. Bloc Québécois member of Parliament Michel Bellehumeur charged that the RCMP's "lack of cooperation" had resulted in Libertina Rizzuto being set free. Herb Gray, the solicitor general, denied these charges, and said that the RCMP's cooperation with the Swiss authorities was "excellent."

In 1992, the body of Joseph Lo Presti, Nicolò Rizzuto's right-hand man, was found wrapped in plastic and canvas alongside a railway track in Montreal's east end. Lo Presti had been a key player in the Rizzuto–New York heroin network in the late 1970s and 1980s. Police had investigated him in 1978 after the Paolo Violi murder, but he wasn't charged. Lo Presti was a longtime supplier of heroin to the John Gotti crew of the Gambino La Cosa Nostra family in New York City. The murder remains unsolved.

At one of his meetings with Caruana and Nicolò Rizzuto, Oreste Pagano was told that Alfonso had an acquaintance in Bolìvar, Venezuela, who owned a gold mine. "And these people, at various times throughout the year, would send the product extracted from the mine to Canada. And together with this, coke could be sent in. They told me to send one hundred kilos of coke to this person. I went to the city of Bolìvar personally and gave [the acquaintance] one hundred kilos of coke."

The man was arrested in Venezuela, and the drugs were seized. When word reached Pagano of the drugs' fate, he discovered also that the man had been shipping 500 kilos of cocaine, and not the 100 kilos Pagano had given him. This angered Caruana, who said the exporter would pay for the shipment and the lost earnings as well.

Other plans to ship cocaine to a friend of Alfonso Caruana's, who owned a Toronto fish market, were discussed, but a scheme couldn't be finalized.

Caruana asked Pagano if cocaine could be provided for shipment to "his cousins" living in Ostia, Italy. Pagano, still stinging over the Bolìvar shipment that fell through, was indifferent. He felt he'd lost the trust of his suppliers, who'd fronted the drugs.

In 1995, Luigi Vella went to Venezuela to meet with Pagano to discuss shipping drugs to Canada. Vella had found a way of getting huge shipments of cocaine into Canada by using Toronto-bound Canadian Airline flights that touched down to pick up tourists in Venezuela. His contacts at Pearson International Airport would put the shipments through. But, he cautioned Pagano, Alfonso Caruana wasn't to know about the method.

"If he finds out about it, he'll keep most of it for himself and only give me . . . a little bit," Vella said.

Vella's scheme was to split the shipments: 50 percent would belong to Pagano and Juan Carlos Pavo, the Colombian back-end; the rest would belong to Vella. Alfonso Caruana didn't figure into the equation at all.

But Luigi Vella had more to worry about than sneaking shipments past Alfonso Caruana.

Toronto, Ontario

Camillo Moro was well positioned to facilitate Luigi Vella's plans to get multi-kilo shipments of cocaine off airplanes and out of Toronto's Pearson International Airport. As a supervisor for Hudson General Aviation Services—a private firm contracted by the federal government to unload luggage from planes at Terminal One—the forty-eight-year-old Moro had access to a fleet of company vehicles, assisted baggage handlers, and could arrange work schedules for staff.

The Calabrian-born Moro lived an agreeable lifestyle in Brampton, northwest of Toronto. He had a comfortable house, a wife, two children, and five vehicles, one of them a late-model Lincoln Continental. In his spare time, he did residential dry-walling. His criminal record was relatively minor: mischief to property, assault causing bodily harm, and, at the time of the investigation, a drunk driving charge, incurred while operating a company vehicle on airport property.

One of the men Moro supervised at the airport was Mario Ippolito Donato, a baggage handler. On telephone intercepts conducted during an investigation called Caviar/Overdate, Moro was "The Tall One" and Donato was "The Little One."

The link between the airport workers and Montreal's Caruana-Cuntrera-Vella group was Giuseppe "Joe" Marchese, a café owner in Toronto. Marchese, whose native tongue is Sicilian, often complained about miscommunication with Moro, who spoke a Calabrian dialect.

In the spring of 1995, Ontario Provincial Police Detective Ron Seaver, a veteran organized crime investigator who had spent years with the Combined Forces Unit, was probing the importation of cocaine into Toronto's Pearson International Airport. He found elements of the Montreal mafia at work, using airport workers to facilitate the removal of multi-kilo loads of cocaine directly off airplanes arriving from South America.

In April 1996, 30 kilograms of cocaine was seized by Canada Customs at the airport. Montreal investigators, who had information about their end of the drug network, went to Toronto, and a project was set up focusing on Francesco Ruggiero, who had emerged as a key player in the scheme. Ruggiero regularly drove five minutes from his house to use a telephone at a bakery. Police wired up the phone and found that Ruggiero regularly called Montreal organized crime figure Gabriele Casale.

The surveillance of telephone calls into Toronto and Montreal began to detect a major cocaine conspiracy involving the Vella wing of the Caruana-Cuntrera. That it was international wasn't in doubt: calls were recorded between Canada and Spain, Germany, and Italy.

By August 1995, the Overdate/Caviar investigators had followed the lines of conspiracy from Ruggiero to Casale on the one side, and from Ruggiero to Marchese to Moro and Donato on the other.

The wires provided evidence that the airport workers were becoming increasingly fearful of continuing to assist the smuggling. At one point they told Marchese and Ruggiero that they had been laid off and wouldn't be able to get the cocaine through the airport. They said they wouldn't be back to work for several months. This didn't sit well with Casale, who continually called Marchese to get them back to work.

In January 1996, a survey of numbers dialed by Ruggiero showed calls to a man named "Luigi" at a telephone listed as belonging to N. Ragusa, at 202 Antoine Forest, Vimont, Quebec. "'Luigi' turned out to be Luigi Vella," Seaver said. "He was married to Antonia Ragusa. Montreal files showed Vella was part of the Caruana-Cuntrera organization."

On February 1, 1996, Marchese called Camillo Moro to find out when he and Donato were going back to work. He told them he was under pressure and had to give "them" an answer right away. Meanwhile, he stalled Casale, who was becoming increasingly agitated that the pipeline wasn't producing.

Three weeks later, Casale flew to Toronto and met with Marchese, Moro, and Donato in the city's Little Italy section. "He met the three guys and really gave them shit," a police wiretap picked up. Frustrated, Luigi Vella called Marchese and asked "if there's any hope" that the airport workers were going back on the job.

"They're going back this week or next week," Marchese said, but he mentioned that things were going to be "different" because cameras had been installed where they worked.

Surveillance and wiretaps continued, with only insignificant results. Ruggiero's brother-in-law was arrested when a courier came through the airport with 2 kilograms of cocaine and delivered them to a local hotel. Another shipment referred to on the wiretaps failed to arrive. Casale made calls to Toronto from Rome; Ruggiero called regularly from Germany where he was temporarily staying.

On March 19, 1996, after meeting with Marchese at a Howard Johnson Hotel in north Toronto, Luigi Vella and an unidentified associate went to an upscale Italian restaurant in midtown, where they met with second unidentified man. When the third man left the restaurant, police ran the license number of his car: it came back registered to Giuseppe Cuntrera, Alfonso Caruana's nephew.

Meanwhile, the problems with Moro and Donato continued.

Luigi Vella called Marchese: "A lot of people are upset, they don't need to hear this. There is Mafia involved and a lot of money."

Under heavy pressure to get back into the game, Donato was heard in April telling Moro, "I'll do it even if I don't make a penny, as long as they leave me alone."

On April 12, Vella had his supplier in place in Venezuela—Oreste Pagano—and his airport people lined up. He called Marchese and told him the deal was on the go.

Marchese pleaded with him to stop the shipment.

"It's too late," Vella told him, describing two wine-colored suitcases that contained the drugs.

At 7:50 p.m., a Canair flight from Venezuela was searched and two bags—exactly as described by Vella and containing 43 kilograms of cocaine—were seized.

Vella, Marchese, Moro, and Donato were arrested and charged with conspiracy to import cocaine. Donato admitted his role, saying that he and Moro had been involved in bringing drugs through the airport for Marchese and Vella for at least two years. All were convicted and sent to prison.

Ruggiero cooperated with the police and testified in court. Charges against him were dropped.

Luigi Vella's end run around Alfonso Caruana was over.

Margarita Island

Although the Luigi Vella smuggling scheme was halted by Ron Seaver and the Overdate/Caviar teams, Oreste Pagano remained in constant contact with Alfonso Caruana. He hadn't told Caruana about the separate deals he had with Vella. Caruana, for his part, wanted to get new projects of his own going. Early in 1996, he asked Pagano to go to the Margarita Island Hilton Hotel to meet a man who wanted to set up a pipeline into Canada.

"He was Italian, about thirty-five," Pagano said, not remembering his name.

The man introduced Pagano to a French-Canadian named Yvon who kept a boat at Margarita Island. The boat had a secret compartment where up to 500 kilograms of cocaine could be hidden. Pagano looked over the boat and called Alfonso Caruana: "It's doable."

He brought in his Colombian contact, Juan Carlos Pavo; Pavo inspected the boat and was pleased.

A 500-kilogram shipment was arranged. In Caruana's usual method, it was divided into thirds: one-third each for Pagano and the Colombians, and one-third to be shared by Alfonso, Gerlando, and Pasquale Caruana—who had finally been freed from an Italian prison—along with two members of the Toronto Cuntrera clan. One of the Cuntreras had no money; he asked Pagano to put in 25 kilos for him, and in return he'd put up a diamond as collateral in case the shipment was lost.

The shipment went through without incident. Yvon, "the boatman," sailed to the edge of Canadian territorial waters, where the drugs were offloaded onto another boat and brought to shore. Yvon was paid off in cocaine.

Two shipments quickly followed.

At Christmas 1996, Juan Carlos Pavo told Pagano that a shipment of 5,000 kilos would arrive in Spain and he was free to buy into it. Pagano told Alfonso Caruana, who immediately bought in for 100 kilos.

Pagano flew to Spain and met with the Triassi brothers, notorious Italian traffickers. In Barcelona he closed the deal with the Triassis, who loaded the shipment onto a truck bound for Italy. The Triassis paid promptly enough—four and a half billion lire—but Pagano had to have his money picked up in Italy. Pagano hired Alberto Minelli to get the money back to Venezuela, but Minelli used a storefront operation set up by the Italian police as part of the American "sting" operation, Casablanca. The money was seized. Other money Pagano was trying to get out of Italy—about US$500,000 he owed to his Colombian suppliers—was also seized, this time by Swiss authorities.

8

The Italian authorities were convinced that Alfonso Caruana, having fled Venezuela, was in contact with family members in Canada. They sent RCMP liaison officer Dennis Fiorido a package of documents on Project Cartagine, the investigation being conducted by the Raggruppamento Operativo Speciale (ROS) into Caruana's South America–Turin, Italy drug network. Fiorido forwarded the documents to the RCMP Quebec division's criminal intelligence office.

As Christmas 1996 approached, the Italians hoped that Canadian police would get warrants clearing the way to wiretap the telephones of Gerlando Caruana, Alfonso's brother. They wanted to get long-distance telephone records for Gerlando, or any other member of the group, to establish if calls were made to Italy or South America. "We believe that the twelve months [from] Christmas 1995 [to] Christmas 1996 may provide useful intelligence that may ultimately assist in locating Alfonso Caruana, the Christmas season being a time when long-distance telephone greetings are usually made," Fiorido wrote. His memo also noted that the Italian authorities had a wide wiretapping project underway in Italy, targeting "the Mafia Family Cuntrera."

In addition, Italian officials requested any new intelligence on Alfonso Caruana that could be used to track him down.

Fiorido was told by the RCMP in Montreal that there was a possibility Alfonso Caruana had been seen in Toronto. Fiorido notified Italian authorities, who were interested but skeptical. Police forces in several countries had tried to find Alfonso Caruana; that he had possibly been sighted in Toronto was too much to hope for.

The ROS sent fresh intelligence from their own ongoing investigations and asked the RCMP to follow it up. They had documentation to prove that millions of dollars of profits from Caruana's cocaine trafficking business had been sent to the Bank of New York and into the accounts of two Canadian companies, one in Toronto and the other in Montreal. Italian police asked for information on Toronto-area telephone numbers called by the targets of their investigation.

Toronto, Ontario

Since April 1996, after turning Enio Mora's telephone conversation about the Caruana-Catalanotto wedding into the beginning of a major criminal investigation, Detective-Constables Bill Sciammarella and Tony Saldutto of the Toronto Police intelligence squad had been reassigned to the Combined Forces Special Enforcement Unit.

Originally called the Special Enforcement Unit (SEU), the CFSEU had been formed in 1977 in response to increased organized crime activity in Toronto and southern Ontario. It was comprised of RCMP, Ontario Provincial Police, and Toronto intelligence officers and detectives, along with members of Peel and York Regional Police forces. Over the years, the fortunes and effectiveness of the CFSEU ebbed and flowed, depending on leadership and financial resources. Under some managers it was seen as a lame duck, a dumping ground for the disgruntled and inept. Under others it shone, taking the lead in high-profile investigations into Canada's most active crime figures. One success involved hiring a television makeup artist to create two "dead bodies," apparent victims of a murder contract, to convince organized crime figures that the murders had been carried out. Another success was breaking a plot between white supremacists and Canadian gangland figures to invade a Caribbean island.

"The SEU wasn't created by consensus," a now-retired officer said. "It was a fight every step of the way. If you look at the management as 'regimes,' you'll find there were kings who fought for their kingdoms and there were lackeys of management who folded their tents and faded away.

"Remember, when the SEU started you couldn't say 'Mafia' without some politician getting flak from a community. He'd roll the rock down onto the police management, who'd in turn take a swing at the SEU. You were fighting a criminal organization that you couldn't even name

147

in public. And we targeted criminals, not specific crimes. This caused a lot of problems for some managers who felt there was enough crimes reported without finding crimes that not been reported at all. But it was the only way to even begin to penetrate the organizations."

Sciammarella and Saldutto, in the months after the Caruana-Catalanotto wedding, remained assigned to the anti-Mafia squad of the Toronto Police Service. Downsizing, budget cutbacks, and the focus on community-based policing had led to wholesale changes throughout the department. The intelligence bureau, where the officers once worked, was being dismantled. Detectives were transferred; some received pager messages from the commander telling them not to report for intelligence duty the following day, but instead to show up at local divisions for regular policing duties. Specialists in financial crime investigations found themselves back in uniform, patrolling neighborhoods or doing daily, general assignment detective work.

"It was pretty grim at Dyas Road [intelligence headquarters]," a detective remembers. "There was nothing mean-spirited about it—the brass said cut thirty or forty or fifty bodies and the commander did it. But the loss of expertise and experience was astounding, and some of the methods used were pretty heavy-handed."

As the seeds of the Caruana project were being sown, organized crime detectives in Montreal were investigating a Mafia conspiracy. There were several of wiretaps on the go, and many avenues of investigation pointed to Toronto. The Montreal detectives needed more "wires" in Toronto and contacted the CFSEU. This brought RCMP Staff-Sergeant Larry Tronstad into the picture. Tronstad was a veteran of organized crime and drug cases going back decades, and officer-in-charge at the CFSEU.

Larry Tronstad—known as "Tromper"—had a reputation in organized crime investigation that was similar to the reputation Alfonso Caruana held in the underworld. As an investigator with the early SEU, Tronstad had partnered with the best of the best of the investigators tracking drug traffickers and underworld figures, including Richard Dickins, a legendary RCMP "drug man" who became assistant commissioner before taking a job with the United Nations Drug Control Program in Asia. Dickins described the early Larry Tronstad as a "policeman through and through. . . . On a lot of cases he was the heart of the CFSEU."

When Montreal came calling for help with their wires, Tronstad readily went to work. He checked the RCMP's wire room and found it already working to capacity, so he went shopping.

"Metro [Toronto Police] had plenty of room at Dyas," Tronstad said. "They were closing down most of their operations and we made an arrangement with them, agreeing to pick up the tab. They were in a tough position: they had to cut back all over the place. I asked for Sciammarella and Saldutto. They *were* the anti-Mafia squad, and I'd worked with them in the past."

With Sciammarella and Saldutto seconded to the CFSEU, it was only a matter of time before the subject of Alfonso Caruana came up. Tronstad, who'd been aware of the Caruana-Cuntrera since the early days when RCMP Sergeant Mark Bourque put Project Pilgrim together, was enthusiastic. "We decided, then and there: let's do the Caruanas."

In a world of policing where big cases can mean big trouble, Tronstad predicted a big case with big results.

"If it wasn't for Larry, Project Omertà would have never got off the ground," Sciammarella said. Saldutto agreed: "He not only saw the possible problems, he saw the possible success."

Preliminary surveillance had shown that Alfonso Caruana was now operating a drug-trafficking and money-laundering operation out of the house on Goldpark Court in Woodbridge, Ontario. The outwardly calm, stocky, dapper leader of the Siculiana/Caruana-Cuntrera organization spent his days in regular contact with members of the city's most notorious underworld clans.

Surveillance at one of the businesses—the Shock Nightclub in Toronto's west end—had caught several organized crime figures attending the club's grand opening. Similar activity was found at a family-operated health club and several restaurants and stores owned by members or associates of the Caruana-Cuntrera organization.

Once basic research and sporadic surveillance possibilities were exhausted, Sciammarella began the painstaking work of filling out an application for a Dialed Number Recorder warrant. A DNR to target telephones was easier to get than a warrant to intercept private communications. DNRs would allow the investigators to find new avenues of inquiry that would allow them to flesh out the emerging drug network.

Meanwhile, the RCMP's Proceeds of Crime section was conducting a money-laundering "sting" operation.

The ability to move cash is a specialty in the underworld, and people with connections to facilitate the transfer and cleaning of money are in great demand. From the corner restaurant that will "commingle," or blend, a small-time drug trafficker's profits with its own cash flow, to the bank manager or brokerage firm employee who accepts funds without identifying their source, money-laundering services are as necessary to drug traffickers as the drugs themselves.

In the days before money laundering was a criminal act and the proceeds of criminal activities were subject to government seizure, drug importation syndicates had only one major problem: getting their product to market. Interdiction at any level of transport was the primary concern of the traffickers. Generally, if they could get their heroin or cocaine or hashish to the street, they would suffer little if any financial penalty beyond bail and legal fees if they were caught. In some jurisdictions, tax evasion might become a problem, but if law enforcement was able to seize the drugs and lock up the traffickers, it was considered a win.

Over the past decade, however, many jurisdictions—led by the United States—have increasingly targeted the financial side of criminal activities. Legislation of varying degrees of significance has been enacted to allow the seizure of assets proven to be proceeds of crime. Those who assist or enable the movement of criminal profits into legitimate financial systems—currency exchange operators, bankers, lawyers, and stockbrokers—themselves become targets of investigation.

Since the 1980s, United States law enforcement has exploited the criminal's need for financial services by conducting sting operations against crime syndicates, primarily the Colombian cocaine cartels. The stings have sometimes been remarkably creative and resourceful. In Operation Green Ice, the Drug Enforcement Administration (DEA) set up an agent in California who got word out that she could launder huge amounts of cocaine profits. Colombian traffickers flocked to the tall, fashionable, blonde trader who drove a flashy sports car and lived in an upscale neighborhood. After they gave her their money, she put it through law-enforcement-controlled bank accounts, leaving a paper trail that exposed the international financial avenues that were used to repatriate the drug profits. Often, after a sting operation, the money would be seized and forfeited to the government.[1]

In Operation Casablanca, the DEA stung Mexican bankers, luring them to the U.S. side of the border, where they were arrested. Similarly, Operation Dinero took a multi-million-dollar bite out of cartel profits. All of the sting operations had international connections and exposed crossovers between several diverse organized crime groups, ranging from Cosa Nostra, the Camorra, and the 'ndrangheta to white-collar laundering syndicates operating in the world's legitimate financial sectors.

Key to the money sting is the setting up of a "storefront," which might be a trading company, a factory, a currency exchange, an investment house, or just an office with a forgettable name on the door. Once a storefront is set up, word is put out to underworld targets that the "front" can launder money, either through its own bank accounts or via contacts in financial institutions.

Former RCMP Sergeant Gabriel Marion, who worked both the drug and financial sides of investigations, described storefronts as "magnets" that almost always succeed drawing in criminals with too much money and no way to get it into the system or out of the country.

"They come in, you talk to them, but you don't just agree right away to launder their money. You say: 'I'll have to check you out, what you are into.' And they'll tell you. You agree at first to move a small amount, maybe one or two hundred thousand. They tell you where they want it sent; you send it there. As a source of intelligence, storefronts are invaluable; as an investigative lead to track the money later, you can't beat them."

Typically, Marion said, police will have made arrangements with a cooperating bank to "launder" illegal profits; the money is traced as it makes its way through the financial system, perhaps resting for mere hours in one country's banking system before it's electronically wired to another, and then ultimately repatriated. As word gets around in criminal circles that a storefront operation is successful, more and more clients show up with hard-luck stories about being too cash rich. Several storefronts have brought out organized crime groups the police had no idea were active.

Not all stings are completely successful. Between 1990 and 1994, the RCMP set up a currency exchange in Montreal that went badly wrong. The covert company, Montreal International Currency Centre Inc., took CDN$141.5 million in drug profits and changed it into American money or bank drafts on behalf of twenty-five criminal organizations. Because of a lack of support, manpower, and funding from police managers, members of only two crime groups were investigated, and US$40 million was successfully laundered to the criminals' benefit. One organization, with ties with the Rizzuto crime family, laundered US$93 million, of which only one-quarter was recovered.

In the early 1990s, U.S. Customs operated a storefront in Atlanta, Georgia—part of an ongoing project dubbed Operation Primero—that was attracting drug money from centers around the United States. Originally a local money sting, Primero had gone through several stages and was now covering the international movement of criminal profits, with clients wanting their cash shipped to several countries. When the investigation into Alfonso Caruana began, investigators with Operation Primero had already arrested 120 people and seized US$14 million in assets, running at about a 50 percent recovery rate for the money they laundered.

In a court brief, Toronto Detective-Constable Cam Durham, who worked for the Proceeds of Crime unit, described Primero's method: "The operation, run out of Atlanta, Georgia, is investigating individuals who are laundering funds from the sale and for the purchase of narcotics from Colombian Narcotic Exporters. In this undercover operation a 'broker' will bid on a contract for a pickup of money in a particular location. In the case of this [Canadian] portion of their investigation, the broker's name is José Tejada. The broker will give his cost of bringing the money back to Colombia and, if rewarded with the contract, he contacts the Atlanta undercover operators through Guillermo Montoya."

Montoya, Durham explained, was an unwitting informant who unknowingly introduced undercover operators to the money brokers.

"Guillermo Montoya will ask if the undercover can make a pickup at a specific location and in this case it will be Canada," Durham said.

"The undercover officers will accept or reject the pickup depending on the location and the control they can have over same. If accepted they will do it themselves or contact a cooperating police force—as in our case—who will do the pickup."

Once the undercover officer has picked up the money, he converts it into U.S. dollars at a local cooperating bank, then wire-transfers it to a Primero-controlled account. The money is then wired to accounts as specified by Montoya.

Those bank accounts, Durham said, are often leased to brokers for a fee; the account holders allow the money to "run" through their accounts.

A crossover between Primero and Casablanca in the United States, Project Omertà in Toronto, and Project Cartagine in Italy put several hands on the hammer hovering above Alfonso Caruana's head if indeed the CFSEU was tracking the right man.

Toronto, Ontario

Staring at the photograph of the man ROS Inspector Paolo Palazzo believed was Alfonso Caruana, Bill Sciammarella shook his head.

It was October 1996 and more than a year had been spent unravelling the activities of a target believed to be one of the most wanted Mafia bosses in the world. His meeting with organized crime figures, his constant use of pay phones, and his elegant lifestyle had been documented by surveillance teams. A thick file was accumulating.

The most direct solution was to take Inspector Palazzo out and show him his Ghost. A CFSEU car set up on Caruana's home and when he came out a detective called for a marked cruiser to pull his black Mercedes over.

Caruana produced his valid driver's license, confirming his identity. The officers let him go, and passed the information on to the CFSEU team.

Alfonso Caruana could have been taken into custody then and there. But extraditing him, a Canadian citizen, back to Italy would be complex with no guaranteed outcome.

On November 5, 1996, Bill Sciammarella took his affidavit for a DNR warrant to court. The application to support the warrant showed the progress of the investigation to date, noting the Italian government's ongoing probe into Caruana's European drug network and his connection to "new businesses in the Toronto area . . . [providing] him and his organization a legitimate route to launder the profits of the criminal enterprise," and pointing out that extraditing Caruana to Italy could take considerable time and allow him to continue importing drugs.

In Judge Sal Merenda's chambers, the DNR warrant was granted for three telephones: one at Alfonso Caruana's Goldpark Court home, and two at other locations—a fish company and the home of a close relative—where he was believed to be conducting drug business.

Sciammarella was granted a sixty-day warrant; the court order also compelled the service providers, including pager companies, to turn over all records relating to the telephone usage and the subscriber. The warrant was sealed to prevent it from becoming public and alerting the targets.

Sciammarella and Saldutto had sixty days to push the rock a little farther up the hill.

That month, RCMP Constable Craig Sorrie, of the Proceeds of Crime (POC) unit in Ontario, was contacted by Special Agent Lorenzo Mesa of U.S. Customs' Atlanta office. Mesa told Sorrie that a contract had come to Operation Primero from a South American broker to move CDN$1 million out of Canada, noting that the Canadian client was "a different criminal organization."

Arrangements were made to have RCMP Constable Ben Fournier, an undercover officer posing as a money launderer with a financial network, connect with a man named "Albert" at the Marriot Hotel, near Toronto's international airport.

A surveillance team covering Fournier spotted Albert as he arrived at the hotel in a car driven, it was later discovered, by Alfonso Caruana. A third man in the vehicle was identified as Caruana's nephew, Giuseppe Caruana. (Gerlando Caruana, his father, was on parole in Montreal after serving a prison sentence for the United Kingdom heroin conspiracy.)

The tall, slim Albert, speaking in broken English, met Fournier but said he wouldn't have the money for several hours. Fournier told Albert that he had to have the money by 2:30 p.m. that day so that it could be processed during banking hours. Apparently that couldn't be managed, so they rescheduled the meeting for the following day at 11:00 a.m. at the Dodge Suites Hotel, where Albert was staying, on the north edge of the city of Toronto.

At the arranged meeting at the Dodge Suites, Fournier had a brief conversation with Albert about the "financial services" Fournier could offer him. Albert said $500,000 in mixed currency would be available the following week. The men discussed wiring the money to the United States, and Albert said he wanted to convert the money to U.S. currency and disburse it worldwide.

"Then I'll have about $350,000 a week for you," Albert told Fournier.

He then put a plastic bag containing Canadian and U.S. currency— fifties and hundreds, bundled and secured by elastic bands—into the trunk of Fournier's car and the undercover agent drove off.

Alfonso Caruana, driving a Mercedes, and Giuseppe Caruana, driving a Volkswagen, pulled up; Albert got into the VW and both vehicles left the area.

A count showed that the bag contained US$271,570 and CDN$114,250. The RCMP Proceeds of Crime unit wire-transferred the money to an account designated by the U.S. Customs Service, operating as part of Project Primero.

During the next month, more money pickups were arranged. Fournier met with Giuseppe Caruana, who said he was Albert's cousin; on December 9, Fournier met him at the Dodge, and a brown paper bag containing CDN$217,424 and US$39,600 cash was placed in the under-cover's car. A week later, another pickup was made at the Dodge: CDN$104,900 and US$47,200. Arrangements were made for a pickup in Montreal, but it was called off at the last minute.

Meanwhile, the funds delivered by Albert were traced through the banking system, sent through according to exact instructions from Guillermo Montoya. A portion of the December 9 pickup, for example, was broken down into four wire transfers. Wire 1 ($80,000) went to the Bank of New York to account 890060336 (Commercial Bank Rossiyskiy Kredit); Wire 2 ($20,000) went to Marine Midland Bank in Buffalo, New York; Wire 3 ($33,528) went to The Hong Kong and Shanghai Banking Corp., in Hong Kong; and Wire 4 ($51,992) went to Citibank in the Colon Free Zone, Panama. Law enforcement netted $13,860 in fees from the transactions.

The appearance of Alfonso and Giuseppe Caruana at the money drop brought the Proceeds of Crime team in contact with the CFSEU. Clearly both the POC unit and the CFSEU had the same targets in their sights.

There's a natural rivalry between the drug investigators, who go for product and arrests, and the sting artists of the Proceeds of Crime units, who go after the money.

The Proceeds of Crime specialists argue that the only way to hurt organized crime figures is to dismantle their financial infrastructure, seizing any assets that can be proven to be proceeds of crime. "If I want to take out the heart of a criminal conspiracy I go for the business office," said former RCMP Inspector Garry Nichols, now with the Canadian government's anti-money laundering center. "You can lock up drug dealers all day long; there's more where they come from. But if you take their profit, it can collapse the organization."

Traditional investigators maintain a more direct vision of policing. "Catch the bad guys and lock them up," Larry Tronstad believes. "Get the bodies, get the dope. If you can get the money too, fine."

The truth is probably somewhere in between, but deciding who gets the lead role—who gets to determine the focus—in investigations depends not only on skills and passion, but also on funding. For the past several years, in Canada, funding has gone into creating financial investigation task forces, like the Integrated Proceeds of Crime (IPOC) units that bring private-sector financial experts, Crown attorneys, and Revenue and Immigration officers under one umbrella.

Tronstad, who managed the field operation of the Caruana case, and Nichols, speak highly of each other's unit, citing teamwork and cooperation. But privately, law enforcement insiders tell of complex jockeying and positioning behind the scenes.

"When Omertà was just a drug-and-money case—emphasis on 'drug'—it was pretty cut and dried," a participant said. "It was a CFSEU project. It had the dope, it had Mafia members, it was brought in by Sciammarella and Saldutto. But when the Americans asked for the Proceeds boys to run a sting, then it got complicated. Caruana was the hottest thing going. At the end of it there was going to be an international success.

"The IPOCS were brought in, to great fanfare, by the Sol-Gen [federal solicitor-general], and they'd spent millions; they needed a case that would justify the money and faith they put into financial policing.

"But the CFSEU's been up and running for twenty-five years; IPOCS are the new kids on the block, and they didn't really have a chance."

Larry Tronstad had been through the turf wars with other police agencies, but they were usually outside the RCMP itself. A stubborn defender of his own turf, Tronstad had in the past been accused of taking over other police forces' investigations. Usually, he won. Several officers from outside police agencies, attached to the CFSEU, ended their secondments with more loyalty to Tronstad than to their own colleagues.

But the problems with the Proceeds of Crime section and the growing international scope of the case—not to mention the budget the CFSEU was burning through at an alarming rate—required a different kind of turf war, something a little more subtle, and at a higher level.

Inspector Ben Soave had known of the Caruana-Cuntrera long before he returned to Canada in July 1996 from his post as RCMP liaison officer in Rome. A former street cop who had worked undercover in the turbulent 1960s, Soave had bounced around the world throughout his career. In addition to the Rome posting, he'd been sent to South America and Asia. He had worldwide contacts and could, with a personal telephone call, circumvent much of the red tape that could choke off an investigation.

He'd been in Italy during the deportation of the Cuntrera brothers. He'd worked with Alessandro Pansa, the Italian officer who first went after the Siciliana family's money, and he was aware that the Caruana-Cuntrera had used corruption to evade capture for thirty years.

"Why did they keep getting away? I'd heard rumors of corruption regarding the Cuntreras in Quebec, I'd heard rumors of political interference in cases relating to the family," Soave said. "When the case came into Newmarket, I was determined none of that was going to happen."

Soave, who was officer in charge of the CFSEU during the thick of the case, believed he could lend his skills, both administrative and international, to the benefit of the Omertà team. "This case was going to be two things," he said. "It would be expensive and it would be global. The cost was going to devour the CFSEU budget, and the international complications to be dealt with would be prodigious. When an investigation is

157

of the size Omertà became, there'd be an obstacle around every corner, and no one would make it easy. I think, for the people working the case, I was lucky enough to be in the right place at the right time."

At the end of November 1996, two weeks after the DNR warrant was approved, the CFSEU and the Proceeds of Crime unit sat down to hash out their interests in the case. It was agreed that the two sides would work together: the CFSEU would continue working up their case, aiming for legal authorization that would allow wiretaps and other high-tech techniques to be used; the POC unit would penetrate the financial side of the case by using undercover officers to conduct stings, as well as identifying assets of the Caruana-Cuntrera for future forfeiture. Revenue Canada agreed to commit officers to the case. Agreement was reached that the Proceeds unit would notify the CFSEU before conducting any physical surveillance on the targets. Immigration Canada would go after any suspects who weren't residents of Canada and attempt to deport them.

As 1996 drew to a close, the Italian police wanted to put some heat under Alfonso Caruana, as demonstrated in memos sent from Rome by RCMP liaison officer Dennis Fiorido: "The Italian investigation has concluded that Alfonso Caruana has been intricately involved in international drug trafficking and money laundering activities while residing in Canada. Police are eagerly waiting for the Italian Ministry of Justice to officially request the extradition of Caruana to Italy. . . . They are equally eager to uncover new Italian and International elements of the criminal organization Caruana has been involved in."

Toronto, Ontario

By January 1997, the Proceeds of Crime unit had managed to penetrate the Caruana-Cuntrera organization. Undercover officers had been collecting large amounts of drug profits, and it looked like the money stream would never end. By depositing the money into a cooperating Canadian bank and then having it forwarded to the Operation Primero accounts, the international money trails were being exposed. But a legal roadblock suddenly appeared: on January 17, the Ontario Court of Appeal, which was hearing the Shirose-Campbell case involving convicted drug traffickers, ruled that police would no longer be allowed to facilitate the laundering of criminal proceeds. This effectively ended Canadian assistance to Operation Primero. The upshot on the Caruana-Cuntrera financial probe was immediate: it stopped dead.

On January 30, the mysterious "Albert" left Toronto after making his first handoffs to Ben Fournier, the Proceeds undercover. He was followed to a Montreal hotel, where he met with members of that city's wing of the Caruana-Cuntrera. At a hotel bar, when Albert paid for a round of drinks, local Proceeds officers got the name Alberto Minelli off his credit card. Checking with U.S. Customs Special Agent Sandra Francis, the Omertà team found an extensive file on him.

Born in Brescia, Italy, the thirty-three-year-old Minelli was well known to U.S. anti-crime authorities as a main player in the international movement of criminal money. Minelli—code-named "Willie" by members of the Caruana-Cuntrera—was an Italian citizen who was a resident of Venezuela. He also maintained a $240,000 home at 10637 54th Street in Miami. Over the past three years, Minelli had filed several currency transaction reports (CTRs) in the $250,000 range. (CTRS are required by the U.S. Government, under money-laundering legislation, when more that $10,000 enters or leaves the country.) The addresses he provided on the CTRs were hotels, and the deposits were forwarded by wire transfer to locations outside the United States. Minelli's documents showed him to be the general manager of the Construction Equipment Company in Venezuela. U.S. Special Agent Francis, who had spent a lot of time working on Minelli, said her investigation showed that he had made several telephone calls from Miami to Toronto, Montreal, and Venezuela. Included in the telephone records were the calls made to the pager used by RCMP undercover officer Ben Fournier.

Cohabiting at the 54th Street home was a man using the name Cesare Petruzziello, a sixty-year-old resident of Venezuela who was also originally from Italy. Intelligence reports showed that Petruzziello—who identified himself as the president of the Construction Equipment Company of Venezuela—had made numerous trips between Miami and Toronto.

Special Agent Francis told Canadian investigators that there were two

$70,000 Jaguars parked in the driveway of the Minelli-Petruzziello residence. Her investigation showed another vehicle at the address registered to Massimiliano Pagano.

In reality, Cesare Petruzziello was Alfonso Caruana's back-end drug man, Oreste Pagano, who, according to several *pentiti* in Italy, was the boss of the Neapolitan Camorra criminal organization in Brescia.

Listed as "armed and dangerous" and under caution for violence, the fifty-nine-year-old Pagano was the subject of a lengthy Interpol circular that listed his past crimes as criminal conspiracy, drug trafficking, Mafia-type criminal conspiracy, armed robbery, fraud, receiving stolen property, violations of firearms law, theft, rape, and forgery. On the run from several sentences, Pagano owed the Italian authorities almost twenty-two years.

The Omertà team had made the Caruana-Cuntrera/Camorra link.

9

The Oreste Pagano Family

Since his first meeting with Alfonso Caruana in the early 1990s, Oreste Pagano had expanded both his family and his underworld connections. By the time Project Omertà was up and running, he had a new common-law wife—his first wife, Mirella Romano, had died in Miami in 1993—and three children: Massimiliano, Gianluca, and Enrica, aged twenty-nine, twenty-seven, and twenty-one respectively. Massimiliano and Enrica, in particular, were part of the financial side of Pagano's criminal operations. He sent them around the world laundering his money and doing his banking. In addition, he had two young children with his common-law wife Belandria Zambrano Milagros Coromoto, known to friends and family as "Milagros."

The purely criminal side of his life was populated with an endless array of accomplices from either Naples or the town of Brescia, the base of his Camorra group. Among them were Alberto Minelli and Riccardo Santin, both with money-laundering convictions, and drug traffickers Luigi Buono, Michele Coppola, and Arturo Tiritelli. It was Oreste Pagano's ability to link up with diverse criminal groups in Colombia, Venezuela, Brazil, Aruba, Mexico, Canada, the United States, Spain, Switzerland, and Italy that made his organization such a powerful asset to Alfonso Caruana.

In Venezuela, for example, Pagano had a relationship with Umberto Naviglia, a Camorrista with connections to Cuban organized crime in Miami. In Mexico he had strong contacts with the Juarez cocaine cartel; in Los Angeles he had ties to the Colombians who moved tons of cocaine into the state every year. In Colombia itself Pagano was in regular contact with the very top of the Cali cartel, and was of such stature that he was able to get multi-hundred-kilogram shipments entirely on credit.

In the early 1990s, Pagano's son Massimiliano had brought young Alberto Minelli from Brescia, Italy, to Venezuela and introduced him to his father. Minelli was exactly the "clean face" Pagano needed. He was ultra-European, could move through the capitals of the world, saw himself as a financier, and was able to adhere to the maxim that money has no smell: dirty drug profits or clean industrial profits, it was all the same to Alberto Minelli.

Together the men created an appliance company called Euro-Machine. Over the following years, Minelli became Pagano's straw man, putting his name to all manner of documents, including the deeds to two houses Pagano owned in Venezuela.

Toronto, Ontario

By the middle of February 1997, the Combined Forces Special Enforcement Unit had run out of first-stage investigative tools. From the start, Larry Tronstad had predicted that the case would be "wires and tires"—eavesdropping and surveillance—and the surveillance had gone about as far as it could, showing that a full-tilt Mafia drug and money-laundering operation was underway of which the main directors were based in Toronto, Montreal, and Venezuela. The Omertà team knew that Alfonso Caruana was replicating the drug networks he'd operated in other countries. Surveillance teams from the élite Toronto Police Mobile Support Services (MSS)—it was an old joke in Toronto that the MSS could enter a revolving door behind you and come out in front—and the RCMP's Special O Surveillance branch had already documented hundreds of hours of Caruana's days.

Each surveillance led to new suspects and new vehicles; meeting locations were monitored and investigated for links to organized crime. Typically, Caruana would leave his home and drive to a series of pay phones along the northwest edge of the city of Toronto. Using prepaid phone cards, he would log calls all over the world, as the Dialed Number Recorders (DNRs) showed. Private homes and companies were used as safe call centers where he'd visit and make and receive calls.

Hundreds of man-hours of surveillance on other suspects showed the cautious, to the point of being paranoid, patterns of operation that usually characterize drug operators. Known, even notorious, Mafiosi were appearing at meetings; a gallery of photographs had been accumulated. Other faces were new, and each of them had to be identified. It was frustrating and time-consuming, and each new discovery raised even more questions.

Surveillance did yield one solid benefit, however: it proved conclusively that Alfonso Caruana was indeed the same man listed on the Interpol warrant. When a team spotted Caruana angrily tossing a crumpled twenty-dollar Bell calling-card into a trash bin, they recovered it. CFSEU Detective-Constable Mike Harvey took it to the RCMP's Forensic Identification Section for fingerprinting. It was treated with cyanoacrylate ester glue fume and fingerprints were recovered from the bottom left corner. The prints, compared against the Interpol report, were a match.

The DNRs also gave a shadowy outline of the Caruana-Cuntrera crime syndicate, showing hundreds upon hundreds of telephone and pager calls throughout the world, many of them made to known Mafiosi or their associates. As each name came up it was added to the conspiracy. Subjects or associates appeared in Montreal, New York, Miami, Venezuela, Italy, and Mexico.

The ownership of several companies and motor vehicles was researched, and yet more suspected conspirators were revealed. Assets owned by the targets were detailed and forwarded to the RCMP's Proceeds of Crime section for possible future seizure in the event that a successful drug case was brought to trial. But getting an informant inside the drug trafficking side of the group was admittedly impossible. "You can pick around the edges of any crime group, but with the Caruanas and Cuntreras you couldn't penetrate to the heart. Blood, marriage and history worked against us. It was impossible to get in," Inspector Ben Soave said.

As the team worked, other jurisdictions began to hear of the investigation and urgent requests for information arrived at RCMP Ottawa and at the Newmarket CFSEU offices. Italian officials regularly demanded updates; an organized crime task force in Montreal conducting Project Falcon sent intelligence reports and wiretap transcriptions; the Atlanta office of U.S. Customs kept close tabs on the case: their Operation Primero had underworld figures demanding that undercover customs officers find a way to get millions of dollars out of Canada, millions that belonged to the Caruana-Cuntrera. Authorities in France were also requesting updated information for a money-laundering probe they were conducting involving profits that were being used to finance the purchase of aircraft by Colombians for the transport of drugs.

What the Project Omertà team badly needed was to know what the conspirators were saying in order to find out exactly what they were doing. They needed a "Part VI Authorization" that would allow them to tap not only the residential and business telephones and pagers of the Caruana-Cuntrera players, but also the several dozen public pay phones the group was utilizing.

"On television it looks easy," Larry Tronstad said. "The detectives go to a judge and the judge signs off on it. But getting a Part VI is a bureaucratic nightmare. The affidavit that has to be filed has to be legally perfect because if it gets shot down later in court, the entire case can go out the window. The Affiant officer has to know the case inside and out and be able to answer every question put to him."

Bill Sciammarella was the Affiant officer for the investigation. He was charged with managing the legal paperwork needed to show that all normal routes of investigation had been tried, but failed, prior to filing for the Part VI.

On February 17, 1997, Sciammarella took his voluminous affidavit to the chambers of the Honourable Justice J. D. McCombs. When he left, he had in hand the first of five Part VI "Authorizations to Intercept Communications" of the Caruana-Cuntrera suspects and their families and associates. The first Authorization, and each of the subsequent four, would be valid for sixty days, after which time a new application could be made to renew it. Under Canadian law the targets of electronic eavesdropping had to be notified within ninety days of the termination of the wiretaps on their telephones.

The Authorization named several targets, whose personal and business hard-line and cellular telephones could be tapped, among them Alfonso Caruana and other members of the Caruana-Cuntrera organization. Relatives were also named as residents whose communications might be intercepted. Six companies, including the Shock Nightclub, and hotel rooms used by conspirators were fair game. As well, cars belonging to the Caruana-Cuntrera or their family members were designated, and nine pay phones used by the targets were also listed. By the time the final Authorization expired two years later, several dozen pay phones, pagers, fax machines, offices, residences, and vehicles had been monitored.

The day after Justice McCombs signed the first Authorization, the CFSEU "went up on the wires." Gone were the early investigative methods that saw policemen climbing telephone poles and attaching alligator clips to the lines—the fondly remembered "clipinskis." Now telephone companies were served with a court order to cooperate with the investigators and the intercepts were conducted electronically.

Right from the first surveillance, it's likely that Alfonso Caruana suspected or intuited that he was being watched. He'd spent a life in international underworlds, and was wanted for arrest in many countries. He had been targeted for murder by the Corleonesi. He'd been hounded by the media. He'd squeaked out of Venezuela just before his expected arrest—some said he had a sixth sense, while others said he had enough government officials in his pocket that he was given a heads-up.

On several intercepted communications, he and members of his organization hinted at suspicions of being monitored and devoted themselves to conducting counter-surveillance. But the vague fears didn't slow down the momentum of the organization.

Family Life

Because of the close-knit nature of the Caruana-Cuntrera family, the Project Omertà wiretaps recorded hundreds of family conversations that had little or nothing to do with drug trafficking or money laundering. Many relate to the day-to-day activities of a family such as internal family finances. Several calls give inside glimpses of a family with plans and dreams: anticipated holidays overseas, college and career goals, and, as with one recorded by a Caruana family member, details of Alfonso Caruana's dream to replicate his estate in Valencia, Venezuela, one of the most peaceful places he'd lived in. "[He] wants to buy some land up north and build a farm, like the one he had in Venezuela," a young relative said. However, the family was hardly typical in that much of its stress came from several ongoing court cases involving imprisoned family members.

Many members of the Siculiana family believed on some level that they were targets of persecution at the hands of police and the media. "They told me that they were always being persecuted," recalled Oreste Pagano. "That the father and the grandfather had already been persecuted, that the grandfather that lived in Brazil had been persecuted, that they have always been labelled 'a Mafia family.'"[1]

This feeling of being hounded is echoed by a Cuntrera who, depressed over personal problems, told a friend: "Why can't they realize that we're just a family like everyone else?"

But being identified as Mafia was something the Caruana-Cuntrera used to advantage on occasion. Returning a message a Cuntrera had left on his pager, a nervous associate asked, "What's going on?"

"I gave you a fucking little heart attack, eh, buddy?"

"Yeah, I thought the mob was calling me," the man said. "But, as a matter of fact they are, actually."

"You better be careful . . ."

"I know."

" . . . the fucking boogieman may be after you."

Some conversations were whispered, at times obscure. A woman, after visiting a relative in an Italian prison, called her son in Canada:

MOTHER: "Listen to me good."
SON: "Yeah."
MOTHER: "Speak to you-know-who . . . Tell him that those two . . ."
SON: "Uh huh."
MOTHER: "They have to tell Frank and Max, they have to go see Pa immediately."
SON: "Okay."
MOTHER: "Now do you remember when Peppe was there and there was that guy we sent you-know-what to? . . . We have to arrange for something . . . Did you get all that?"

The family's reputation as a major Mafia organization could not be denied. A woman spoke of keying her name—Cuntrera—into the Internet and finding her family history in a series of articles on organized crime. A man told his girlfriend not to let her mother watch the Italian news broadcasts on a particular day: "She shouldn't be watching that, because sometimes they say stuff you wouldn't want her to hear." A young Caruana told friends that his father said if he's ever hassled by "the bikers" he has only to mention the family name.

"I know your father 'wears pinstripes,'" a friend said.

"So what's wrong with that?"

"Oh, he does, eh? Mafia, for sure. We can't talk to you any more, because we're afraid that you might kill us. . . . What does your father do?"

"Oh, he deals drugs to young children."

"Your father killed everyone."

"At least people respect him."

Ultimately a family life that was, in the main, not unlike that of other families. Babies were held up to telephones to gurgle "Happy Bird-day" to long-away grandfathers; there were discussions of what kind of fish to bring home for dinner; the frustrating crises of far-away family members in difficulty were discussed. It was unique, perhaps, to the Siculiana family that the absent grandfathers were international fugitives who couldn't travel freely, or that the fish shop was a front for drug smuggling, or that the far-away family members were in foreign prisons.

The men discussed their cholesterol, sugar-readings, and hair transplants. The women discussed trips, shopping, and their children.

There were weddings and baptisms and funerals. Proud fathers behaved like proud fathers, bringing their underaged sons to manhood, urging them to smoke cigars and drink *grappa* to the point of hilarious intoxication. New-born babies were worried over, their health discussed and advice given.

Life in the family was a constant hustle, a persistent effort to make good in the face of the family's position of adversity. Police uncovered a tireless effort to make business deals: plans to open Italian sandwich shops in Toronto; the purchase of prime waterfront development property in the Caribbean; starting up a company to import cigars; opening nightclubs in Calgary. Small-business loans were applied for, impending bankruptcies carefully evaluated. Even the most innocent chat could sound sinister. Vague references to "that guy there we met last week at that place" turned out to refer to a legitimate real estate broker doing a legitimate business deal.

Several calls related to the purchase or lease of luxury automobiles, $24,000 Harley Davidson motorcycles, jewelry, and trips to casinos, where losses were shrugged off and winnings bragged about.

The wheeling and dealing seemed non-stop, the complex plans of a group of people with unlimited funds at their disposal and a frenzy to create a financial empire.

Discussing plans to bankrupt his company, a Cuntrera was indifferent when told business was slow: "It's supposed to be slow."

"You're the captain of the ship."

"And I am an expert at fucking sinking them."

The taps on the business phones brought calls from neighboring firms, warning the Caruana-Cuntrera that police were in the area. One businessman detailed where the police cars were set up on surveillance, describing the vehicles and their occupants.

Other calls were strange. "You're all dead," a man told a female employee at a Cuntrera firm before hanging up. Another caller, a creditor owed money by one of the family companies, said in frustration: "Tell them to launder some more money and pay their bills."

Alfonso Caruana's role as head of the Siculiana family was defined throughout the investigation and in interviews and documentation. As the Caruana-Cuntrera family expanded over the century, the key "father" role shifted from a Caruana to a Cuntrera, then back to a Caruana and then to a Cuntrera. It can't yet be determined if this movement back and forth was meant to alternate from one side of the family to the other. Certainly it appears each generation had its turn; in fact, one Cuntrera, despondent over his collapsing marriage, was overheard saying, "When the family offers 'it,' I'll turn it down."

The father role is one of great responsibility—whoever holds the position is de facto responsible for the well-being of all.

An example of this responsibility was evident in Alfonso Caruana's dealings with a family member who was in jail in Italy.

"He was supporting Pasquale's entire family," Oreste Pagano said. "In fact, many times I would see Pasquale's wife at Alfonso's house because she would come to get money, or even when she'd be leaving to go to Rome to see her husband. Alfonso would give her what he had to give her, always in terms of money."

Families who had fathers in prison, or fathers who had died, continued to receive assistance from the organization. Asked where he got his money, a young Caruana whose father was in prison said his "uncle" (Alfonso) gave him a $200-a-week allowance. Vito Genco, Alfonso Caruana's cousin, described how he felt about him: "I look upon you as a savior."

While property might belong on paper to a particular family member, it ultimately belonged to all and was funded by the profits of the group as a whole. The understanding of ownership was more binding than contracts or deeds.

"To me [a person's] word is worth more than a power of attorney," Alfonso Caruana once told a friend.

According to Oreste Pagano, who had several long intimate talks with Alfonso Caruana in Venezuela, much of the property and businesses owned on paper by family members was actually paid for by Alfonso Caruana, and Pasquale Cuntrera's drug activities and in earlier generations by the elderly Giuseppe Caruana. The drug profits were cleaned and reinvested in a host of businesses, all in the names of other family members.

Pagano said the Siculiana boss purchased houses for each of his daughters as they got married, although his name never showed up on any paperwork.

A Caruana youth told a friend, "My mom has a new convertible Mercedes, but it's under my sister's name." Alfonso Caruana's Cadillac STS was "bought under the company," a Cuntrera told a banker.

A Cuntrera involved in a divorce found himself in difficulty because of this pattern of indirect ownership. At issue was his net worth. Much of the property he had under his name was actually owned by other family members, who could not admit the fact that they had assets fearing they'd be seized as drug profits. "The majority is in Zia Pina's name and my name, and Peppe with his brother there . . ." He feared if his wife went after half of the couple's assets on paper, it would be discovered that he didn't own most of them.

To the outside world—Pagano included—Alfonso Caruana was a master at crying the blues. "He always said to me . . . he always complained that he didn't have money . . . that the family was expensive and all this. . . . The money, where did the money go? Money doesn't just disappear. Alfonso doesn't gamble, he doesn't womanize, he doesn't stay out all night." (Alfonso was aware, apparently, of the benefits of using other people's money—when Project Omertà was all said and done, he owed Pagano US$7 million.[2])

Alfonso freely dispensed advice. When his son-in-law Carlo Napoli complained mildly about a factory he was operating in Venezuela, Caruana told him: "Why the fuck are you struggling with this fucking factory? Sell it and get out of it. Do you need this factory in order to survive?"

Discussing a drug deal, his cousin Vito Genco moaned to Alfonso about how broke he was and how he needed some profits from a drug deal. Alfonso told him: "It's not just for us—it's for everybody." And when Genco complained about the pressure he was under, Alfonso told him he was "an old woman": "Because you should take life as it comes, what else can you do. You're a fifty-year-old man now, aren't you? Try to take problems in stride, we all have them."

Some women in the family clearly practised willful blindness when it came to the criminal side of their husbands' and fathers' careers. They could be heard passing messages in a manner that showed they were aware of the secret dealings the men were involved in.

The Caruana-Cuntrera technique of corrupting—or attempting to corrupt—bank employees and politicians came through clearly in the wiretaps. Female tellers at Toronto banks were given passes to fitness clubs and nightclubs in return for putting aside Canadian $1,000 bills for the Cuntreras. Some of the conversations showed the women being romanced by telephone, engaged in long personal discussions about their lives and their plans for upcoming nights out.

Local politicians were heard on several tapes discussing campaign contributions. One politician's daughter was given a job answering telephones at a Cuntrera business. Alfonso Caruana's pager showed messages from employees at Canada Customs. A free meal for a senior local politician at a family-owned restaurant was arranged—including "a small birthday cake"—the bill going on a Cuntrera's account.

Food was an important factor in the lives of the Caruana-Cuntrera. One Cuntrera passed on recipes for preparing an Italian dish; long discussions were undertaken about what kind of fish to buy and what to serve it with. Quail had to be prepared in a specific fashion. Telephone calls were interrupted because one of the speakers had to "look to the pasta."

McDonald's was a regular stop, and not only for the children, who liked the pancakes. In the middle of a drug shipment, two Caruanas arranged to meet in Montreal.

"Where are you?"

"Having the breakfast."

"I'm on my way. I'll be there—"

"After eleven?"

"Yeah, get me a hash brown before it [breakfast] closes."

Family infighting was rampant. Alfonso Caruana was seen variously as cheap or generous, approachable or intractable, a father or a devil. His wife was generally seen as being as tough as her husband. Snipes were directed at relatives' mates—she's too young, he's too old, her wedding dress wasn't appropriate.

On overseas calls it emerged that the "Canadian" family was seen as not doing enough for the family members in prison. This apparently was a widespread belief and had been the subject of much conversation in the days before the wiretaps were installed.

"He speaks badly about all of us," a Cuntrera said of a relative living in Venezuela.

"What does he say?" a Toronto member asked. "What the fuck did we do?"

"You did nothing for that one [in Italy] and that we only think of ourselves." He added: "He said all we think about is the money."

Members of the Vella family, related to the Caruana-Cuntrera, were often discussed as being lazy. "[He's] a Vella, completely. A Vella through and through, one-hundred-percent Vella. People go hustling here and there and he just sits. . . ."

Montreal, Quebec

The ghost of Sergeant Mark Bourque continued to haunt Alfonso Caruana.

The RCMP's Proceeds of Crime investigator's persistent assault in the 1980s on the finances of the Caruana-Cuntrera hadn't ended well for him. He'd been effectively sidelined and assigned to protection services for VIPs visiting Montreal. His voluminous case file had gone nowhere in the Canadian criminal justice system. But the data proved to be of great use to Revenue Canada.

At the end of his financial investigation, Bourque had successfully proven that in an eight-month period in 1981 Caruana had put bank drafts worth CDN$21,608,605 through his bank account at City & District Savings Bank's Dollard des Ormeaux branch. The drafts were paid out to several people, including Pasquale Cuntrera, Gerlando Caruana, and Alfonso's uncle, Salvatore Vella. In addition, he wrote another CDN$6,000,000 in drafts. No taxes were paid on the money.

In 1995, Alfonso Caruana had filed for bankruptcy in order to avoid the Canadian government's demand for payment of $8.6 million in unpaid taxes and $21 million in interest and penalties on the money that flowed through his accounts. He claimed assets of only $250.

The government had contested his claim, pointing out that Caruana had, after making the bankruptcy declaration, purchased a brand new four-wheel-drive vehicle. (The sales manager at a local Suzuki dealership told investigators that Alfonso Caruana had been "recommended by a good customer" and had been allowed to take the vehicle without any payment.)

In late February 1997, after seven years of investigation, Revenue Canada brought Caruana before the Quebec Superior Court in Montreal to contest his bankruptcy.[3] Lawyer Chantal Comtois, representing Revenue Canada, pointed out that Caruana had left Canada in 1986 to avoid paying his tax bill. Before leaving for Venezuela, she said, he and his wife had sold two businesses and a vacant lot in Montreal for more than CDN$1.2 million.

Called to testify, Caruana was at a loss to explain the source of the money that passed though his bank account in 1981.

"The money wasn't all mine," he said.

"But twenty-one million dollars in your name. That's a lot, isn't it?" Comtois asked.

"I did it that way to provide services to others."

When Comtois asked for details, he replied: "That's it. To provide services to people."

When a frustrated Judge Derek Guthrie asked why he provided the "services," Caruana answered, "I don't have any other explanation. I provided those services."

He admitted that $800,000 of the money was his own—it came from the sale of a herd of pigs in Valencia, Venezuela—and said he lost the money in 1984, when he tried to relaunch his business. The rest of the money, he testified, went to "certain people" in Venezuela.

When a visibly angry Comtois asked him if he was the "Godfather of the Italian Mafia," the judge made her retract the question.

Showing him a magazine article stating that the Caruana-Cuntrera owned 60 percent of Aruba, he denied it: "If only that were true."

When asked by the Crown attorney if he owned 160,000 square kilometers of land near Colombia, Caruana told her: "It's all false." He said his life since returning to Canada—he'd stayed briefly in Montreal before moving to Toronto in 1993—had been fairly spartan.

He said he lived in Woodbridge, Ontario, in a home owned by his nephew, Giuseppe Cuntrera; he paid $1,500 a month in rent. For employment, he said, he "washed cars. . . . I move them around." His wife Giuseppina worked at a discotheque, and between them they scraped by on $3,500 a month.

Giuseppina Caruana said she couldn't remember where the money came from to buy the property in Montreal she sold in 1986 for CDN$1.2 million. Judge Guthrie commented: "It surely didn't come from the sky?"

It came, she said, "in little bits from Venezuela."

She testified that she had purchased a small supermarket in Toronto, investing $300,000 that her son-in-law had lent her. "I still have that debt," she added. And a relative also generously lent her $17,000 to buy the 1996 Golf GTI she drove.

At the end of the hearing, Judge Guthrie flatly stated that he wasn't buying Alfonso Caruana's testimony: "I don't believe a word he said. . . . I don't believe the bankrupt [Caruana] and his wife, whose testimonies were full of holes, hesitations and incomplete explanations, but I must render my judgment based on proof, not suspicions."

He said he had to accept the Caruanas' financial assessment because Revenue Canada was unable to demonstrate that Alfonso Caruana was wealthier than he claimed.

Judge Guthrie ordered Alfonso Caruana to pay $90,000—$2,500 per month over a three-year-period—to the federal government.

Caruana and his wife returned home to Toronto. He didn't appeal the $90,000 judgment against him. In fact, the government promptly received its first installment of $2,500 a month later.

10

On March 11, 1997, money man Alberto Minelli called Ben Fournier on his cellular phone. An undercover officer answered and told Minelli that Fournier wasn't available. Later in the day Giuseppe Caruana tried; he was told Fournier was in Geneva. The undercover gave him another phone number where, he believed, a man named Robert could provide laundering services. When Giuseppe Caruana called Robert, he was told to bring the money across the border to Detroit. Caruana declined.

Money was backing up in Toronto. Repeated efforts by the Caruana family to contact their facilitator, Fournier, were frustrated. Unless the money could be repatriated to Oreste Pagano or the Colombians, it would be difficult to continue the cycle of drug shipments.

On March 31, an American undercover agent with Operation Primero in San Juan, Puerto Rico, received a page to call a Toronto area telephone number. The subscriber for the number was a hair salon located in a shopping plaza north of Toronto, where Alfonso Caruana made regular use of public pay phones. The undercover called the number. Alberto Minelli answered the phone and said he had about $975,000 to be picked up. The agent tried to lure Minelli and the money over the border to northern New York State. Minelli refused, and the agent said, in that case, he couldn't help him.

Other storefront sting operations run by American authorities received urgent calls for assistance in getting Caruana-Cuntrera-Pagano money out of Canada.

"The callers were getting increasingly panicky," an American undercover agent said. "We were hoping they'd get desperate enough and

175

come across [the border], but they seemed to have a phobia about crossing. They obviously felt safe laundering money in Canada."

Handcuffed by the Shirose-Campbell legal decision, RCMP undercover agents were ordered not to return the telephone calls begging for assistance.

The pipeline was plugged.

At the end of March 1997, two messages on Alfonso Caruana's pager showed that Alberto Minelli was back in Toronto. He had checked into the Dodge Suites Hotel. Unable, in spite of numerous attempts, to get someone to send the cocaine profits out of Canada, Minelli was beginning to panic. Almost $1 million was ready to go, money that needed to be in Pagano's hands to pay for shipments of cocaine Alfonso Caruana was sending to Italy and Canada.

On April 2, intercepted phone calls revealed that a frustrated and angry Oreste Pagano was coming to Toronto to straighten things out.

On April 3, at 10:30 p.m., flight 608 from Port of Spain, Trinidad, put down at Toronto's Pearson International Airport. Pagano was traveling as Cesare Petruzziello-Grella. He was steered into secondary inspection. Customs Inspector Eric Wheeler later reported to Detective Cameron Durham that Pagano was traveling on a valid Venezuelan passport in the name of Petruzziello. When asked how long he'd be in Canada, Pagano said he intended to spend about a week in Toronto and a second week in Montreal, staying in hotels. Wheeler photocopied Pagano's passport: it showed extensive international travel. Pagano was allowed into Canada.

A surveillance team followed him to the arrivals area, where he was met by Alfonso Caruana and Alberto Minelli. The three left the airport in Caruana's car and drove to 38 Goldpark Court in Woodbridge. The next day the trio drove back to the airport and Minelli caught a flight to Montreal.

Surveillance teams meanwhile followed the remaining targets to various locations around the Toronto area. One team watched Alfonso Caruana meet with Ignazio "Ian" Genua and saw Genua put a black duffel bag into the trunk of Caruana's Cadillac. Genua, investigators noted, was the son of Nicola Genua, a notorious Canadian heroin trafficker convicted a decade earlier. Three weeks later another surveillance team watched as Alfonso Caruana and Giuseppe Caruana again met Ignazio Genua. This time a large shopping bag was put into the trunk of Caruana's car. Alfonso Caruana was also seen meeting with Domenic Rossi, a colorful underworld character who had been arrested with Nicola Genua and had a heroin trafficking conviction of his own.

The meetings and intercepted conversations from that first Part VI Authorization set the tone for the rest of the preliminary stages of Project Omertà: meetings, handoffs, double-talk, and an array of familiar underworld faces.

"It had all the makings of a drug operation fully underway," Larry Tronstad said. "We were getting a handle on the players, but we didn't know what was in the bags, money or dope. And, where was it coming from and where was it going?"

Oreste Pagano checked into the Dodge Suites where he and Minelli made several calls to South America, preparing a cocaine shipment of as much as 2,000 kilograms, some destined for Canada and some to be transited to members of the Caruana-Cuntrera in Italy. Another shipment, to an unknown destination, was to total an astonishing 5 tons.

Minelli flew to Miami and then on to Caracas to coordinate the finances of the cocaine shipment; from there he was to fly to Italy to sort out a problem over some funds he had transferred.

For the next several days Pagano chafed, waiting for arrangements to get his money out of Canada. Traveling by stretch limousine, he and Alfonso Caruana visited Niagara Casino. Pagano won $7,000 but, he complained, "Every day I'm here costs me a thousand." He spent hours shopping for his common-law wife, Milagros, a chic young Venezuelan woman with a voracious appetite for consumer goods. In one conversation, Milagros feigned sexual excitement as Pagano listed the presents he'd bought for her.

PAGANO: "I bought Rocco Barocco [perfume] for you."

MILAGROS: "Rocco Barocco? You bought Rocco Barocco for me! You bought Rocco Barocco for me! How many did you buy? I don't just want one."

PAGANO: "I bought you two."

MILAGROS: "Ohhh, my love."

PAGANO: "I bought you [makeup] for the eyes . . ."

MILAGROS: "You drive me crazy."

PAGANO: " . . . and for the mouth . . ."

MILAGROS: "Son of a bitch! Don't tell me any more. I'm going to . . ."

PAGANO: ". . . three bags of perfume, eau de cologne, cream, everything . . . Valentino day and night cream."

MILAGROS: "Stop, stop. Enough. Enough."

PAGANO: "Wait, I haven't finished—"

MILAGROS: (Making sobbing noises) "No, no."

PAGANO: "Lipstick, eyeshadow . . . Lilla from Alain Delon, for you . . . I bought you Dolce & Gabbana, Shalimar, Clinique . . ."

MILAGROS: "Enough, I'm sweating! . . . I'm going to . . ."

PAGANO: "Versace jeans, white with pink designs, and two black suits, complete ones with skirts . . ."

MILAGROS: (pause) "What else?"

The intercept gave the Omertà team one crucial fact: in addition to being Neapolitan—an outsider to the Caruana clan—Oreste Pagano had a weak spot, a vulnerability that might one day be exploited.

In another call, Pagano told Juan Carlos Pavo, his Colombia supplier, to send couriers to get the money out of Canada. Pavo said he'd send two men, Temistocle and Rodrigues Torres, to Toronto. And it was the Torres connection that gave the Omertà team the break they needed.

Toronto, Ontario: RCMP Wire Room

For the CFSEU team, cracking the coded telephone numbers the Caruana-Pagano group used was critical.

Codes have to be both complex and simple at the same time. A code that's too complex, if it's one that many people have to be able to under-stand and use, is as useless as no code at all. A code that is too simple can be easily cracked.

"It was a problem," Larry Tronstad remembered. "We'd get half the message on one line, and then they'd say call me at such-and-such a number. But the number wasn't an actual phone number."

While several pay phones were wired up, Alfonso Caruana was mostly using random lines that hadn't been identified. More important was the technology being used to tap the calls. Rather than needing a wiretap on a specific telephone, the Omertà team had an arrangement by which they could have any call to or from a number intercepted remotely.

For example, even if there had been no wiretap on Alfonso Caruana's home line, any long-distance call to or from that number would still be recorded automatically and the number at the other end identified. Then that number could be added to those covered by the Part VI warrant, and calls to or from that number would also be picked up.

On April 12, 1997, Oreste Pagano was still lodged at the Dodge Suites Hotel. The line in his room was bugged, and there was a room probe installed in the suite. A command post was set up in a room nearby and the Omertà team listened to conversations as they occurred.

In a conversation with Juan Carlos Pavo, the Colombian supplier, Oreste Pagano was given a telephone number to call in order to reach the couriers sent up from South America to transport his money out.

Pagano: "Okay, I'll repeat it to you . . . The code is four hundred and sixteen. The number is six, three, six, eight, three, three, three."

"Exactly." The man told Pagano to call the number and ask for "Temis."

After hanging up, Pagano called the Hotel Victoria in downtown Toronto and asked for Temis, one of the two Torres brothers.

Tony Saldutto, in the wire room at the Newmarket RCMP office, looked at the transcript. He picked up the telephone book and looked up the number for Hotel Victoria: 363–1666. He began playing with numbers, remembering an earlier reference to "the nines." On the wiretaps, a caller would say "Give it to me in the nines, or, "Is this the 'other way'?"

"In baccarat, a total of nine is the best hand you can be dealt," Saldutto said. "The [callers] referred to getting telephone numbers in 'the nines.'"

Saldutto played with the two phone numbers and eventually found the key: each digit in the telephone number would be adjusted to add up to nine. For example, 1 became 8 $(8+1=9)$; 2 became 7 $(7+2=9)$; 3 became 6 $(6+3=9)$, and so on.

"That was it," Tronstad said. "Once we had the code and we knew what numbers were in use, we'd made the largest step forward possible."

At the Shock Nightclub, Pagano met with Alfonso Caruana, Big Joe Cuntrera, and Little Joe Cuntrera. Pagano was given two heavy sealed, sky-blue gym bags containing CDN$750,000 in $20 bills.

Pagano headed downtown to deliver the money to Juan Carlo Pavos's couriers. Quickly he realized that he was being followed. A heavy rain had forced the Omertà surveillance team to tail him too closely. In panic Pagano returned to the nightclub.

Another attempt to get the bags to the couriers at Hotel Victoria also ran into difficulty. Pagano went into the hotel and told the Torres brothers to meet him at a restaurant in a few hours. He was again unable to shake the surveillance. He gave the two couriers $5,000 and sent them back to South America.

Back at the nightclub, Pagano told Alfonso Caruana that he was being followed and gave him the bags. Alfonso drove him back to the Dodge Suites Hotel. There, as Pagano recounts, "In the morning, opening the door, I saw two people coming straight toward my room. I thought it was the police. I called Alfonso and told him this."

Little Joe Cuntrera went to the hotel to verify Pagano's fears. After a brief stint of counter-surveillance, he agreed with Pagano's assessment: "The hotel's surrounded."

Arrangements were made to get Pagano out of town. At eight o'clock that night he paid his bill at the front desk and said he'd be checking out the next day. He returned to his room, packed, turned up the volume on the TV, and slipped out of the building. Big Joe Cuntrera picked him up and took him to the airport, where he caught a flight to South America. But the bags he was desperate to deliver to Pavo's couriers remained behind.

In the world's law-enforcement circles word was spreading of the growing investigation targeting Alfonso Caruana and his drug trafficking activities out of South America. Governments and law-enforcement agencies around the world were slowly getting wind that a major initiative, based at the CSFEU offices near Toronto, was showing signs of finally putting the elusive Mafia boss behind bars.

In April 1997, an agent of the British intelligence service passed on information that a 46-meter fishing vessel, the *Zeeland*, was being retrofitted to carry cocaine out of Colombia. The RCMP found the *Zeeland* was registered to C.I.C Group Inc., of Montreal, was further registered in Belize, Central America, and was owned by Montrealer Joseph Ali Chedid.

Aware of the Caruana investigation, Tim Manhire, the liaison officer for British Customs in New York City, contacted Larry Tronstad. He told Tronstad intelligence indicated the *Zeeland* would be fitted to carry seven tons of cocaine. It had been in port for four months and curiously the crew kept to themselves and did little socializing.

The *Zeeland* with the cocaine hidden on board, was expected to leave South America the following month, destination unknown, except for information from an intelligence source who said two tons of cocaine would be dropped off "somewhere in the Caribbean" and the rest would go either to Italy or Canada.

This fit with what was turning up in the Omertà case, Tronstad said, where several bits of information indicated a shipment for the Caruana-Pagano operation was imminent. Montreal wiretaps were showing Alfonso and Gerlando Caruana discussing renting storage space for $1,000 a month for a year, and Oreste Pagano talking about a large importation deal at about the time the *Zeeland* was to set sail.

The U.S. DEA and the Miami-based Joint Intelligence task force, of which British Customs was a part, would monitor the progress of the *Zeeland* and, when it hit international waters or U.S. territory, would take it down.

And, coincidentally, Alfonso Caruana's pager during that time showed

The Canada Customs number was checked and an employee interviewed. She said she had worked for Canada Customs for twenty-five years, including at the international airport and in the small vessels department. She told investigators a pager had been given to her husband—who operated an import company—by a man who worked at a Toronto restaurant owned by a Siciliana family member. Asked who her husband's "friends" were, she said: "That's a good question."

several pages from a number subscribed to by Canada Customs. No record was found of Caruana returning calls to the number.

Venezuela

Of constant concern to the Caruanas and Cuntreras were the legal battles family members were waging in other countries. Sheila Dagwell was obsessed with getting her husband, Pasquale Caruana, out of prison in Italy. Conversations show the anguish that she and their son, Carmelo, went through as they calculated exactly when his sentence would end. At issue was whether the eight months spent awaiting extradition from Germany, where he'd been arrested with Giuseppe Cuffaro, would be counted as time served on his Italian sentence.

For Paolo Cuntrera's daughter, Maria, anger was the dominant emotion. Her father, and her uncles Pasquale and Gaspare, had been "deported" from Venezuela in 1992 after their lawyer was detained incommunicado. The men had been flown to Italy and imprisoned there on drug and Mafia-association charges. The Cuntrera family filed a constitutional injunction with the Venezuela Supreme Court of Justice to overturn the stripping of Pasquale Cuntrera's Venezuelan citizenship.

In April 1997, a letter written by former minister of the interior Luis Pinuera Ordaz appeared in the Caracas newspaper *El Universal*. He said he had lawfully sent the Cuntreras back to Italy instead of to the United States, and that he had lawfully revoked Pasquale Cuntrera's Venezuelan citizenship. It wasn't arbitrary, he said, and didn't violate human rights.

This was too much for Maria Cuntrera. She wrote a letter to *El Universal* that the newspaper declined to publish. In it, she pointed out that the police raid that had rounded up the brothers was a farce.

"My father, Paolo, and my uncles were arrested in a blitz-like raid," she wrote, adding that members of the raiding party were dressed as commandos. "My father and my uncles were held in isolation for three days. And then they were extradited. My uncle Pasquale had just had a surgical operation and couldn't move—he was confined to a wheelchair."

Maria Cuntrera noted: "They cannot be accused of any crime as then-President Carlos Andres Perez publicly admitted. . . . They never committed anything punishable in Venezuela. My uncle has Venezuelan citizenship and would not be extraditable."

She said a decree revoking Venezuelan citizenship was illegal. "When they put Pasquale Cuntrera on the airplane this decree was not yet published in the Official Gazette. My uncle was still a Venezuelan citizen when he was deported."

Pinuera Ordaz, she said, was the "architect of a campaign of libel against my relatives."[1] (In 1998 the Venezuelan attorney-general said the constitutional injunction was inadmissable.)

Maria Croce Cuntrera (1963) is the daughter of Paolo Cuntrera (1939) and Antonina Caruana (1940). She is married to Nino Mongiovì (1957), a convicted narcotics trafficker. Another Maria Croce Cuntrera (also born in 1963) is the daughter of Liborio Cuntrera and Maria Nobela Cuntrera, according to Italian police files.

"Absolutely fearless and loyal," a source familiar with the Cuntreras in Venezuela says. "If the power in the family could flow directly to any woman, Maria would be the one." The source added: "It doesn't matter how many judgments go against him (her father, Paolo), Maria will spend every Bolivar for his freedom as long as he's alive."

Hamilton, Ontario

Project Pipe, the police operation that led to the crucial wiretap on Enio Mora's telephone in April 1995, took a murderous turn at the end of May 1997.

The investigation had uncovered an investment scam that left leading members of the Canadian Mafia defrauded of millions of dollars. Rumor had it that much of the money lost belonged to members of the Montreal faction of the Caruana-Cuntrera, and other mobsters in southern Ontario.

One of the men who ran the scam had earlier been kidnapped by Enio Mora, crammed into the trunk of a Cadillac, and taken on an hour-long drive to Hamilton, Ontario, to meet Mora's boss, John

Papalia. The elderly Papalia, it was said, doused the investment broker with gasoline and flicked his lighter repeatedly as he emphasized that he wanted his money back.

Papalia, something of an icon in the Canadian underworld, was the son of an old 'ndranghetista whose business had thrived in the early days of Prohibition. Papalia had turned his back on his Calabrian roots and was now the Buffalo La Cosa Nostra's representative in southern Ontario. A heroin trafficker in his early days, the high point of Papalia's career had been as a player in the French Connection heroin pipeline, which in the early 1970s had inspired the most prominent international drug investigation of its time.

While Toronto fell into Papalia's sphere of influence—the former La Cosa Nostra boss, Paul Volpe, having been murdered in 1983—it was control of the narrow Niagara Peninsula, from the city of Hamilton down to Niagara Falls on the U.S. Border, that was key to his criminal network. In Toronto, with its international financial center, Bay Street, and its many ethnic communities, Papalia profited from much of the illegal gaming, extortion, stock promotion, and loan-sharking. But the short stretch from Hamilton south to Niagara had for a century been an important strategic piece of geography for La Cosa Nostra. Cocaine, heroin, illegal immigrants, smuggled cigarettes, and myriad rackets produced tens of millions of dollars each year for organized crime groups on both sides of the border.

Papalia was essentially in the same position and role in the 1990s in Hamilton as Vincenzo Cotroni had been in Montreal in the 1970s when the Caruana-Cuntrera-Rizzuto rose to power. Papalia was the Buffalo La Cosa Nostra man, as Cotroni had been the New York Bonanno LCN's man. Both felt protected by their American overseers, and both were of Calabrian descent, steeped in a similar tradition. Where Cotroni had used the hotheaded and loyal Paolo Violi as his second-in-command, Papalia had Enio Mora in Toronto and Carmen Barillaro in Niagara Falls.

On the last day of May 1997, as the Omertà project was fleshing out the activities of Alfonso Caruana in Toronto, a low-level Hamilton street hoodlum, Ken Murdock, shot John Papalia dead. Two months later Murdock murdered Papalia's man in Niagara Falls, Carmen

Barillaro. Murdock confessed to the murders—and a third, carried out several years earlier—and testified that he'd done it on behalf of the Musitano family, a notorious local crime family with Calabrian roots.[2]

No public mention was made of any involvement by the Caruana-Cuntrera, although police speculated privately that the coincidence of Alfonso Caruana setting up shop in Toronto was startling. And Murdock never mentioned a Sicilian connection, but he was too far down the food chain in organized crime to know.

Similarities to the events in Montreal twenty years earlier were apparent. The Sicilians would have come to town and made alliances. If the alliances were rebuffed, as they certainly would have been with Papalia, an old-timer of Vincenzo Cotroni's generation who would never have given up any of his power voluntarily, then more direct action would have been taken. The removal of three of the top La Cosa Nostra players in an eight-month period—first Mora, then Papalia and Barillaro, all occurring during the formation of the Toronto Caruana-Cuntrera drug network—gave rise to speculation that the Siciliana family, as they had in turning the Rizzuto wing of the Cotroni-Violi clan against their masters, had found a hungry ally in the Musitanos.

When reports later surfaced that Vito Rizzuto of the Montreal Sicilians had conducted meetings in Toronto with members of the Musitano family two weeks after the murder, recorded by police on surveillance video, the theory of Montreal Sicilian involvement was given more credibility. While this didn't prove that the Rizzutos ordered the two killings, they clearly benefited from them: southern Ontario crime groups would now answer to the Montreal Mafia, and no longer to La Cosa Nostra in the United States.

Project Omertà's surveillance notes bring to light a strange coincidence. Just weeks before John Papalia was murdered, Alfonso Caruana had been followed to Pearson International Airport, where he'd met a Sicilian-Canadian, a former banker the family had corrupted years earlier. This man lived in Hamilton. After the meeting, Caruana introduced the ex-banker to Vito Triassi, who was traveling with his wife, the daughter of Sicilian Mafia trafficker Santo Caldarella. They had just arrived in Canada. Triassi has arrests for drug trafficking which are still before the courts in Italy. He planned to move his entire family to Canada and to settle in the Hamilton area. After the meeting, he and his wife went to Hamilton to check out some real estate.

Palermo, Italy

In the summer of 1997, the Palermo Court of Appeal, Third Penal Section, passed sentences for international drug trafficking on thirteen members of the Siculiana family. The court recognized the existence of the Siculiana family as a part of Cosa Nostra.

Seven *pentiti* had testified about the Siculiana family as had John Costanzo and David Lorino, the U.S. Drug Enforcement Administration agents who'd penetrated the Cuntreras in Venezuela in 1990.

Alfonso Caruana was found guilty *in absentia*; he received a sentence of almost twenty-two years. Paolo, Pasquale, and Gaspare Cuntrera were sentenced to fifteen years and two months, twenty-one years and ten months, and fifteen years and two months, respectively. Giuseppe Caruana, Alfonso's elderly father-in-law and uncle living in Brazil, received five years *in absentia*. Various other members of the Siculiana family also received lengthy sentences.

The prosecutor had asked the judge to give Paolo and Gaspare twenty-seven years each and thirty to Pasquale. After the sentencing, Paolo turned to his brother, Gaspare, and said: "Gaspare, we got a discount." The courtroom solemnity turned to laughter.

According to a memo written by *Carabinieri* Major Benedetto Lauretti of the Raggruppamento Operativo Speciale in Rome, the testimony at the Palermo appeals court detailed much of the infrastructure and workings of the Siculiana family: "This branch of Cosa Nostra consisted of (the elder) Giuseppe Caruana who, before forming the branch, had asked permission from the Sicilian Commission and the American La Cosa Nostra.

"In subsequent years Pasquale Cuntrera became head of the 'Venezuelan family' . . . and Alfonso Caruana was second-in-command."

Major Lauretti's memo detailed the activities of the Caruana-Cuntrera: smuggling drugs into and out of the United Kingdom; setting up money-laundering operations in the Pizza Connection case in New York; the 'ndrangheta cocaine cartel; and laundering money through Montreal banks in the 1980s. Giuseppe Cuffaro traveled throughout the world on behalf of the family to facilitate the many conspiracies. The memo relied heavily on information from Sergeant Mark Bourque's huge Project Pilgrim file.

The Siculiana family members in Canada were angered at the sentences.

"It's a half-a-death penalty," one man said. "Pasquale is already reduced to a wheelchair, diabetic." He went on to discuss getting a Toronto lawyer "with big balls" and one in Ottawa and another in Italy, also equipped with "big balls." The Ottawa lawyer would attempt to have the Cuntreras brought to Canada to serve their sentences, "even if it costs a million dollars," the man vowed.

In Colombia intelligence agents kept track of the *Zeeland*. In June, two months after Larry Tronstad was tipped off by British Customs, information came in that the ship was ready to set sail. A shipment of narcotics—of unknown quantity—had been hidden on board. But dock fees hadn't been paid and Colombian officials were refusing to let it out of harbor. The crew had revolted and abandoned ship: they hadn't been paid their wages to date. The owners of the ship were trying to find a new crew.

The missing component of Omertà—drugs—remained just out of reach.

Toronto, Ontario

The network of tapped phones in Toronto continued to map out the players in the Caruana-Cuntrera organization. In one phone call, Alfonso Caruana had a long talks with a relative in Venezuela. There were obscure references to numbers and "paper" and "the crazy one." Another call, between Alfonso Caruana and Oreste Pagano, who was now based in Cancun, Mexico—taped off a wired-up pay phone north of Toronto—had a drug-related message in code. Pagano wanted to know when Caruana was going to send the "architect to see the apartments."

Surveillance teams followed Omertà targets to Montreal where they held an hour-long meeting with eight other men after the restaurant they'd been eating in had closed. Other targets spoke of trips to Italy, South America, and the southern United States. Alfonso Caruana made plans to travel to Calgary, Alberta, to look for investments.

All the sudden activity convinced Project Omertà investigators that the Caruana-Cuntrera were on "a spend." Alfonso Caruana and Little Joe Cuntrera had been followed to area casinos, where they'd gambled heavily.

"During the last week of August the targets have been busy paying up their outstanding debts, purchasing new vehicles, and setting up new businesses," an RCMP analysis read. "It is unknown where this new found money has come from but investigators believe this is a result of drug proceeds."

On August 8, 1997, Bill Sciammarella again made the trek to the chambers of Justice McCombs of the Ontario Court of Justice. The case file had now reached thousands of pages.

"Billy was just shrinking," a fellow detective said. "For an investigator working Mafia, this Caruana thing was huge, and it was getting bigger every day."

In chambers once again, Sciammarella was granted a further Authorization, this one under Canada's new Criminal Organizations legislation.

Calgary, Alberta

On August 19, 1997, Alfonso Caruana—casually dressed for travel in a light gray checked sports jacket—Big Joe Cuntrera, and Mike "Mike Hammer" Azzopardi, an employee at Shock Nightclub, flew from Toronto to Calgary, Alberta.

The Shock Nightclub wiretaps had indicated that the men had plans to look for commercial real estate in western Canada. CFSEU believed that Alfonso Caruana was looking for other, lower-profile areas in the country in which to invest his money. Calgary, in the richest oil province of the country, had an uneven economy, but when it boomed it boomed large. Aside from local crime groups in the city, several eastern and Vancouver organized crime groups maintained outposts there.

When Air Canada flight 117 arrived at the Calgary airport, six members of the Calgary Strike Force Unit—experts in surveillance—were waiting.

After retrieving their luggage, the three men climbed into a taxi and went to the Delta Bow Valley hotel. In the lobby, police overheard them rent three rooms on the twelfth floor—rooms 1202, 1204, and 1206—for five nights. The rooms weren't all prepared yet, so they went to Caesar's Steak House for lunch, then to the Royal Liquor Store near Caesar's to check Alberta liquor prices.

At 3:45 p.m. they were back at the Delta Bow, where they met an unidentified businessman and conducted a meeting in the hotel, listening intently to the unknown man as he read aloud to them from a brown leather portfolio. After shaking hands with the man, Caruana, Cuntrera, and Azzopardi went up to their rooms.

The Strike Force set up an observation post in room 1211, just along the hall from the targets' rooms. When the three emerged for a late dinner, they were followed to La Dolce Vita Restaurant, then taken back to the hotel, where they remained for the rest of the night.

At 9:30 a.m. the next day police watched Big Joe Cuntrera come out of his room and knock at Alfonso Caruana's door. Still in his underwear, Caruana chatted with Cuntrera, arranging to meet for breakfast in the hotel's Garden Patio Restaurant. After breakfast, the Strike Force lost them in the hotel until they emerged at 12:45 p.m., climbed into a taxi, and were taken to the Eau Claire Market area, where they priced wines. They lunched on the patio at Joey Tomato's Restaurant. After lunch—Azzopardi paid—the men picked up a Budget rental car and visited liquor and wine stores, not making any purchases. After looking at houses in Patterson Hills, they had dinner at McQueen's Restaurant and returned to the hotel for the night.

The following day was much the same, with some sightseeing, a visit to the Imax theater, and lunch back at the hotel. That night the men went for dinner at La Dolce Vita, visited a local bar, and drove to the casino at Stampede Park. The Strike Force team—now more than a dozen officers, rotating shifts—put them down for the night just before midnight.

Most of the next day was spent shopping at the Eaton Centre and pricing wines and liquors, strolling Chinatown, and dining at La Dolce Vita before looking at some vacant commercial space and visiting the casino.

On Sunday, August 24, the men checked out of the Delta Bow. Alfonso Caruana paid for the rooms with money he snapped from a large wad of cash. Then they headed for the airport.

The visit, including the inspection of businesses and pricing of liquors and wines, confirmed for the Omertà team that Alfonso Caruana planned a western move. Telephone calls recorded during the western trip showed inquiries made to the provincial liquor and gaming commission, to the labor board, and to liquor and wine stores for local prices for alcohol.

"Intercepts also revealed that they were also interested in the opening of a new Sheraton Hotel in Calgary, and they were going to inquire about renting space within the hotel to open a nightclub," RCMP reports said. "The trip by Caruana and associates definitely confirms that (he) was looking to move into Calgary and continue with purchasing of businesses to facilitate . . . money-laundering operations," RCMP documents noted.

During the trip, police later learned, Caruana managed to slip away to Banff, Alberta, a mountain-resort town, to look at business possibilities there.

A request was sent to the RCMP Calgary criminal intelligence section to monitor local agencies to determine any future purchases of properties or businesses, and to investigate any associates that might emerge in the western initiative.

Toronto, Ontario

Back in Toronto Alfonso Caruana was on a binge of meetings and telephone calls, being surveilled having meetings and exchanging bags with targets of the investigation. Members of his group made plans to travel to Mexico and Florida.

Dialed number recorders put in place by the U.S. Drug Enforcement Administration showed Alberto Minelli making regular calls between his home in Miami and numbers in Montreal, Venezuela, Mexico, and Colombia. As the CFSEU had done, the DEA was hoping to use information from the DNRs to apply for a Title Part VI wiretap authorization that would put them deeper into the American side of the case. Members of the Caruana-Cuntrera were burning up the telephone lines, talking in roundabout fashion about deals in the works.

For months the organization appeared to be gathering money to put together a cocaine shipment. Minelli traveled to France, Switzerland, London, and Miami—often in company with Oreste Pagano's daughter, Enrica. Police in each of those countries kept them both under surveillance, documenting meetings with money launderers and monitoring their telephone calls.

It looked to Larry Tronstad as though the cocaine needed to pull together an airtight drug case was hidden in a ship sitting thousands of kilometers away.

Several times during the late summer and early fall of 1997 police overheard Alfonso Caruana and Oreste Pagano talking on the phone, apparently making drug and money transport arrangements. Caruana told Pagano he would be sending him "two"—two million dollars—and "not to worry." Pagano had a voracious appetite for money and constantly pestered Caruana to send him cash shipments. Caruana, for his part, seemed to resist sending money for new cocaine buys and appeared to be trying to put Pagano in the position of having to spend his own money.

Omertà surveillance teams spent weeks watching Alfonso Caruana's days unwind in a series of telephone calls from public booths, meetings with other targets and associates, and the suspicious passing of packages or bags. The telephone calls could be listened to, and the meetings could be photographed. But the contents of the bags was a riddle.

One week in September 1997 was typical. Caruana drove to a home owned by one of his childhood friends from Siculiana. As officers watched, Caruana carried a red duffel bag into the man's home. A few minutes later Caruana left the home without the bag. It was one of several "mystery bags" in the case.

The next day, surveillance by the Toronto Police Mobile Support Services followed Alfonso Caruana and his wife, Giuseppina. The couple went shopping, returned home, then went out again. Caruana stopped at a pay phone and made a call; after another short drive, he again pulled over and made another call from a public phone.

Two days later, surveillance by Mobile Support followed Caruana to 4646 Dufferin Street, where the Cuntreras maintained the Shock Nightclub and Autobahn Car Care, where Caruana ostensibly worked. A short while later he left 4646, returned home, and then was followed to a meeting with his son-in-law, Anthony Catalanotto. After briefly returning to 4646, he went to Genua Fine Foods, a shop owned by the Genua family on Spadina Road. Leaving there, he returned to 4646. Then he drove to a bakery, where he used a public phone. He chatted with Ignazio Genua. Leaving the bakery, he returned to his car and drove to a Tim Horton's donut shop, followed by Genua. From there they proceeded to an ice cream shop where they met with Genua's father, Nicola. After a brief meeting, Caruana returned home for the day.

The following day Caruana followed his usual pattern. He left the house and drove his gold Cadillac to 4646 Dufferin Street. He later left 4646 and drove to the Columbus Centre, an Italian community recreational and cultural facility, where he met briefly with Ignazio Genua. After Genua left the parking lot, Caruana went back into the facility. Two men approached the gold Cadillac, opened the trunk with a key, and placed a bag inside. Slamming the trunk shut, the men walked off.

The surveillance team called Larry Tronstad and brought him up to date.

"We still had no idea what was being passed around," Larry Tronstad said. "We figured it was either dope or money. In any case, it was suspicious."

There was much hand-wringing at the RCMP's Newmarket offices over what to do. Tronstad wanted to have a marked Toronto police cruiser pull the car over on a false pretext and try to get a look into the bag in the trunk. "Drugs or money, we had to know."

The Proceeds of Crime unit wanted nothing to do with it. They felt that, following a recent court decision, a pretext search would be deemed illegal.

"It was a chance, I'll admit," Tronstad recalls. "But if there was money [in the trunk], it would indicate there was a shipment of cocaine on the way."

The surveillance team called for a marked cruiser. Caruana was pulled over and told that his car matched one that had been used in a nearby sexual assault. He readily agreed to cooperate. In the trunk, inside the bag, police found pairs of running shoes.

"If it had been money, we'd have let it go," Tronstad said. "If it was drugs, we had our case."

Since the beginning of the investigation, the Proceeds of Crime unit had wanted to seize one of the money shipments, but the Omertà team had held them off. It had caused bad blood in the Newmarket offices.

The pretext search led to the exit of the Proceeds of Crime unit from the case. One Proceeds of Crime officer telexed a memo to RCMP Divisional headquarters in London, Ontario, saying that the pretext was illegal and would jeopardize future criminal prosecution.

Larry Tronstad was philosophical about the search. "It was a chance we had to take, to see if there was cocaine or cash in the car. The memo sent to headquarters pointed out that all evidence arising from the pretext search would be poisoned. The memo went into the case file and could cause us problems with defense lawyers down the road at trial. It would be Christmas Day for the defense. The proceeds boys removed themselves from the investigation. That's okay, it went ahead anyway."

11

The Project Omertà case was plagued with crisis after crisis—and most of the problems came from within the RCMP itself. In the fall of 1997, the issue was money.

The RCMP budget is a contentious political football. Over the years the federal government's allocation to the force had diminished. In hard costs, not counting the salaries and usual day-to-day expenses of running an investigation, Project Omertà was eating up the funds at an alarming rate. Wiretaps were expensive to maintain; lines had to be leased from the telephone companies. Surveillance was racking up overtime expenses, and translators were working around the clock. The money that had been made available for Omertà was now gone, and the investigation was just hitting its stride. At one point, RCMP Inspector Ben Soave, needing a printer to output a 6,200-page affidavit, had to borrow $4,000 from another RCMP unit.

Soave headed to Ottawa. After showing the significance of the Omertà investigation—one of the biggest, if not the biggest, in Canadian history, and one that certainly had global implications—Soave managed to get a little more funding, enough to keep things going into the new year.

"It was tight, no doubt about it," Soave said. "But Ottawa was receptive, finally, to the significance of this case. They came through."

When, four months later, the budget again ran out, Soave went looking for more funding. He went to see Chris Lewis, who headed up the Criminal Intelligence Service of Ontario (CISO). Soave didn't have much hope. "CISO wasn't into funding permanent joint forces projects, which the CFSEU was. I arranged a meeting with the joint management team and when Chris heard about Omertà, he jumped right in."

After the meeting, Soave walked out with $100,000 in his pocket.

Switzerland

Italian police, actively hunting Alberto Minelli, recorded a conversation he had with his father in Italy. Minelli was emerging as a key player in the Pagano organization. During 1997, a money courier named Riccardo Santin had been arrested trying to deposit US$2 million into a Swiss bank. Unaware that he was dealing with undercover police, he said the money belonged to Massimiliano Pagano and his father, Oreste, and that both were associates of Alberto Minelli. The funds were to be transferred to the Marine Midland Bank in Buffalo, New York.

When, in October 1997, Alfonso Caruana was making arrangements to move money to Pagano, Pagano said they could continue the discussions when Minelli returned from Italy.

By tracing the phone call between Minelli and his father, Italian police found him checked into a hotel in Lugano, Switzerland. Video and audio surveillance was set up and caught him meeting with Enrica Pagano, Oreste's daughter. The two went to Paris for a day, then back to Switzerland, where they made plans to fly to London, England. British police were notified and were waiting to keep tabs on the couple when they arrived. British agents watched Minelli as he met with money launderer Santin at the L'Incontro Restaurant in London. Meanwhile, Italian police wiretaps overheard Minelli ordering airline tickets to Miami for October 14; he also asked the travel service about connecting flights to Caracas.

Toronto, Ontario

The tapped telephones at Little Joe Cuntrera's Shock Nightclub were gathering evidence that the club was the nerve center of the organization. All the major players met there regularly, and Alfonso Caruana visited on a daily basis. He spent hours on the telephone and sitting around dreaming up ways to solve his drug and money problems. The wires were pulling in all kinds of insider information: who was traveling where, and when; business schemes, including one that involved two female bank employees gathering thousand-dollar bills for Little Joe; and general gossip about who was doing what.

Project Omertà had days' worth of wiretaps and miles of surveillance. The only thing missing from the drug case, the thing that would put the icing on the case, was drugs. Enter Richard Court and John Hill.

The Eastern U.S.–Canada Border

In January 1995, Richard Court found himself in deep snow on the American side of the border between Maine and New Brunswick with 50 kilograms of cocaine, a half-frozen armed Sicilian drug smuggler—known only as "Giovanni"—and Nunzio LaRosa, an out-of-shape Mafia courier with a bad heart and big dreams.[1]

"Nunzio became faint halfway there. I think it was either his heart or it was actually fatigue," Court said later, noting that LaRosa had foolishly not eaten before making the border run; he'd drunk coffee instead. "Maybe it was his heart, I don't know. But what I do know is that he had to sit down on a trail and sit on the bag. . . . I gave him some apple juice and just tried to make sure he kept breathing, because it seemed pretty serious."

The cocaine was wrapped in carbon paper and divided into three army duffel bags: Court and Giovanni split the bulk of the load between them, and LaRosa had only a small quantity in his bags, because of his awkwardness on snowshoes.

Court took LaRosa's duffel bag and strapped it to his own body, and the three men trudged on through the snow. They finally crossed the forty-ninth parallel into Canada a couple of miles from a customs post. According to directions they'd been given, Court looked for a stand of trees where the men could stash the drugs; the plan was for Giovanni to wait on the Canadian side, while Court and LaRosa snowshoed back to the little Maine village where they'd left their vehicle. They would then drive through customs into Canada, circling back to pick up Giovanni and the 50 kilos.

Equipped with a cellular phone, a small bottle of liquor, and a gun, Giovanni made himself comfortable on the bags and watched Court and

LaRosa, moving quickly now with the stiff wind at their back, disappear back into the United States.

Electronic commerce, the Internet, and remote instant banking have made the commercial side of the drug trade almost boring, nothing but mundane criminal chores carried out by men with briefcases. Crooked bankers, brokers, and lawyers shoot money all over the world over wires and bounced off satellites, instantly transmitting hundreds of millions of dollars at the stroke of a key. These gray men are not much different from executives who conduct legitimate business, and they often don't even think of themselves as criminals. Even "smurfs," who spend their days laundering small quantities of cash at banks and trust companies, and the bulk currency smugglers who physically carry millions of dollars across international borders, are ultimately just the blue collar workers of crime.

But the product itself—drugs or contraband or even illegal aliens—can't be transmitted anonymously; someone has to bring the goods to market, has to run the risk of being caught red-handed.

When Richard Court successfully brought Alfonso Caruana's cocaine shipment to Montreal in the January 1995 operation, it wasn't his first time running the border. Some of his earlier trips had been unsuccessful. In October 1994, he was traveling in Florida with LaRosa and a 50-kilogram pickup failed to materialize. So the men bought a couple of kilos from some Colombians. They stuffed the cocaine into a plastic grocery bag and drove back to Montreal. Court was paid about $1,500 for his work. Another drug transport to California yielded only two traffic tickets, one for speeding and one for tailgating. Several trips were made carrying money out of Canada, always to Fort Lauderdale, Florida. If drugs were available, they were to be brought back into Canada.

The planning of the trips made it clear that Court was the stooge in the scheme. Nunzio LaRosa would follow him down in a separate vehicle and arrange the pickup, then Court would drive in his own car back into Canada, carrying the weight of the drugs and the burden of the risk. His payment ranged from a little under $1,000 to as much as over $10,000 per run, depending upon the success of the venture.

In the middle of the Caruana organization, between Alfonso Caruana at the top and Richard Court at the bottom, a layer of middlemen acted as middle managers. One of these was Court's contact man, Nunzio LaRosa, a forty-eight-year-old importer of food products from Italy. The Italian-born resident of Montreal had no criminal record in Canada, but he knew a lot of people. A manager of the couriers for the Caruana-Cuntrera organization—moving bulk cash out of the country and cocaine back in—LaRosa was constantly on the lookout for fresh, brainless bodies to staff his network, fools to do the riskiest work for the least amount of money. Playing the role of a major Mafioso plugged into the Rizzuto wing of the Siculiana family, LaRosa's value to the organization would increase as he brought people in under him.

A sideline business for LaRosa, police suspected, was providing forged passports for Sicilian mobsters on the run—notably Vito Genco, Alfonso Caruana's cousin hiding out in Venezuela, and, later, Caruana's uncle, Pasquale Cuntrera, both convicted drug traffickers.

Playing the mobster role, with his black hair dye and girlfriend stashed outside Montreal, LaRosa wasn't above trying to make his own way as a drug trafficker. Oreste Pagano, to whom LaRosa delivered money from the Caruana-Cuntrera, often commented that LaRosa was always trying to get a load of cocaine to bring back on his own.

LaRosa was helped in his schemes by his twenty-year-old son, Antonio, and fifty-one-year-old Montreal resident Marcel Bureau. Bureau looked up to LaRosa, who played the part of a gangster with international connections.

Richard Court had met Nunzio LaRosa in 1994 when he'd worked in a Montreal bar part-owned by LaRosa. Within a year the men had established a friendly relationship. LaRosa, constantly on the lookout for someone to do his risky business, mentioned that he had some criminal activities on the go and Court, with a minor criminal record for assault, expressed interest in making some extra money.

Without mentioning the Caruanas or Cuntreras by name, LaRosa made it clear that Court was going to be working in the big leagues. "He said we were dealing with some very, very powerful people, not just nationwide in Canada, but globally," Court said. "He had mentioned to me that even though we were in Canada, we were not—we were not part of something that was small. We were part of something that was quite great." LaRosa dropped enough broad hints for Court to deduce that the "organization" was the Caruana-Cuntrera.

Court then brought in his childhood friend John Hill, with whom he'd gone to school in Sault-Ste. Marie, Ontario. Hill wasn't a great admirer of Nunzio LaRosa; in fact, Hill gave him the nickname "E-Coli" after he and Court got stuck with an expense from one of their aborted money runs and LaRosa refused to pay it.

Court and Hill made several cash runs for LaRosa, ranging from a one-time low of $900,000 up to $2 million. On some trips they carried the cash down to Florida, where the stash compartment in their vehicle was emptied of money and then filled up with cocaine.

LaRosa seemed to have a need to impress him, Hill recalled, and wasn't shy about dropping names. "He would talk about the Mafia a lot . . . and he also at one occasion identified somebody that was . . . the name Rizzuto was mentioned."

The Canada-U.S. money and drug pipeline was working well. Hundreds of kilograms of cocaine were successfully making it into Canada, and millions of dollars of profit were going out, an estimated average of US$1 million weekly.

Florida

In mid-November 1997, a multi-agency task force meeting was held in Fort Lauderdale. Information from Project Omertà's wiretaps showed that the *Zeeland*, currently in port in Cartagena, Colombia, was going to run a massive load of cocaine to a destination as yet unknown. Sifting through the intercepted conversations of Alfonso Caruana, Oreste Pagano, and Alberto Minelli brought police to the conclusion that the shipment's arrival was imminent. It was expected that Pagano and Minelli would link up in Miami to finalize the deal. The FBI noted that the CFSEU wanted any arrest of Pagano to be postponed until the drug shipment had been seized. The FBI agreed not to arrest Pagano for six months, to give Omertà a chance to take down Alfonso Caruana.

Alfonso Caruana's organization included several members who came from outside the core of the family. Most were Sicilian, and some even came from Siculiana, but ultimately they could be trusted only to a certain degree. His brother Gerlando was an integral part of the Montreal side of the network, but Gerlando's parole prevented him from moving freely outside Quebec. There was always a danger he could be picked up on a violation.

In November 1997, Pasquale Caruana, Alfonso's younger brother, was due to be released from prison in Italy, where he had been serving a sentence for drug trafficking. A skilled drug trafficker, Pasquale had learned at the knee of Giuseppe Cuffaro, with whom he'd been arrested in Germany in 1988. And Pasquale was completely trustworthy. He would be able to move freely from Montreal to Toronto and back again.

Like any nieces talking about a long-lost uncle, Alfonso Caruana's daughters were excited about his release.

"He's out!" Francesca Catalanotto said.

"Poor thing," her sister Anna Maria Napoli replied.

"Mum talked to him. She said he is out."

"Oh, poor thing," Anna Maria said. "He must be happy."

"She asked him how he feels. 'Drunk with liberty,' he said."

A week later Pasquale Caruana arrived in Canada and, with his wife Sheila Dagwell, stayed at Alfonso Caruana's house in Woodbridge.

The RCMP's Liaison Officer in Miami, Corporal Varouj Pogharian, was sending updates to the CFSEU about the status of the mystery ship, the *Zeeland*. In November Pogharian sent a fax: the *Zeeland* was suddenly in play, receiving a new paint job and the new crew was working frantically to make the ship ready to leave port. A week later another fax: the *Zeeland* had been moved and was now sitting in the middle of the bay at Cartagena and was undergoing engine tests.

In Toronto Larry Tronstad waited. "Seizing thousands of kilos of cocaine would be a fantastic takedown by any standards," he said. "It would be the icing on the cake for Omertà."

Venezuela

For Vito Genco, Alfonso Caruana's cousin and the man who had operated the Italian end of 'ndrangheta cartel's cocaine network in the early 1990s, things were rough. Genco, who had been held in custody in Italy until he'd escaped to Venezuela, needed money to get a cocaine shipment to his relatives in Italy.

In a long conversation with Alfonso Caruana, Genco lamented his lack of funds. "Listen, do me a favor. See if you can send me some money because I'm really—"

"Who should I send it with?"

Genco suggested that some relatives might be coming from Toronto.

"Who told you this bullshit?" Caruana demanded.

Caruana went into a long rant about his own situation, the pressure he was under and the difficulty he had filling requests for money: "Do you people think that I'm vacationing here? I don't know how you people think. . . . You tell me how I can do it. They're always crying, they are begging me, to please this, please that. I can't do miracles and I can't ruin myself to do everybody favors. I find myself in a very delicate position here and he thinks that I'm here vacationing in the sun.

"You're starving? What can I do about it, damn it! Everybody is starving. I don't know what to do any more. Everybody asks me. You have to organize your life, damn it. How can you live there like this? I don't understand you any more. I am in deeper shit than anybody else. Try putting yourself in my shoes."

Genco asked: "So, where is mine? Nothing is due me, then?

"Yes, but how can I do it [send money]?"

"Listen, can't we buy someone a ticket or something?"

"Fuck, you're sick in the head. You tell me who."

Toronto, Ontario / Montreal, Quebec / Miami, Florida

By January 1998, Alfonso and Giuseppe Caruana—his nephew, the son of Gerlando—were regularly recorded on the wiretapped telephones.

The Omertà team knew that Caruana needed to get cash to Pagano, and in turn he needed a fresh infusion of cocaine.

Just before noon on January 2, 1998, the day after Alfonso Caruana's fifty-second birthday, the wires started humming with calls between Toronto and Mexico. Pagano left his coded telephone number on Caruana's pager. Six minutes later Caruana was at what he believed was a safe phone.

"Everything's okay, thank God," Caruana said.

"When is he leaving?" Pagano asked anxiously, referring to the courier who would bring him the money that was backing up in Toronto in various stash houses both inside the city and in the countryside.

"We'll see this coming week."

"Compa[re], see if you can send me a couple for now," Pagano said, referring to hundreds of thousands of dollars. "We have all those things . . ." A multi-kilogram shipment of cocaine—between 30 and 50 kilos— was ready to be shipped to Canada. Whoever brought down the money would return with the shipment, and the cycle could begin again.

After the call, Alfonso Caruana called his nephew, Giuseppe, in Montreal, and told him to activate a courier. In turn, Giuseppe spoke to his father, Gerlando Caruana, who contacted Nunzio LaRosa.

For several days police recorded numerous phone calls between Caruana and Pagano, and among members of the Caruana-Cuntrera in Montreal and Toronto.

By January 19, a shipment of cash was accumulated in Toronto— CDN$1.5 million. A surveillance team watched Alfonso Caruana in a plaza parking lot, where, after carefully looking around, he went into a store and stood in the front window, studying the traffic and activity outside. A few minutes later a white Chevrolet Malibu driven by Ignazio Genua pulled up. Caruana left the store and climbed into the passenger seat. Surveillance followed the Malibu to the home of Caruana's newest son-in-law, Anthony Catalanotto. Upon leaving the Catalanotto residence, Genua drove Caruana back to the plaza parking lot, and Caruana went into a store. Genua parked the Malibu and walked off, leaving the keys inside.

"That car was hot," Larry Tronstad says. "It was money. Had to be. They had to get a payment down to Pagano and this was how they did it, minimizing their own risk, handing it off blind to the courier."

Within minutes gray-haired Domenic Rossi walked into the parking lot and climbed into the Malibu. He immediately drove to Highway 401 and headed east, towards Montreal.

Alfonso Caruana called his nephew in Montreal, Giuseppe. "Listen," he said, "the big guy is leaving now. Understand? From seven to seven-thirty have someone be there [to meet him]. And tomorrow morning you meet again."

Surveillance teams in Quebec were waiting for Rossi and the Toronto team was relieved at the Quebec-Ontario border. In Montreal, at 8:30 a.m. the following day, members of Montreal's Project Falcon anti-organized crime unit saw Domenic Rossi meet with two unidentified men. Rossi handed over the Malibu's keys to one of the men and, when the car was returned a few minutes later, he headed back to Toronto. Back at his home just outside Toronto's city limits, Rossi took a plastic bag and a large cardboard box from the trunk and carried them inside. After changing his clothes, Rossi left the house and drove to a midtown restaurant, where he picked up Ignazio Genua.

After the Montreal delivery was made, Pagano, still anxiously waiting for money, paged Caruana, who soon called him back.

Pagano complained of not being kept up to date on developments.

Alfonso Caruana, under crushing pressure to keep the drugs and money moving and obviously feeling the day-to-day stress of running an international drug ring, snapped: "Hey, you think I'm on vacation here? You know, you're making me fight with everyone."

"Why?"

"Because the roads are so bad, so people don't want to drive, to do anything," Caruana said, referring to a severe ice storm that had basically shut down Quebec and eastern Ontario. "I have to force them."

Jokingly, Pagano shot back: "It's not like it's my fault! You want to blame me for that, too?"

Alfonso Caruana had sent $1.5 million in cash to Montreal, where Nunzio LaRosa rounded up a courier team—John Hill and Richard Court—and completed a run from Montreal to Miami.

But quickly, problems developed. The $1.5 million had, between leaving Montreal and being delivered to Massimiliano Pagano in Florida, somehow become $1.4 million. Someone had sticky fingers.

For Pagano, who always absorbed the loss of some shrinkage along the way from each bulk money shipment, this was unacceptable. "Sometimes, perhaps [it was] two or three thousand dollars less. I never really communicated [complaints to Alfonso Caruana] about that. I didn't find it a significant sum. But this time—"

He called Alfonso Caruana.

"It's one-four . . ."

Incredulous, Caruana asked: "It's one-four?"

"Yes."

"No."

"Yes."

"It's one-five—not one-four," Caruana assured him.

"It's precisely one-four."

Alfonso Caruana told him to check again, and Pagano agreed to have the money recounted. Forty-five minutes later Caruana called him back and Pagano told him: "It's one-four, *Compare*."

Caruana exploded: "Fuck, this situation is driving me nuts now."

Pagano told him the same person did the count each time in Miami: his son Massimiliano. Alfonso Caruana told him one of his brothers always did the count before the money left Canada. "Now we have to see how the fuck . . . we have to find these fuck-ups. This can't be. Now we have to wait until the guy returns at the end of the week and we'll see what the situation is. Because this can't be. It's not a question of a thousand. One hundred . . . but fuck, here. . . . It's a lot we're talking about, *Compa*."

Pagano's immediate solution was to have future packages of money sealed, with "writing on the top."

"What are we doing here," Caruana exploded, "playing games? When this gentleman [LaRosa] returns we will see how the fuck the situation is. Because if it was a question of a thousand, two thousand, one could say fuck it and . . ." His voice trailed off.

Pagano, like any good businessman, agreed that minor theft was part

RCMP sergeant Mark Bourque, who exposed the financial side of the Caruana-Cuntrera operation.

(below) Alfonso Caruana is pulled over by police for identification on October 10, 1996, in Toronto, Ontario. With a positive I.D., the net surrounding him began to close.

A police surveillance photo of Alfonso Caruana and his nephew, Giuseppe Caruana, February 19, 1997, just north of Toronto.

Police surveillance photos of Alfonso Caruana during Project Omertà, taken in 1996 and 1997.

Police surveillance photos of Alfonso and Oreste Pagano, when they were discussing ways to get bulk currency drug money out of Canada.

Police surveillance photo of Alfonso and his brother, Pasquale, taken on March 31, 1998 in Toronto.

Giuseppe Caruana and Alberto Minelli under police surveillance.

Nicola Genua in a surveillance photograph.

The takedown: Alfonso Caruana is arrested at his home at 38 Goldpark Ave. in Woodbridge, Ontario on July 15, 1998 by the Omertà squad. Arrests were also made in Mexico and Montreal.

(left) Giuseppe Caruana, arrested at Alfonso's home. *(below)* RCMP escort Gerlando Caruana to a waiting car after he was flown to Toronto. He was arrested in Montreal on July 15, 1998.

RCMP sergeant Larry Tronstad (*l.*) and Bill Sciammarella (*second from right*) send Oreste Pagano (*in baseball cap*) to Italy to face Italian authorities. Pagano was arrested on July 15 at his home in Cancun, Mexico, along with Alberto Minelli, and they were brought to Toronto.

Anna Staniscia-Zaino is released on $200,000 bail.

Domenic Rossi at the time of his arrest.

RCMP inspector Ben Soave at a press conference announcing the takedown of the Caruana-Cuntrera crime family. He later was promoted to Chief Superintendent.

of the cost of doing business. "That would be a normal thing."

"However, we're going to find it. That's no problem."

The following day Alfonso Caruana got his nephew, Giuseppe Caruana, on the phone.

"Listen, how much did you give that guy? One-four or one-five?"

"One-five."

"Because that guy says it's one-four."

"No. I sent one-five."

"Now," Alfonso Caruana said, "we have to see who the fuck is not telling the truth."

Giuseppe Caruana was adamant. "I counted it ten thousand times."

After hanging up, Giuseppe immediately called his father, Gerlando. "I need to speak to you, urgently." The men met for a meal and tried to determine where the money had disappeared to and who had it. A half hour later they reported back to Alfonso Caruana, who in turn contacted Pagano.

"We are waiting for this guy to arrive to see what the fuck—"

Pagano had done some interviewing of his own, questioning his son Massimiliano and his daughter Enrica. "They tell me that the guy had it in a duffel bag. It's not that he took it out and put it somewhere else. *Compa*, I give you my word of honor about that. I'm telling you this and I'm one hundred percent sure. Enrica confirmed it to me. She said, 'Dad, I counted it myself.'"

Frustrated, Caruana said, "These things should never happen, they shouldn't happen."

Pagano mentioned previous cases of missing money. "But sometimes it has happened. I'm telling you this. Now I'm telling you this because even the last time when you sent me yours, two thousand five hundred American were missing."

"No, *Compa*. When I sent it to you I sent even more than what I supposed to."

"What?"

For several days the Caruanas tried to unravel what had happened to the $100,000. LaRosa was questioned several times. Each person along the chain was interviewed, but Alfonso Caruana had his suspicions: "I don't want to doubt anybody, but every time there is 'that guy' in the middle of things, there are always problems."

Exhausted, he called Oreste Pagano.

"I have to pay for this out of my own pocket. Now, I don't trust anyone. What am I supposed to do now? I'm supposed to trust. Until the truth is told, I can't trust anyone any more. These things should never happen."

He told Pagano the breakdown of the money shipment: "They were 730 in twenties, 440 in hundreds, and 330 in fifties."

Pagano, misunderstanding, multiplied 730 times 20, 440 times 100, and 330 times 50, and came up with $75,100. "How can this be, *Compa*? It can't be. Because 730 times 20 is 14,000 and . . ."

Caruana picked up on his problem right away. "No. Seven hundred and thirty of twenties—understand?"

Pagano, feeling stupid, realized that he meant $730,000 of the money was in twenty-dollar bills. "Ahh. I understand."

"Fuck then, how much did you think I'd sent you?"

Both men laughed and began putting together another shipment.

It was never determined who took the missing money. Some thought it was Nunzio LaRosa; others thought it was one of the younger Caruanas in Montreal; still others thought Pagano and his kids had cut up the $100,000, if only to make up for the consistently short shipments in the past.

In any case, Oreste Pagano reached into his own pocket: "In order not to fight with him [Alfonso Caruana], I put in the money myself."

Colombia

The sheer amount of cocaine the CFSEU hoped to tie into the Caruana-Cuntrera operation—the thousands of kilograms stashed aboard the *Zeeland* in bay at Cartagena, Colombia—was never far from the minds of the investigators. Geographically, it was so far from the heart of the case that even the greatest hopes had to be tempered with a sense of reality. British authorities had a source aboard the ship and regular updates were being funneled through the FBI, the DEA, and Customs, to the Omertà team.

In mid-January 1998, hopes of putting a big seizure into the middle of Omertà were dashed. The *Zeeland* had departed Cartagena, bound for Trinidad and Tobago, when the Colombian army struck, raiding the ship and seizing 1200 kilograms of cocaine wrapped into 60 kilo bundles. Nine crew members were arrested. The captain declined to provide any information, but a review of his cellular telephone usage showed calls to Montreal and Miami.

After the raid, reports circulated that one crew member, believed to be an intelligence agent who had been providing information to British authorities, was murdered and his body dumped into the bay.

In Toronto, Larry Tronstad listened carefully to the Omertà wires, looking for some reaction from Alfonso Caruana or Oreste Pagano. "Nothing. Not a word. They didn't even seem aware of it, going about their business. Some other organization, some other case. But for a while it looked close."

12

At the same time Oreste Pagano was digging into his pocket to make up the missing $100,000, he was close to being arrested by American authorities—a move that might have scuttled Project Omertà.

Joseph Genovese, at the Office of the Legal Attaché for the American Embassy in Ottawa, sent a memo to RCMP commissioner Philip Murray on January 26, 1998. In the memo he said that U.S. authorities wanted to take Pagano down: "Our [FBI] Miami Office and the Miami DEA are both of the opinion that now may be an appropriate time to apprehend Pagano and wishes to hear from the CFSEU on their position of this strategy."

Nine days later, Larry Tronstad replied with a memo marked "Urgent" to Legal Attaché Genovese. Tronstad pointed out that, at a meeting hosted by the FBI in Miami in November 1997, a consensus had been reached that arresting Pagano and Minelli prematurely would result in the Caruana-Cuntrera going deeper underground.

"This would seriously obstruct our collective success," Tronstad wrote. "History has proven . . . that they will not risk detection. Caruana has recently been convicted 'ex parte' in Italy on a variety of narcotics/Mafia offences and he, like Pagano, has been sentenced to a significant jail term.

"To disrupt this at this point would be a serious setback as our wiretap expires on 98–04–08."

While continuing cooperation from the U.S. agencies would be helpful, the main target outside Canada, Oreste Pagano, wasn't even in America; he had relocated to Mexico. Tronstad noted: "Suffice to say, if this were a simple arrest we are more than capable of doing this with the assistance of our LO [liaison officer] in Mexico." He added yet another reminder about the agreement made the previous November: "In the Miami meetings we and the F B I placed a six-month moratorium on the Pagano arrest."

Tronstad was used to outside forces trying to get a piece of Omertà. The French government had sent memos asking for information to be used against Alfonso Caruana concerning money funneled through banks in France. German authorities were also closely watching Omertà unfold, building a case of their own. The R C M P had successfully fended off the requests for information—politely but firmly—arguing that if Omertà was successful, everyone would get a piece of Alfonso Caruana. Too often, they believed, Caruana had managed to evade capture because of leaks in foreign government agencies.

Project Omertà had the makings of a successful initiative against the Caruana-Cuntrera, and it even showed signs of doing what had for years seemed impossible: bringing Alfonso Caruana before the courts.

Rome, Italy

While Larry Tronstad's memo had effectively calmed the situation in Miami, plans were afoot in Italy to stir things up. Working through the Italian drug enforcement team, the Direzione centrale per i servizi antidroga (D C S A), the F B I again forced the issue. On February 10, 1998, the R C M P's liaison officer in Rome, Dennis Fiorido, received a memo from the D C S A that a meeting on Omertà was "urgently requested" for the following day.

When Fiorido arrived at the meeting, having no idea what it was about, he was confronted by representatives from the Italian police who were involved in the case, including the Raggruppamento Operativo Speciale (R O S), and the D C S A.

According to Fiorido's report on the meeting, it was clear that the F B I had "orchestrated" the meeting through the D C S A to procure more information about Omertà. In fact, the F B I had flown two investigators from Miami solely to be present at the meeting. "The approach utilized by the F B I in this case has undoubtedly frustrated the D E A representative in Rome," Fiorido wrote. "A number of participants present at the meeting were left with the impression that an intensive struggle for power is currently taking place among agencies in the United States, and the F B I in Rome chose to exhibit their leading role in this investigation."[1]

When Fiorido asked the participants if there were agencies communicating information about the investigation to the Colombian authorities—he had the surprise seizure of the cocaine-laden ship, the *Zeeland*, in mind—the FBI was quick to point the finger at the DEA. They said they themselves had never discussed the case with the Colombian government.

"Some animosity surfaced at the beginning of the meeting when Italian authorities questioned the reason why the FBI was leading this investigation in the United States, since it was a drug investigation," Fiorido noted.

The Italians also questioned why the FBI was "entertaining a direct relationship" with the *Carabinieri* and the ROS in exchanging drug-related information. "The DCSA indicated that their department is the coordinating body in Italy for drug investigations, and the FBI should not try to circumvent the current structure in order to achieve their agenda."

The response from the FBI was quick: "[They] stressed that they took great exception that someone would tell them as to who they should do business with," Fiorido wrote.

When the FBI said they had been unable to get authorization for wiretaps in the United States because they had received no information that targets in Canada or Italy were calling suspects in America, Fiorido suggested that they review the information they had been sent. "I brought to the attention of the FBI representative that the investigating unit in Toronto is submitting a periodical report every fifteen days and that this report is being disseminated by their Legal Attaché in Ottawa."

Fiorido's memo squarely took aim at the FBI and its motives: "In conclusion, I believe very little has been achieved with this meeting, if it is with the exception of the FBI trying to muscle their way into the lead role in this case. It is my opinion that there is a major problem with the dissemination of information within the FBI itself; however, by trying to blame other agencies in this case has only contributed to a source of embarrassment from their part."

Upon receiving Fiorido's report, Larry Tronstad replied: "The attitude expressed by the FBI Miami rep at Rome meeting is no different than what CFSEU has experienced to date during this investigation."

Tronstad, noting several successful joint investigations with the FBI in the past, expressed surprise at the bare-knuckle session in Rome. "This is not characteristic of our normal relationship with them. . . . We view their/DEA cooperation as critical."

A senior Canadian official who monitored the progress of the case summed up the situation: "When we told the Italians in the first instance we had him here, they were skeptical. Then they became believers and got on board. They didn't crowd us. They were supportive and supplied a massive amount of documentation. When we crossed [our investigation] with Primero [the U.S. Customs' sting operation], they were cooperative, even in light of the decision that the RCMP couldn't continue to directly assist their operation [because of the Shirose-Campbell decision prohibiting the RCMP from laundering money]. The DEA committed full resources and assistance. But the FBI was another story. Omertà had become huge and it was being directed by a relatively small task force in Newmarket. Some of those guys thought Toronto was a backwater— and they'd never heard of Newmarket. If they could jump the case, they were gonna. Whoever walked in with a successful case against [the Caruana-Cuntrera] was walking up the food chain."

Montreal, Quebec

It's all too easy to project the face of a monster onto people and view them only in the thin light of the stereotype, to think of all Sicilians as Mafiosi, of all Asians as Triad members, of all drug traffickers as single-facet individuals who don't have the common problems and disappointments of life. But in the midst of the talk of missing money, lost trust, and drug shipment plans, a lopsided and quirky love story showed a human, vulnerable side to the Caruana-Cuntrera family.

Gerlando Caruana, Alfonso's older brother, had been caught red-handed in Montreal in 1986 with the heroin shipment from the United Kingdom. Sentenced to twenty years, he was a model prisoner, as are most Mafiosi in custody, and he was released at the end of March 1993. He immediately returned to the trade he'd been raised in, drug trafficking. Restricted to Montreal by his parole conditions, he was the anchor of Alfonso Caruana's drug network there. Brother Pasquale Caruana was in prison in Italy, as was the Caruanas' mentor, Giuseppe Cuffaro. Nicolò Rizzuto was serving a cocaine sentence in Venezuela and hadn't sufficiently bribed authorities there to gain his release.

In Montreal, Gerlando Caruana lived with his wife, Vincenza—also his first cousin—and their children.

Having learned the hard lesson of his brother Alfonso—who was now practicing the same wisdom in Toronto—Gerlando Caruana appeared to own no property of any kind. Forty surveillances conducted by Montreal police between March 1997 and May 1998 revealed that he had no regular employment. He drove vehicles registered to his wife or other associates. He used cellular phones and pagers registered to several people.

On paper, through a numbered company, a woman named Anna Staniscia-Zaino owned the Piano Bar Zacharie, a hangout for underworld figures in Montreal. Dozens of wiretaps, though, showed that the bar was actually owned or controlled by Gerlando Caruana. He was heard giving orders, advice, and suggestions concerning the bar's operations. The Zacharie bar was managed by Aldo Tucci, the man who, in the 1980s, had laundered Caruana-Cuntrera drug profits through Montreal banks.

Anna Staniscia-Zaino was married when she met Gerlando Caruana. Her marriage, she told friends, was an unhappy one. A relationship developed between Anna and Gerlando. Through wiretaps and room probes, police heard an underworld paperback romance of love and loyalty develop, of plans for a future free of their families and the obligations of life in the family business.

"Gerlando was absolutely in love with her," an officer who reviewed tapes and transcripts said. "She'd had a tough life and she felt she deserved a break. If he wasn't a Mafioso trafficker and she wasn't a front for his business, I'd bless them myself."

Gerlando called Anna regularly, and their personal conversations were peppered with romantic comments and sweet pet names. They constantly tried to find time to be together, away from their spouses—a few minutes here, an hour there.

In February 1998, Gerlando Caruana was at the Burger King restaurant in St. Leonard. He called Anna and said he was waiting for someone.

"What are you doing?" he asked.

"I'm exercising," she told him.

"Then I guess you can't come down here."

She read something in his voice. "Why? If you need me, I'll come."

"Because—here there are things, ah, in front of the door, from far away."

She picked up on it right away—he'd spotted police surveillance. "Oh, my God! What do you want me to do?"

He told her a "document" was at his house.

"Pass by and give it to me," she said. "I'll take care of it."

"I don't know if that's good or bad to do."

Anna, referring to his parole, said, "I'm telling you it's good, better me than you."

A few minutes later he called her again on his cell phone: "I'm leaving now."

"Are they still around?"

"I have it in back of me."

"Make a couple of turns and have a look."

He called again from the end of her block and said he'd lost the surveillance. He handed off the "documents" to her.

Compared to some of the whining women in the Caruana-Cuntrera family, who often complained about constant telephone calls, late-night meetings, and absentee husbands, Anna Staniscia-Zaino was a breath of fresh air. She was loyal to Gerlando Caruana and she was, by all accounts, even tougher-minded than some of the Caruana men. On one wiretap she mentioned that three policemen had been at the bar, and she wished that she'd had some laxatives to put into their drinks "so they'll go to the toilet for a week."

In a conversation with a friend she described her relationship with Gerlando: "I found, and I'm very lucky to have found, this man that as the days go by, he's more and more attached [to me]. It's three or four years we know each other, it's only a year, a year and a half now that we talk about our future, and whatever we do for our future, we do it together." She respected him, she said, and he respected her right back.

But she was pragmatic in her feelings about Gerlando; in fact, she said, she'd told him straight out that she had no intention of getting involved with anyone until she had a certain amount of money in her bank account.

Her friend was shocked at her pragmatism: "Oh, my God!"

"Oh, yes, I was always open. Well, my dear, I have it. I could honestly say that I could tell everyone to fuck off tomorrow and I have my security, security that I could give up everything, even what I have now instead of working my head off. . . . I don't need to break my head right now. I could live comfortably for the rest of my life if I wanted to."

For Gerlando Caruana it was a good deal. When he had problems to discuss, he could turn to Anna. For the first time in thirteen years his diabetes was under control because she watched his diet and took him to doctors.

When she told Gerlando that she wanted to have children, he immediately agreed that they should adopt. And as soon as Gerlando Caruana's children were all married off, she said, she'd leave her husband and she and Gerlando would be free.

Their exit strategy was to disappear and make new lives in Belize. Anna was recorded calling the Belize government office, discussing opening bank accounts, getting credit cards, and buying property there. Gerlando estimated that they would have enough money saved to give them $3,000 a month in interest; they'd live on $1,000 a month and bank the remainder, letting the money build up in their bank accounts.

He explained how he'd prepare his children. "When the time comes—I'll say this is the situation, accept it as it is. The important thing is I won't leave anybody. I won't leave anybody in the street. If they accept, if they don't accept, they tell me and they can each do what they want to. Because once that I have everybody settled, I have to talk, especially with Alfonso."

He expected them to make their move within a year: "It's clear—after 1999 I don't want to be here any longer. We have come to the point that we have to do something because life is passing us by, and soon we won't let it slip by any more."

Toronto, Ontario

As ever, Oreste Pagano needed money to feed the voracious Colombian cartel he dealt with. It seemed to be both Pagano's and Alfonso

214

Caruana's constant purpose in life, to always have a deal in the works, and money had to be made to buy more cocaine to make more money.

On February 16, 1998, Caruana called Pagano in Venezuela. Caruana knew that police activity was heating up, and he didn't have the freedom to make moves as quickly as Pagano was demanding. In Pagano, Caruana had a good thing: an offshore supplier who'd proven reliable and who had increasingly greater access to sources of major cocaine supplies. He was a middleman who, when he had to, was willing to believe Caruana's sob stories about having no money and would dip into his own pocket to make deals. Caruana needed shipments, not only for Canada, but also for his customers overseas in Italy. But Pagano needed cash.

In their conversation, Pagano got right to the point: "Send me some green."

"I don't know, *Compa*. It'll be difficult."

"Because I have to pay those people; otherwise, we'll lose a lot of money in the exchange."

"It's difficult, it's difficult. The situation is a little critical here. I can't move around as much as I could a while back, you understand me? There is more pressure than ever."

Alfonso Caruana was clearly telling Pagano that there was lots of money available, but it couldn't be moved from one place to another because of the surveillance. But he'd try.

Project Omertà officers, watching Caruana make his rounds, believed he was gathering a shipment of money to send south. He was aware he was under almost constant surveillance, but he practiced nothing more than rudimentary evasion. He was like some kind of criminal stockbroker, practicing the art of the deal, sweating to bring all the elements of the transaction together in a pressure cooker. He drove to Shannonville, Ontario, where he picked up a duffel bag from the country home of a childhood friend from Siculiana. He conducted several meetings with Ignazio Genua. His nephew, Giuseppe Caruana, came to Toronto from Montreal and took bags of money back with him. In a matter of a few days, $800,000 was ready to be sent south.[2]

But, as usual, there were problems. One courier broke his leg and couldn't drive; LaRosa wouldn't be able to get a team together until the following month. Some of the problems were mundane to the point of being ridiculous: when Nunzio LaRosa was on his way to pick up the money, Gerlando and Giuseppe Caruana could find only a small "purse" to hold the money. They thought of running over to the local Price Club to get a larger bag, but the Price Club was about to close for the day, and LaRosa was put off until the next day.

The question of who had dipped into the previous $1.5-million shipment was still nagging at Caruana. And it didn't help to have policemen watching his every move.

When the drug money was ready, he and Pagano spoke. Caruana said: "I am a wreck. . . . I was a little sick, not with the diabetes. Fuck, here they are driving me crazy. A mess, fuck, I am going nuts, if I end up in a hospital this time, damn it."

Pagano, expansive now that money would soon be on the way, laughed.

They discussed the pending shipment and possible future ones; then Caruana returned to the subject of his health: "Because I am already tired. Fuck, you wouldn't believe, here I can't make it any more, I am falling ill."

Pagano laughed again: "The only thing that we shouldn't lose is our health."

They talked about the finances of the next deal, about 500 or 600 kilograms of cocaine. They were going to pay US$4,000 per kilogram, and after shipping and expenses their total cost would be $9,000 per kilogram. Each kilogram would sell for up to $35,000 in Canada. Both men would have to put up about US$2.5 million to cover the entire shipment.

A few days later Pagano told Caruana that he wanted to increase the shipment, paying up front for half and getting the other half on credit. His Colombian suppliers wanted to know how soon he'd pay for the credited portion.

Caruana was incredulous—he didn't like Colombians in general, and he seemed to be unhappy with Pagano's latest supplier in particular. "How are you going to pay for it ahead of time?" Caruana asked. "Only give, if anything, what it costs there. What do you mean pay ahead of time! *Compa*, what kind of reasoning is this? What if it doesn't arrive?"

"If it doesn't arrive they'll give me the money [back]."

"One cannot pay for it before it arrives. Fuck, how do these people work? I don't know. I don't understand a thing. I have never heard of this being done."

Pagano calmed him: "Maybe I didn't explain it right. Since I had problems last time . . . "

Caruana chided him. "You're going to have to excuse me for saying this, but you go looking for problems."

A cash shipment was put together, but it was far short of what Pagano needed, less than a million dollars.

"How much?" Pagano asked.

"Eight hundred."

"Ohhh . . . "

"*Compa*, please, don't be like that, because you don't know all the problems I have here, the difficulties."

By the end of the first week of March 1998, Oreste Pagano had told Caruana that the shipment would soon be underway: "Next week the architect will be leaving for where the little boy is, you know?" The cocaine, he meant, would arrive in Miami, where Pagano's son, Massimiliano, was living. The key was to have Alfonso Caruana's money shipment arrive at the same time so both the money and the drugs could be quickly moved out.

Turin, Italy

In mid-April, Alfonso Caruana got some good news from his sister-in-law in Italy. The Court of Assizes of Turin had "absolved" him of charges arising from Project Cartagine, the investigation into his shipments to Vincenzo Mazzaferro's 'ndrangheta cartel. Antonio Scambia had provided detailed information on the mechanics of the scheme to supply the cartel in Calabria with tons of cocaine. Scambia had told police of his meetings with Caruana, laying out the financial trail used by Vito Genco to get Caruana's profits out of Italy. The prosecutor had asked for a thirty-year sentence for Caruana.

But in March, Scambia had suddenly decided not to testify. Both Caruana and Genco were acquitted. Neither had appeared at the trial: Caruana remained in Canada and Genco in Venezuela.

The news reached Oreste Pagano first. He immediately called Alfonso Caruana.

"I always get the good news from others," Pagano complained, jokingly. "Why do you never call me when there's good news?"

"Why, what's going on?"

"The good news from Turin." He said he'd heard it from "the whimsical guy": "That guy was jumping up and down on the phone."

Toronto, Ontario / Montreal, Quebec / Miami, Florida

In the last week of March 1998, police intercepted several calls between Alfonso Caruana and Oreste Pagano indicating that two shipments were likely being planned: one for Caruana and the Genua crime family, the other for Caruana, Pagano, and a man named Luis. At least one of the shipments—"apartments"—was in Mexico City and would be moved to Miami. Whoever went to Miami to pick up the drugs would drive down with a stash of money Pagano badly needed. From the wiretaps it also appeared that drugs were backing up in Florida; there were indications that as much as 800 kilograms of cocaine was stashed in Miami, waiting for distribution. The plan was to move the cocaine to Canada in 60- to 80-kilogram lots and, as payment was made, send the same amount every week or two.

The network had to get moving again. Arrangements were made to do a run after Easter 1998.

Meanwhile, in late March, Montreal's Project Falcon wiretaps intercepted Nunzio LaRosa speaking to a man he called "John." LaRosa asked John if his truck was ready. He was told the truck had been in an accident and was in for repairs. Speaking in vague terms, John asked LaRosa if he had some drugs; LaRosa asked John if he knew any women who could accompany him on the trip. Analysis of the conversation led investigators to conclude that either a drug transport or a money run was imminent.

After reviewing several other John-LaRosa intercepts police identified "John" as John Curtis Hill, a resident of Sault Ste. Marie, Ontario. An investigation of Hill led to his boyhood pal, Richard Court.

Nunzio LaRosa swung into action, lining up John Hill to make the

Miami run. Several attempts were made to get a second courier, but most fell through. Richard Court wound up taking the job.

On April 17, 1998, LaRosa—whose code name on the telephone was "*Baffetto*," "*the Mustache*" was told to get a money run set up for Miami. He called John Hill in Sault Ste. Marie and told him to bring his pickup truck to Montreal where a stash compartment was to be installed to bring a shipment of drugs back. When the body shop hired to do the job couldn't get the right materials, the planned trip went ahead anyway.

For Toronto Police Detective-Constable Mike Harvey, being part of the Caruana case was a dream come true. Seconded to the CFSEU, Harvey was designated surveillance coordinator, focusing his efforts on whoever was the target of the day. He knew all the players and their vehicles, knew the back alleys and surveillance points around their homes and businesses, and once they were in motion could "take them by the nose"—follow them from in front.

When LaRosa arranged for John Hill and Richard Court to take the run to Florida, Harvey was set up on Hill's home in Sault Ste. Marie. At dawn when Hill came out of the house and climbed into his pickup truck, Harvey swung in behind him. It was the start of a seemingly endless surveillance.

"He drove to Montreal in the morning and by eleven o'clock that night we were back in the Soo," Harvey recalls. "He had Court with him, and LaRosa and his gofer, Marcel Bureau, were following in a sedan with the shipment of money. He never shut off the car; he went into the house, came out, and away we went."

With Harvey on their tail—Court, LaRosa, and Bureau in the sedan; Hill alone in the truck, now in possession of the money—the mini-convoy drove across the border into the U.S. Hill, whose truck had been flagged on the U.S. Customs computer was pulled over for a secondary inspection. Harvey managed to advise the inspector that a "play" was underway. Hill was allowed to pass.

"The DEA had units waiting along the way, at each state line," Harvey said. "They switched off vehicles so the license plates of the cars matched the state we were driving in."

As Harvey followed the two vehicles down through the United States, he fought exhaustion, watching as the pickup and the sedan pulled over in rest areas or behind gas stations to grab some sleep. In Chattanooga, Tennessee, the vehicles stopped at an all-night car wash; in Florida they drove down a backroad and watched a strip show.

In Florida some of the pressure of maintaining visual surveillance was alleviated when the DEA put up an airplane to assist.

Things were looking good: a successful money delivery would free up another cocaine shipment and maybe the Omertà squad would finally get their "powder."

Just before noon on April 21, a frantic Oreste Pagano called Alfonso Caruana:

"I'm really worried because Willie [the code name for Minelli, in Miami] said that there are people following him. . . . God damn, he said they were at the house, then he went driving around town and they were following him. He went to another place and they followed him there too." Pagano said his son Massimiliano and his girlfriend were in the house with money. "They can't be moved."

Both men began cursing, but immediately talk turned to the second shipment: 200 kilos; 100 for Caruana and Pagano, the other hundred for the Colombian suppliers.

Caruana: "*Compa*, I'm completely broke. I gave everything I had, I gave to . . ."

Pagano: "There is no need for me to give the money. For the first time they will give it to me, one hundred for them and one hundred for us."

A decision had to be made about where to pick up the next cocaine shipment—Houston, Texas, or "where the actors are," in Los Angeles, California.

An hour and a half later Pagano called again: the money couldn't be moved from the house. But without it, the next shipment of cocaine couldn't be picked up. After Minelli had left the house, Pagano said: "He said the stuff is well hidden but can't be moved. We'll wait a week and then do it."

Again, accepting that the situation was out of their control, they began to discuss other shipments.

When word of the Miami "burn" on the surveillance outside Minelli's house reached Larry Tronstad, he immediately called the FBI and told them what was going on.

The FBI said it wasn't them.

"Bullshit," Tronstad told the agent. "They've got everything—the make and colors of your cars, everything but the license plates."

The agent denied it was them. Tronstad persisted.

Finally, the agent called back and said a "renegade surveillance team" had set up at Minelli's and they would be pulled off. But it was too late for the Omertà team to catch their suspects with the only thing lacking to make their case: cocaine.

LaRosa repeatedly contacted Gerlando Caruana in Montreal: should we stay or head back? Hill and Court were getting antsy. They told LaRosa that if they had to return empty-handed—losing much of their salary—they weren't "going anywhere for anything any more."

LaRosa: "These guys here told me it's useless . . . They've lost faith in me, you understand? They've lost trust in me, this is the problem."

Gerlando Caruana said he hadn't heard anything about retrieving the drugs or making up a replacement shipment. He, too, was left hanging.

Alfonso Caruana was concerned about the predicament Hill and Court were in. He told Pagano that the failed shipment "was an enormous mess with these guys who came empty-handed, and they still want their expenses, this and that."

PAGANO: "It isn't our fault."
ALFONSO: "They made the trip, understand?"

Several more calls were recorded in anticipation of the next 200-kilogram shipment. Caruana and Pagano discussed getting someone to make the trip and commiserated about the problems in their lives.

ALFONSO: "Fuck, he already doesn't want to do this any more. I have to find someone else."
PAGANO: "Why don't you tell him not to break the balls because they're already swollen?"
ALFONSO *laughs*: "What can be done?"
PAGANO: "All the others try to look good and we always end up with the problems."

Nunzio LaRosa now had a problem of his own. The failed pickup in Miami had caused him to lose face with Hill and Court—especially Court—and their role as couriers was a crucial one. Finding, then grooming, then getting control over people willing to carry millions of dollars and hundreds of kilograms of cocaine across the U.S. border was a long process that tested La Rosa's people skills. His risk was significant. If the couriers got caught, the only person they could offer to police was him.

A new shipment had to be picked up in Houston, and Hill and Court were perfect for the job. But getting them back onside after the disaster in Florida would be tough. LaRosa called Gerlando Caruana from Miami a half-dozen times, telling him that Hill and Court were regularly telling him to "fuck off."

The Caruana-Cuntrera weren't unsympathetic to LaRosa's position, and they were willing to give the angry couriers more money, but they weren't going to get muscled. Discussing the situation with his brother Gerlando, Pasquale Caruana noted, "We're interested in them and they know it. Hey, they're looking out for their own interests."

"It's logical," Gerlando replied. "Everyone looks after their own. I'll try to come up with an agreement with them, even if I have to give them a little more, understand?"

Pasquale agreed, showing a steeliness. "We're interested in them, but we don't want them to grab us by our throats."

Gerlando said, "No, I understand this. That's why I called you, to find out if we really need them or not. If there are—if there is someone else—I'll tell them to fuck off right away."

"As I was saying," Pasquale continued, "if we are, if it is something realistic, then yes, otherwise, if they have to grab us by the throat, then it's no. We are not going to let anyone do that."

Gerlando: "I'm not letting anyone grab me by the throat."

As long as Hill and Court's demands were reasonable, they agreed, they would pay them something.

"They can be replaced," Pasquale said.

"I know that, but to find others—"

"I know, I know."

"That's the fucking thing. Everything is difficult," replied Gerlando.

Italy

Getting narcotics out of South America was only half of Oreste Pagano's business. Moving money, often hundreds of thousands of dollars at a time, was the other half. It was time-consuming and required a trusted network of people. His main money mover was Alberto Minelli.

Minelli was the modern equivalent of an old-time bagman. But rather than driving from bar to bar to pick up or deliver money, he jet-setted across the world. A review of his flights into the United States alone shows that the energetic and elegant money launderer spent a lot of time in airports as he moved Oreste Pagano's and Alfonso Caruana's drug profits.

Computerized records show that Minelli arrived at Miami's airport twenty-eight times between February 3, 1995 and April 28, 1998; in between he had flights into Toronto and Montreal. Most of the flights originated in Caracas, Venezuela, and Canada.

Oreste Pagano wasn't above carrying his own bag, when necessary. Currency Transaction Reports—required by the U.S. government when more than $10,000 enters or leaves the country—show that he filed several times, for amounts ranging from $20,000 cash to $260,000.

Pagano's daughter, Enrica, also traveled on her father's business. Records show that she flew from Amsterdam to Detroit on December 13, 1997; she had no luggage, but she did have $13,464 in cash that she did not report and it was seized by U.S. customs. Her brother, Massimiliano, who also used the name Giuseppe Carmelo Salma, showed high travel mileage but never reported any cash imports or exports.

Massimiliano Pagano didn't confine himself to the financial side of the operation. A trace on his debit card—in the name of Giuseppe Carmelo Salma—tracked his movements from Miami, Florida, to Houston, Texas, in the days before the 200-kilogram cocaine shipment was to be picked up for Alfonso Caruana. After the drug shipment left Houston, the debit card shows purchases as the young Pagano made his way back to Miami.

During his rounds in Europe, Alberto Minelli walked into the Italian component of the U.S. sting operation, called Operation Casablanca. The Americans had found out that drug money from Italy, Spain, and Holland had passed through Italian banks as it left Europe. Major Benedetto Lauretti of the ROS set up a company, Enterprise Consulfin s.r.l., and staffed it with young, energetic *Carabinieri* officers. Through informers, they put out the word that they were in the business of laundering money.

On May 19, 1997, using the code name Alex, Alberto Minelli delivered 784,550 *lire* to Enterprise Consulfin. The money was directed to the Operation Casablanca bank account at the Bank of America in Los Angeles. Three days later, Minelli returned to the storefront, accompanied by his associate Giambattista Rivetta, and turned over another 1,194,350,000 *lire*.

The contracts were negotiated through the U.S. Customs undercover storefront in Los Angeles. The clients needing the pickups in Italy were three Cali cartel money brokers: Carlos Cock, Herman Villagas, and Oscar Ortiez. The money was delivered to the Italian storefront by Minelli and Rivetta, who had instructions from Cock on where to wire the funds.

Over a two-day period, the money was wired to bank accounts in Tampa, Miami, Minneapolis, New York, Colombia, Taiwan, Manchester, Israel, and Mexico. Unaware that he was speaking to an undercover ROS officer, Rivetta confided that he had been hired by Minelli to collect money all over Italy for Minelli's Colombian "friends."

Timing his arrests with the rest of the takedowns of Operation Casablanca, Major Lauretti arrested Giambattista Rivetta on money-laundering charges. Alberto Minelli, who seldom remained in one place for long, was gone.

He wouldn't have been arrested, in any case. In cooperating with the Omertà team, Major Lauretti had made an agreement with the RCMP not to arrest Minelli immediately. According to the Omertà wires, there was a chance to catch the Caruana-Cuntrera with quantities of cocaine, and arresting Minelli would have ruined the opportunity.

Cancun, Mexico

With Miami too hot to safely do business, Oreste Pagano quickly made arrangements to find some cocaine. Operating now from his real estate office in Cancun, Mexico, he arranged in May for a 200-kilogram shipment of cocaine to be delivered to his contact, Luis Humberto Rivera, in Houston.

"He was the one who was dealing my stuff there," Pagano said. "My son had gone a couple of days earlier to give money to Luis."

In Canada, the Caruana-Cuntrera scrambled to get couriers to Houston to pick up the load.

Montreal, Quebec

Thinking he could cool down his couriers, Nunzio LaRosa gave them $1,500 each in expense money. Hill accepted the payment calmly—he was, after all, getting cocaine from LaRosa and was making some extra money—but Richard Court was angry. LaRosa had deducted $560 from his share because Court owed it to him. He refused to take the thousand dollars.

"Richard's impossible," LaRosa told Hill. "I can't work with him, he's fucked up."

Hill said Court was "disappointed."

Nunzio, impatient, replied: "Everyone's disappointed."

Hill, who obviously had a different arrangement with LaRosa than Court, alluded to a private deal—a drug transaction—they'd made. "Hey, ah, that lunch you packed me before I left [Montreal]. . . . I'm gonna need more. That was a great sandwich, man. Everybody up here said 'Where'd you get that salami, man?' Half the lunch is gone already."

LaRosa, needing Hill, if not Court, for the upcoming Houston drug run, romanced him a little and appeared to be preparing him for some future action regarding Court: "John, listen, I like the way you act, that you work. Now I want you to think about—we have problem with this guy. He's not completely reliable any more. I don't like the way he's talking. He's nervous, he's paranoid, he's really unreliable. Anyway, think about it and we gonna talk after."

But in a later conversation, LaRosa, speaking to his son Antonio prior to the Houston trip, complained that he couldn't reach Hill by telephone. "Fuck, is this guy stupid!"

Antonio, in reply, said, "He's a real idiot."

In the end, John Hill and Richard Court did the run to Houston. Hill had wanted nothing to do with this one; in fact, the previous year he'd called the RCMP anonymously and told them that LaRosa was "with the Mafia, cocaine trafficking and money laundering." But there was no one else to go to, and LaRosa muscled them; after the problems in Miami, the Houston run was critical for the family. LaRosa told them that the Mafia was relying on the shipment: "You're playing with your lives."

Toronto, Ontario/Houston, Texas

The Project Omertà wiretaps in Toronto showed a sharp increase in calls between Alfonso Caruana and Oreste Pagano as they discussed several deals. Cocaine shipments were ready to go in Los Angeles and Houston, and the men also alluded to three container loads to be shipped to New York City, totaling 900 kilograms.

Caruana and Pagano decided to do the run through Houston.

Larry Tronstad wanted to install a Global Positioning Satellite (GPS) on John Hill's pickup truck to ensure that it could be located if the surveillance teams lost it. RCMP Special I officers took a truck identical to the one driven by Hill to the garage at the Newmarket office and took it apart. The GPS required a clear line of sight to an orbiting satellite. Also, finding a secure place to hide the device meant identifying a space large enough to hold the several batteries needed to power it. Once the hiding place was found, a team flew to Sault Ste. Marie, where they went to Hill's home and, in the middle of the night, quickly installed the device on his truck.

On May 9, 1998, Tronstad and a team flew to Houston to set up an operational plan with Miami and Houston FBI agents, DEA and U.S. Customs agents, and the Texas Department of Public Safety. "We thought about doing a controlled delivery, letting Hill and Court bring the drugs to Canada, but the Americans thought it was too risky," Tronstad said. "We decided to have a traffic stop made, take the drugs and arrest Hill and Court, and let LaRosa and Bureau return to Canada."

Surveillance teams monitored Nunzio LaRosa and Bureau from the airport in Detroit to Houston. At a Shamrock gas station in Houston, agents watched the cocaine being loaded into Hill's green pickup. Another surveillance team saw LaRosa meet with Alberto Minelli and Pagano's son, Massimiliano.

On May 15, 1998, the Omertà wiretaps picked up Alfonso Caruana and Pagano confirming the Houston shipment. Pagano said: "The documents have already been handed over." Caruana replied, "Perfect."

On Saturday, May 16, LaRosa and Court picked up Hill at the airport in Houston and drove to a designated spot where Bureau was waiting with the green pickup. With LaRosa and Bureau traveling behind in the sedan, and Court and Hill in the pickup—"loaded to the roof," according to Hill—all four headed back to Canada.

Court later said he knew that the shipment, propelled by LaRosa's urgency to complete the contract for the family, was doomed from the beginning. "I thought that Texas was a hot spot; I thought that the timing was rushed—I thought that the preparations were forced, and I thought that his idea and his basic plan were dangerous. . . . It was almost like not even concealing [the drugs] . . . throwing them into the vehicle."

About an hour outside of Houston, when Hill failed to signal a lane change on Highway 59, Texas Department of Public Safety troopers C. E. Kibble and John Hart pulled him over to the shoulder of the highway. Kibble told Hill that he was being stopped for an improper lane change; Hill agreed and produced his driver's license. Kibble smelled a strong chemical odor coming from the bed of the truck and saw a black sleeping bag draped over several large, bulky items. Hill got out of the truck and allowed himself to be patted down.

Kibble, who describes himself as having received specialized training in Kinesic Roadside and Field Interviewing, asked several seemingly innocent questions and noted subtle signs of deceit in Hill's answers. Kibble escorted Hill to the cruiser, then returned to the truck to talk to

Richard Court. It didn't require an expert interviewer to recognize the not-so-subtle signs of deceit there: Richard Court was wet with sweat. "Court was extremely nervous to the point he was barely able to maintain composure," Kibble said. Casually, he asked Court about the drug situation in his neighborhood, then for his opinion about how the court system should prosecute people found to be in possession of dangerous drugs, or found transporting dangerous drugs.

Court—shaky, perspiring, and clearly aware that the jig was up—began babbling: "Well, I feel that they should be . . . ah . . . punished to the full extent of the law."

Satisfied, Kibble went back to Hill and chatted with him about the Highway Patrol's criminal interdiction program, checking for weapons or drugs or other contraband being transported.

"Hill was being very deceptive; that is, evasive eye contact, sweating, pulsating jugular vein, patting clothes, adjusting clothes, change in speech rate, vocal skippers, bargaining statements, and non-verbal body language," Kibble said.

He asked permission to search the truck; Hill agreed and signed a voluntary consent. Kibble looked under the black sleeping bag and found more than a dozen large black plastic trash bags. Inside were brick-like packages wrapped in tape and cellophane.

Kibble and his partner pulled their guns, handcuffed Hill and Court, put them in the ditch, and read them their rights. Hill was offered the opportunity to speak to a State narcotics investigator; he said he would.

"How much cocaine is in there?" Kibble asked.

Hill in turn asked Court: "How much is it?"

Court said he didn't know, that he'd thought the bags contained money.

The truck contained eleven bags of cocaine, totaling 200 kilograms.

By this time, Nunzio LaRosa had driven past the arrest scene with Marcel Bureau. He kept going for twenty kilometers, found an off-ramp, and then turned around to go back for a second look. Believing they were clear, they headed back to Canada.

"We let LaRosa and Bureau go," Larry Tronstad said. "It would look to Alfonso Caruana that the lost load was just the cost of doing business. We were hearing they were planning loads from California and we didn't want to spook them. There was a flight risk regarding LaRosa and Bureau, but ultimately it was worth the chance."

Finally, Project Omertà had its "powder."

Oreste Pagano in Mexico and the Caruanas in Canada were in a dead zone. Confirmation of the delivery and shipment should have come. Oreste Pagano repeatedly called, looking for updates.

"I'm confident," Pasquale Caruana told him. "What do you want me to tell you? I'm confident . . . we'll wait."

"That's all we need," Pagano sighed. "It's not the time to take it all back."

"Those are well-said words."

Pagano, philosophizing: "I know. What can we do? We were born to suffer."

An hour and a half later, Pagano called Pasquale Caruana again. There was still no news. Pagano knew something had gone badly wrong. "It's dead," he said, "and we have to die."

"Let's hope nothing is wrong." Then Pasquale Caruana laughed bitterly.

Pagano concluded the conversation by saying, "We have died here enough for many years."

When he arrived in Montreal, LaRosa called Gerlando Caruana and told him, referring to the Hill and Court arrest: "I think they got poisoned. They might be in the hospital."

Lee Anne Hill called her husband at Polk County Jail in Houston. Of Nunzio LaRosa she said: "I'm going to kill him with my bare fucking hands."

Natalie Boucher, Court's girlfriend, had a similar opinion of LaRosa: "That motherfucker."

In the wake of the Houston seizure, the Caruana-Cuntrera had to first reassure themselves that the incident was just bad luck and that Court and Hill wouldn't turn on them. And then the organization had to bring in another load.

A week after the arrests, Oreste Pagano called Alfonso Caruana to discuss strategy regarding Court and Hill, and to arrange another shipment.

Pagano said he had "350 apartments"—code for 350 kilograms of cocaine—for Caruana, but Caruana wanted to talk about the Houston arrests first. He asked for Court and Hill's case number.

Pagano said, "What do I care [about Court and Hill]?"

Caruana replied, "It's not like I'm going to go there and go to jail for them, *Compa*. Tell them to find a lawyer and send him—how the fuck—that way these people see that there is someone who is thinking about them."

Toronto, Ontario/Parma, Italy/Fuengirola, Spain

Following the arrest of Hill and Court, the continuous wiretap campaign brought a bonus, far from the epicenter of Project Omertà. Alfonso Caruana's uncle, Pasquale Cuntrera, who with his brothers had five years earlier been unceremoniously kidnapped in Venezuela and flown to an Italian prison, got lucky. Paolo and Gaspare Cuntrera had been released on February 25, 1998, but both had been picked up instantly on fresh warrants. An oversight in the Italian justice system, however, led to Pasquale, now confined to a wheelchair, being set free.

The release caught the Italian government completely off guard, but it was no surprise at all to Alfonso Caruana. The night before, he had phoned Vito Triassi, and told him to go to Parma, where Pasquale Cuntrera was being held. The old man, Caruana told Triassi, would "be coming out."

The next day, in the shadow of Parma's prison, Pasquale Cuntrera's wife, Giuseppa Vella Cuntrera, waited. Sixty-eight-years old and bursting with energy and joy, she embraced her husband and they kissed. Those who know the couple say their marriage was strong and their commitment deep.

Impatiently, Vito and Vincenzo Triassi escorted them to a waiting vehicle and took them

The Triassi family is part of the Caruana-Cuntrera organization. Brothers Vito and Vincenzo are married to two daughters of Santo Caldarella, a Mafioso who was convicted in Italy *in absentia* for Mafia association. Santo Caldarella remains at large. The Triassi family has several relatives in Canada—notably in Montreal and southern Ontario—and family members have visited Canada several times. Vito and Vincenzo Triassi have been charged by the Italian police for trafficking hashish that was shipped to North America and Italy, via Spain. They also received large cocaine shipments from Oreste Pagano's organization in Venezuela.

to seclusion in Ostia, a small city about twenty kilometers east of Rome.

Famed for its ancient Roman baths, Ostia is a tourist mecca where tens of thousands flock yearly. The city has been called "Rome's Pompeii." For the Caruana-Cuntrera, Ostia has been a nerve center of the family's activities on mainland Italy for decades. Family members own a lot of real estate in the city; properties bought in the 1970s remain in their hands to this day. The wives of the imprisoned Cuntrera brothers live in apartments whose ownership can be traced directly to the heroin trade of the 1970s. Italian police records of the Siculiana family indicate that most members have either lived in or paid extended visits to Ostia. With the constant flow of tourists through the city, Ostia is a prime hiding place for members of the Siculiana family on the run.

On May 6, Little Joe Cuntrera called Vito Triassi to ask after his uncle. Pasquale, Little Joe was told, was fine, and meals were being prepared for him.

The following day Alfonso Caruana called and spoke to Pasquale Cuntrera. "How are you?"

"Not bad. I'm here," Pasquale Cuntrera said.

"Damn." They both laughed. "How are you feeling?"

"My legs are bad."

"Let's not let them get us any more, damn it."

Chaos in the Italian government was meanwhile reaching a fever pitch. The government's embarrassment was heightened by a similar bungle involving another prominent criminal. Lucio Gelli, the eighty-one-year-old former grandmaster of the outlawed *Propaganda Due* group within the Masonic Lodge, had been serving a twelve-year sentence for the multi-million-dollar bankruptcy that led to the collapse of the Banco Ambrosiano in 1982. He was free while his case was on appeal when he apparently just vanished from his Tuscan villa.

Pasquale Cuntrera, meanwhile, had a five-day head start on authorities—the time it took for documents that would have held him in custody to arrive from Palermo. When the story broke, a storm of controversy immediately arose. Much was made of the fact that Pasquale Cuntrera had been confined to a wheelchair at the time of his escape. Minister of Justice Giovanni Maria Flick announced his resignation; the opposition also demanded the resignation of the minister of the interior, Giorgio Napolitano. The government faced several uncomfortable days under media scrutiny.

After the escape an Urgent Secure Fax arrived at the RCMP International Liaison Branch in Ottawa from Bruno Saccomani, the assistant liaison officer in Rome: "We have received urgent requests from the Italian authorities on information regarding CUNTRERA Pasquale (B:7.5.1930, in Siculiana (Ag) and his wife VELLA Giuseppa (B: 10.06.1933) in Siculiana (Ag) as follows: '1: Do the above-named subjects hold Canadian passports which are presently valid? 2: Through your collaboration of police officials, would you know if there is a possibility that the above-named are currently in Canada? 3: Can you verify any communications between subjects operating in Canada and the above-named subjects which would indicate any trace on Cuntrera?'"

For the Italians, finding a lead in Canada was a long shot, but the Omertà wires were already humming.

Alfonso Caruana regularly spoke on what he thought were safe telephones to Vito Triassi in Ostia. On May 20, he went to a pay phone at Yorkdale Shopping Centre in Toronto and reached Triassi. Caruana told him that he'd spoken to the "kids" in Toronto—likely meaning Pasquale Cuntrera's young relatives—and he wanted Triassi to keep some control over the situation in Italy while he sorted it out. He urged Triassi to exercise caution.

"Now you give him [Pasquale] a call, too. You tell him to be careful when he goes out, to be aware. Understand?"

"Yes. I called him this morning," Triassi said. "I am calling him again now. I said that everything is okay there, because I was alarmed."

Alfonso Caruana alluded to getting a passport to allow Pasquale Cuntrera to leave Italy, possibly to be smuggled into Canada. The same channel had already been used to get documents for Vito Genco. "But I need a little bit of time," he said.

Triassi suggested getting Pasquale Cuntrera to either Venezuela or Canada: "The only thing for him if he wants to go to the other side [is with] an original certificate. There's no other way."

"I had another idea," Caruana told him. "But I need more time. He must not go out, understood? And then I'll bring him to the other side so he's protected, you know?"

"Okay."

"Then," Caruana said, "we'll organize a big party."

Triassi passed the telephone to a man identified as "Uncle Leone" for a brief greeting. Uncle Leone asked Caruana how he was.

"Ehhh. Nice, rich. Damn the Madonna. Fuck if you made money. God damn." Then Caruana laughed. "What can you do? Let's try to keep our eyes open and we'll see what the fuck we have to do, because we are all in the shit."

In a later call with Oreste Pagano, Caruana discussed the fallout from the escape. Pagano knew Pasquale Cuntrera personally. In fact, long before he'd met Alfonso Caruana, the old Mafioso had come to him with photographs to be used to make up false Venezuelan documents.

"Did you see what a fucking mess over there, fucking ministers and . . ." Caruana asked.

Pagano said, "Oh yeah! But, is the uncle safe?"

"Yes, for now, yes. We'll see. I'm trying to settle something a bit better." He asked Pagano for assistance in getting documents for the fugitive. "It's just that he would need a valid document," Caruana said.

"No problem, no problem."

Pagano warned him that the authorities believed Cuntrera was trying to make his way back to Venezuela. "In Caracas they have put in something special at the airport. They have set up a special group there just to find out about this."

But it was a call from his son, "Venezuelan Joe" Cuntrera in Toronto, that proved to be Pasquale Cuntrera's undoing. The Omertà team notified the Italian government that, through their wiretaps, they now had a fix on Pasquale Cuntrera.

"They didn't believe us," Larry Tronstad said. "The government in Italy was going crazy—there were resignations demanded; it was a nightmare over there."

Skeptical, the Italians believed that the CFSEU officers were mistaken about their information. They flew an Italian investigator, who was working in Miami, to Toronto. He listened to the tapes and blanched.

"In about thirty seconds he was on the phone to Rome," Tronstad said.

The Omertà tapes revealed that Pasquale Cuntrera had gone to ground in Spain. Working from the Omertà transcripts, the authorities placed Cuntrera and his wife in or near the town of Fuengirola, on Spain's Costa del Sol, a playground for celebrities like Antonio Banderas and Sean Connery. The area was also known as the "Costa del Crime" for the criminals on the run who went there, notably Charlie Wilson, one of Britain's "Great Train Robbers," who was killed there.

As a hideout, Fuengirola was ideal. A fugitive could quickly and easy make his way to nearby Gibraltar—a first-class offshore financial center—to access funds. Coincidentally, the prime minister of Gibraltar was named Peter Caruana—no relation.

"We told the ROS and the Special Anti-Mafia Squad of the State Police (SCO) that Pasquale Cuntrera had reached the Costa del Sol in a car driven by the Triassis," CFSEU Inspector Ben Soave said.

On May 21, 1998, four members of the ROS and SCO units initiated a stakeout in Fuengirola and began inspecting passersby. They received information from Toronto that Cuntrera had abandoned his wheelchair and that he and his wife were living in an apartment rented by Fabio Di Francesco, another member of the Caruana-Cuntrera-Triassi Ostia group. Then more specific information pointed to a particular neighborhood.

Over the next few days the geographic circle tightened to five square kilometers. Within the area was the Residencial Las Camelias, an elegant building with high arches, wide balconies, and wrought-iron handrails, built around a spacious courtyard of flowers and palms. For Major Benedetto Lauretti of the ROS, the situation grew more tense as the days passed: "I felt sure that Cuntrera was staying at the Las Camelias, but we didn't know in which flat. There were over eight hundred. Almost all of them were occupied. We couldn't search floor by floor: we would have risked spoiling the operation."

On May 24, a member of the team suddenly burst out: "Here he is."

They watched an older gentleman, leaning on a cane, strolling arm in arm with his wife along the palm-tree-lined boulevard. Looking like any of the retirees along the Spanish coast, Pasquale Cuntrera wore a white shirt, dark pants, a rough cardigan sweater, and shoes without socks. The unit moved in. As befit his status as one of the most prominent

Sicilian Mafiosi in the world, he was unarmed. Polite, almost amused, he was arrested without incident.

His first request was typically protective: "If you allow my wife to leave immediately, I'll go as well. I accept immediate extradition to Italy." Authorities agreed and the next day Giuseppa Vella Cuntrera was back in Ostia, grief-stricken and telling her relatives that she would never be allowed to grow old with her Pasquale, who presumably would die in prison, paying the sixteen years he still owed.

True to his word, when Pasquale Cuntrera—frail and barely able to walk, even with his cane—appeared before a Spanish judge, he said, "I go back to Italy, even if I'm innocent." He formally accepted extradition and was flown back to Italy under heavy guard in a Spanish air force jet.

"Pity," he was heard to say, "in Spain I could hug my wife after so long. It was like a second honeymoon. I choose to go back to Italy because there my wife and other relatives will be able to visit me."

He told ROS Colonel Mario Parente: "I'm an old man; I hope not to stay in jail too long."

The Italian government, feeling some of the heat lifting, praised international cooperation in capturing Pasquale Cuntrera.

A jubilant Alessandro Pansa, who'd been hunting Cuntrera for decades, said, "He is a man who always used his brain rather than a gun. He always handled money, not weapons."

To keep Project Omertà secure, it was kept secret that the arrest came about because of information from Omertà wiretaps. Nevertheless, some Italian media referred to information that came from Canadian authorities. Fortunately, the Caruana-Cuntrera in Canada didn't pick up on the reports.

On May 25, just twenty-four hours after Cuntrera was captured, Oreste Pagano and Alfonso Caruana spoke over cell phones.

PAGANO: "What did he do, that fucking Pasquale? He let himself be caught again."
CARUANA: "Eh, I know, I know, I know."
PAGANO: "Damn the Madonna. But anyway, he really never got his act together. Instead of hiding and staying indoors and not—"

CARUANA: "I know. There is so much to say about this, so it's better not to make any comments."

PAGANO: "He caused so many problems for us all that I have never had before."

CARUANA: "Eh, eh, that's life."

PAGANO: "They are still continuing with the searches there [in Italy]—[Pagano giggles]—at the house of my poor friend [Alberto Minelli] in Milan. As a matter of fact, his father has a tumor and I don't know, but, he doesn't have long to live. Why don't they go fuck themselves?"

Larry Tronstad was pleased when he read a transcript of the conversation. "It was good. They thought Cuntrera had been caught because he wasn't careful. Actually, it was Alfonso who was careless.

"We couldn't have been happier."

Project Omertà had about fifty days to run.

Washington, D.C

Just days after Court and Hill were arrested, on May 20, 1998, the U.S. Justice Department announced the success of Operation Casablanca, their initiative against the Colombian and Mexican cocaine cartels and corrupt bankers who facilitated the laundering of drug money.

Casablanca, underway for three years, was deemed by the Treasury Department to be "the culmination of the largest, most comprehensive drug money-laundering case in the history of U.S. law enforcement."

Thirty-five million dollars had been recovered, with another estimated us$122 million still to be seized, and 22 Mexican banking officials were charged in the Casablanca indictment. Two tons of cocaine, four tons of marijuana, and a total of 112 people were arrested.

The Mexican bankers, some representing the largest banks in that country, were lured into the United States by undercover customs agents and arrested.

One name wasn't on the publicly released documents: Alberto Minelli.

In Toronto, CFSEU Inspector Ben Soave breathed a sigh of relief.

Listening to Alfonso Caruana on the bugged telephones, one might have believed that his organization was ready to collapse, even without the efforts of Project Omertà. A pay phone picked up Caruana and Vito Genco having another of their lengthy conversations.

CARUANA: "What can I tell you, my brother. I'm in bad shape over here. I don't know what the fuck to do here, I'm going around in circles. . . . Something has to be done. I'm completely ruined. I am completely ruined, physically, morally and financially. Can you image how I've become?"

GENCO: "You have to stay calm."

CARUANA: "How can I stay calm? At this point a person gets demoralized."

Cancun, Mexico

After leaving Venezuela, Oreste Pagano moved his base of operations from Caracas, Venezuela, to Cancun, Mexico.

Cancun was no different from much of the rest of Mexico when it came to corruption. It was the closest thing to a narco-state. From the highest political levels down to the underpaid policeman on the beat, protection could easily be bought. Few officials resisted being corrupted. The drug traffickers of Mexico would always offer a bribe first, then immediately follow up with threats of deadly violence if the bribe didn't work. The rule of thumb in Mexico was that if an official turned down a bribe, it was only because it was too small and he or she had already been bought for a larger sum.

Pagano, like the Caruana-Cuntrera, was aware of the etiquette of bribery. In certain countries it's a subtle "man's game" in which corruption is viewed with a cosmopolitan sophistication and conducted with a smile or a shrug.

In Cancun, Pagano's corruption reached the highest level: the

In April 1999, twenty-four hours after leaving office, Villanueva was charged with drug trafficking and involvement with organized crime. Charged with permitting Quintana Roo to be used as the gateway for the movement of cocaine from Colombia, Villanueva is the highest-ranking elected official to be investigated for drug trafficking while in office. He responded that the allegations were politically motivated because he was engaged in political warfare with Mexican President Ernesto Zedillo. He fled Mexico. American and Mexican authorities are unravelling his financial dealings and believe as much as US$73 million is hidden in bank accounts around the world.

governor of the state of Quintana Roo, in which Cancun is located. Mario Villanueva was key to the success of many domestic and foreign drug traffickers who resided in his area of influence. He reportedly took tens of millions of dollars from Mexican cartels to facilitate and protect their trafficking operations. A much sought-after service the governor offered was the use of government aircraft hangars as transfer points for cocaine shipments.

Particularly close to Villanueva was Ramon Alcides Magaña, known as "El Metro." El Metro was the leader of the Juarez cartel, a violent network of drug traffickers.

On June 2, 1998, a young Mexican army lieutenant—part of a secret CIA-trained anti-drug task force—was keeping surveillance on El Metro. The lieutenant was investigating links between Mario Villenueva and the notorious Juarez cartel boss.

At midnight, the lieutenant stopped at a traffic light and his vehicle was quickly surrounded by local police officers, who dragged him from the car at gunpoint; he was turned over to members of Magaña's cartel. The lieutenant was tortured for several hours. Other cartel members broke into the lieutenant's office and looted it of the documents he'd accumulated tying the governor to the drug trade.

When word of the kidnapping spread to Mexico City, Defense Minister General Enrique Cervantes reacted with stunning decisiveness. He sent a unit of soldiers, backed up by armored personnel carriers, to Magaña's home in Mexico City. The soldiers surrounded the residence, trapping Magaña's wife inside. A message was sent to Magaña that unless the lieutenant was freed, the armed convoy would open fire on the home.

At the same time, hundreds of black-clad commandos were sent into the enclaves of the wealthy drug traffickers to hunt for the lieutenant. Documents and faxes were seized showing that State police officials had been tipping the Juarez cartel traffickers off to the activities of federal drug agents in the area.

Under the pressure brought by Cervantes, the Juarez cartel released the lieutenant.

In Toronto, Larry Tronstad watched events unfold with trepidation. "The Mexicans were going nuts," he said. "They were going to raid the homes and businesses of every suspected drug dealer in the province. They wanted that lieutenant back." It was likely, he said, that Oreste Pagano would be swept up in the roundup.

Tronstad contacted Ben Soave and told him of the impending crisis. Soave, who had become the troubleshooter for the increasingly complex investigation, immediately called a contact in Italy, who had a good relationship with the Mexican officials. The Italian called his contacts in the Mexican government. Leaning heavily on the favor done by the CFSEU in the recapture of Pasquale Cuntrera, Soave managed to get Pagano excluded from the dragnet.

"Too many things outside our control were happening," Soave said. "First the Casablanca sting, and now this. We came close to the edge with the arrests in Houston, but that could have gone either way."

Mexico/Toronto, Ontario

Alfonso Caruana was certain now that police were closing in on him. His greatest fear wasn't being arrested in Canada—he was, after all, a Canadian citizen with a considerable array of rights—but being extradited to Italy to serve out the twenty-one-year, and ten-month jail term awaiting him would be a death sentence.

"He felt very pressured," Oreste Pagano said. "He was telling me that, ah, he felt the police were about to do something."[3]

But Caruana's fear of arrest did little to stop his need to successfully complete a shipment. He had 500 kilograms of cocaine hidden in the secret compartment of a sailboat owned by a French-Canadian smuggler that was destined for Canada. The division of the shipment was skewed in Caruana's favor; he needed some extra kilos of cocaine for one of his nephews. Pagano was out on a limb on this one. With the surveillance on him, Caruana didn't want to expose the financial side of his network by gathering the money together, and Nunzio LaRosa wasn't available to take it to Miami, in any event. Pagano put up the money for the Colombians about US$750,000.

Hamilton, Ontario

Any shred of anonymity Alfonso Caruana might have believed he still had disappeared when on June 5, 1998, *The Hamilton Spectator* carried a front-page headline: "Canadian haven: Alleged Mafia boss living quietly near T.O."

While several other Canadian reporters had known about Alfonso Caruana, CFSEU Inspector Ben Soave had quietly discussed the case with each of them, pointing out the danger of alerting Caruana to the fact that his whereabouts were known. All had agreed to hold the story until Caruana's arrest.

But Italian anti-Mafia prosecutor Gioacchino Natoli, who had been tracking the Caruana-Cuntrera for several years, gave an interview to *la Repubblica*, an Italian daily newspaper, saying, "We have reason to believe [Alfonso Caruana] is hiding in Canada."

Crime reporter Adrian Humphreys of the *Spectator* quietly went after the story and located Caruana living in the Goldpark Court house. When Soave saw the piece, he knew too many crises had been narrowly averted, and if the *Spectator* story was any indication, anything else that could go wrong, would go wrong. He began making plans for the take-down.

Italy

Alfonso Caruana, now feeling incredible heat from police and fearing he'd be arrested within days, if not hours, was working on an exit strategy. He had his brother Pasquale Caruana contact Alwan Raffat, a master Iraqi forger Pasquale had met while in prison in Italy.

Raffat's services had been requested a month earlier during Pasquale Cuntrera's escape, but before he could come up with documentation, the old Mafioso had been arrested in Spain. When Raffat's phone number came up on the Omertà wires, the Italian police paid him a 4:30 a.m.

visit, seizing false documentation, all perfectly forged, and four cellular phones. Italian investigators also found he'd been in contact with the Qatar Embassy in Rome.

"If I were you, I know what I'd do," Pasquale Caruana told him over a tapped phone on June 30, 1998.

"Yes."

"Right away, right away, right away. Just leave right away, understand me?"

Raffat said he'd go to Holland.

Pasquale Caruana told him: "Right away though. I don't see why you are still there. Just leave that damned country."

Raffat promised to call Caruana when he'd settled in Holland. He said he had meetings planned that would have the false passports ready within days.

To the Omertà team, it was clear that Caruana was arranging documents that would allow him to flee Canada.

Toronto, Ontario

Alfonso Caruana made it clear in a conversation with Oreste Pagano that he expected to be arrested. In a phone call on July 10, he told Pagano, "*Compa*, you wouldn't believe it. I'm being watched twenty-four hours."

He said there were four or five "of them" on him around the clock. "I don't call because these bastards are following me. As soon as I hang up the phone, they're checking to see who I call and who I don't call."

Cancun, Mexico

Oreste Pagano was anxious about the fate of the latest 500-kilogram shipment. He'd sent pager messages to Alfonso Caruana in Toronto, but had received no callback. He'd called Pasquale Caruana, but the phone line sounded dead. He'd called Carlo Napoli to find out how to reach Alfonso; Napoli wasn't able to help him.

The latest cocaine shipment should have arrived in Montreal by now, but he'd had no confirmation. He was effectively isolated.

At 5:00 p.m. on July 14, he went to a public telephone, called Alfonso Caruana's lawyer in Montreal, and asked if Caruana had been arrested. He was told everything was fine. Pagano got the lawyer to give him Gerlando Caruana's telephone number. Gerlando Caruana told him all was well, that the shipment had arrived successfully.

13

The Omertà raids were coordinated for dawn on July 15. Plans were made in Toronto, Montreal, and Cancun, Mexico. All arrests would occur at 7:00 a.m., Toronto time.

An RCMP aircraft was assigned to pick up the Montreal suspects and bring them to Toronto. Oreste Pagano would be arrested by Mexican authorities, who would then execute a provisional arrest warrant allowing him to be held pending an extradition hearing. CFSEU Detective-Sergeant Steve Perrow and Detective-Constable Tony Saldutto were sent to Mexico to assist in the raids on Pagano's home and office.

The night before the raids, Perrow called Larry Tronstad in Toronto: "It's a go: the Mexicans are going in at 7:00 a.m."

Cancun, Mexico

At 2:00 a.m. on the 15th—five hours before the time set for the coordinated raids—Oreste Pagano was two hours into the day of his sixtieth birthday. Dozens of armed men smashed into his house and crowded into his bedroom.

"Oreste, Oreste, how are you?" one officer asked, adding, "Happy birthday."

Alfonso Caruana's cocaine connection, dazed and disbelieving, struggled to wakefulness, his common-law wife, Milagros, lying frightened and quiet beside him. Outside, the front yard was crammed with police cars; overhead, helicopters buzzed. The noise was deafening.

It appeared to Pagano as though there were between forty and fifty armed men in his bedroom. He asked what the problem was, and in response he was dragged from his bed and handcuffed. When he asked to call his lawyer he was told he wasn't calling anyone.

Pagano was taken to a military jail and kept incommunicado. When authorities tried to take mug shots of him, he struggled and was beaten into submission. Three hours after his arrest he was put into a car with Alberto Minelli, who, unluckily, had stayed over at Pagano's home in anticipation of attending Massimiliano Pagano's upcoming wedding. With a military truck in front and one behind, each containing dozens of soldiers armed with machine guns, they were driven five hundred kilometers to a small airport, where they were put on a small plane and flown to Mexico City.

Mexico City, Mexico

In Mexico City, Steve Perrow was waiting for them. Things were going sideways and, on a technicality, the Mexicans had decided they weren't going to act on Canada's provisional warrant of arrest. A meeting had been held between Dr. Samuel Gonsalves, of the Procura Generale della Repubblica (PGR, the Mexican equivalent of the Department of Justice), Perrow, Saldutto, and representatives from Italian police, the FBI, and the DEA. The Italians wanted Minelli; Perrow wanted Pagano. The Mexicans had them both, and there was little Perrow could do except let events unfold.

Perrow asked: "What is the status of our provisional arrest warrant?"

A Mexican official told him that they wouldn't act on the warrants because they were not in possession of the actual arrest warrant, only a copy.

In his mind's eye, Perrow watched the arrests melt away. "Are you saying that we have no say in this matter?"

"Yes."

However, in a burst of creative law-enforcement technique, the Mexicans said they were expelling Pagano and Minelli as "undesirables." The men were being sent back to Italy, via Toronto, said Dr. Gonsalves, and if Perrow wanted to arrest them when the plane stopped in Toronto for refueling, he could do it there.

It was clear that the Mexicans were circumventing any difficulties that might be presented by an extradition hearing, or the involvement of lawyers for Pagano or Minelli, and that they hadn't just picked Toronto out of an atlas. The idea of flying a Gulf Stream from Mexico City to Italy via Toronto was ridiculous, and everybody in the room knew it.

Pagano and Minelli were loaded aboard the Gulf Stream. Mexican efficiency, Perrow and Saldutto believed, might not extend to airplane maintenance, so they took a commercial red-eye flight.

The Gulf Stream stopped short of the U.S. border, refueled, and, with several members of the Mexican military on board, continued north. About fifty kilometers outside of Toronto, the pilot notified Pearson International Airport that he was coming in. He was asked what his flight plan was.

"I don't have a flight plan."

"Well, if you don't file one, you're not landing here."

The pilot, with his jet running on fumes, quickly filed a plan, saying that they were en route to Italy. They were permitted to land.

A large group of foreign officials bringing two prisoners in handcuffs into a civilian airport close to midnight was a little much for Immigration officers. One officer asked Pagano: "Why have you come to Canada?"

Pagano was flustered. "I guess this is a joke. I don't wanna come into Canada. You don't want me to come to Canada, and therefore, what shall we do?"

The Immigration officer refused to admit Pagano to Canada. CFSEU officer Ken Hand then showed up, told Immigration what was going on, and arrested Pagano and Minelli.

No one should have been surprised at the Mexicans' ingenuity. A memo, sent by the Mexico City liaison officer and dated May 19, two months prior to the Omertà take-down date, clearly noted the possibility of taking Pagano early. "Workable compromise might be to have him routed to Italy via direct flight to Toronto."

Arresting Pagano and Minelli five hours ahead of the schedule agreed on with the CFSEU was another example of Mexican law enforcement exercising a bit of creativity.

"We'd asked them to hold off until 7:00 a.m., to secure the office. We wanted to get into the safe and we wanted to seize the hard-drive from Pagano's computer," Larry Tronstad said. "We believed there was a lot of money in the safe, and the computer could provide sensitive information about Pagano's drug-trafficking and money-laundering operations."

When CFSEU officers arrived at Royal Mott Real Estate, Pagano's Cancun real estate office, at 27 Calle Quetzal, they found several members of Mexico's élite U.S.-trained anti-drug squad having a bit of a party. They were wearing "Royal Mott Real Estate" T-shirts, and had helped themselves to Oreste Pagano's supply of beverages and food. The floor safe had been drilled open, its door left ajar to show it was empty. It was later determined that there was between $350,000 and $800,000 in cash and jewelry in the safe. The computer was gone.

The Mexican officers involved in searching the office were the pride of American anti-drug foreign policy. All had been handpicked for bravery and honesty, had undergone extensive training, and had been given polygraph tests before being put to work. After the early-morning raid on Royal Mott, the supposedly incorruptible officers were transferred to other duties.

Toronto, Ontario

At 2:00 a.m., two hours before the scheduled briefing for the Omertà takedowns, Larry Tronstad received his second call from Detective-Sergeant Perrow in Mexico: "They already did it."

Tronstad scrambled a team to Caruana's home. He feared if word got back to Toronto that Pagano was in custody, Caruana would bolt. Surveillance was set up around the home while search teams were briefed at a nearby McDonald's restaurant, each member having read and initialed the warrants. At 7:05 a.m., as scheduled, CFSEU officer Mike Harvey led a convoy of marked and unmarked police cars into Goldpark Court.

Harvey, who had overseen the surveillance part of Omertà, knew Goldpark Court as well as he knew his own street. Within seconds, Goldpark was a parking lot for police vehicles. A marked cruiser blocked the entrance to the street, cutting off a dozen media vehicles; reporters left their cars in the intersections and many began hopping fences down the block.

At 7:07 a.m., Mike Harvey rang the doorbell at 38 Goldpark Court. Giuseppina Caruana let the officers in, and they quickly fanned out throughout the home. In the upstairs hallway they found a bleary-eyed Alfonso Caruana, clad in shorts and a T-shirt. He was read his rights in English and Italian. Asked if he understood, he muttered, "*Sì.*" He was allowed to inject his leg with insulin.

Giuseppe Caruana, Alfonso's nephew, was visiting from Montreal. He was arrested too.

Downstairs, Giuseppina Caruana made her husband a breakfast: two pieces of toast, a grapefruit, half a toasted-cheese sandwich, and a glass of water.

After Caruana had said goodbye to his family, RCMP Criminal Intelligence officer Mina Alborino told him that the media were waiting outside the home. She asked, "Do you want to cover your head?"

"I don't care," he shrugged. He was then handcuffed.

He walked calmly to a waiting police cruiser. As a cameraman and two photographers took pictures of him, he looked neither left nor right and kept his head up, exhibiting the greatest of dignity. He gave no sign of anger or shame.

After the cruiser had departed, one of the photographers shook his head: "Wow. Now that's Mafioso."

A simultaneous raid was carried out at Pasquale Caruana's home in Maple, north of Toronto. He answered the door, identified himself, and was told that he was under arrest. Calmly, and with no agitation, he said he understood, "Yes." He read both the warrant to search and the warrant to arrest. He was then taken to a local police station, hand-cuffed, to be booked and held. Met by a media scrum, he staggered around, doubled over, trying to hide his face, until he could be taken into the building and lodged in a cell.

Domenic Rossi was quietly arrested at his home.

Raids were carried out at the Shock Nightclub and several other business where Alfonso Caruana and members of his crew spent much of their time. No drugs were found, but RCMP Sgt. Reg King, one of the raiding party at Shock, decided to sit at a desk to have his lunch. The office had already been searched, but King noticed a ceiling tile slightly out of alignment. He probed above the ceiling and found a bag containing CDN$200,000 in cash.

Later in the day the suspects from Montreal arrived: Nunzio LaRosa, Gerlando Caruana, Marcel Bureau, and Anna Staniscia-Zaino. As they were led from the RCMP aircraft to police vehicles, they appeared dazed. Then Anna Staniscia-Zaino, Gerlando Caruana's mistress, showed the spirit her lover liked: she held her cuffed hands out to the photographers and gave them the double finger. An officer laughed and said, "I wanna marry that girl."

Nunzio LaRosa, the man who wanted his own Mafia family, was allowed his one phone call. He asked Omertà squad officer Mike Harvey to reach out to his wife, Rita.

"You really did it to me this time," his distraught spouse said.

"It's useless to recriminate! Advise your son [Antonio, vacationing in Italy], because he's included as well."

"All the house is upside down."

"Did they take things?"

"The guns. The computer," she said. "The thing to distill the wine."

"Well, what can I do?"

"And you're on TV," she told him. "It's since this morning that you're on."

"You seen me on TV?"

His son Antonio later returned to Canada and surrendered.

Ignazio Genua, the son of Mafioso Nicola Genua, "the Little Old Cheese Maker," was also in Italy when the arrests went down. His mother, Lucy Genua, called him and said she'd gone to his house, thinking there'd been a burglary, that robbers had gone in. "Domenic Rossi's been arrested, along with Alfonso and his brother." She said she'd call him back after they spoke to a lawyer.

Antonio LaRosa and Ignazio Genua later returned to Canada and surrendered to police.

The Omertà arrests offered the Venezuelan government a much-needed polishing of its tarnished reputation. With the Cuntreras long gone, and the prospect of recovering tens of millions of dollars in criminal assets, Venezuelan officials got down to work.

In October 1998, police raided Centro Nacional de Finanzas, a Caracas firm run by Exequiel James and his son, Rodriguez Edward Jesus. The Centro Nacional de Finanzas, they said, was a front company used to set up and direct money-laundering operations for Oreste Pagano and Alfonso Caruana. Both father and son were arrested. Graziano Di Mauro, described as the Mafia's contact man with "international narco-traffickers," was arrested; Pagano's common-law wife, Milagros, was also picked up. Warrants were issued for Maria Isabel Ortiz Jimenez, Alberto Minelli's common-law wife.

Among the assets seized were 880,000 acres of prime land in Bolívar State. Six apartments, a dozen luxury cars, two yachts, and several bank accounts containing us$14-million were also seized.

Canadian information was also used to capture Vito Di Maria, a sixty-year-old Italian fugitive wanted for eight Mafia-related homicides. Di Maria, a member of the Siculiana family, had been hiding in Venezuela for twenty-five years. Using the name Giuseppe Di Maggio, Di Maria had built up a huge fortune and was the owner of two of the most profitable ranches in Carabobo State, as well as liquor stores, bakeries, and other companies. Di Maria was held at a clinic because of ill health; after a public outcry, he was taken from the clinic to prison. Di Maria, at whose home Alfonso Caruana had been a frequent guest, died of a heart attack before he could be extradited to Italy.

Luciano Gregoriani, another wanted Sicilian underworld figure on the run from organized crime charges in Italy, was also picked up and was jailed pending extradition to Italy.

For several months after the arrests, it looked as though there would be a Great Canadian Mafia trial. News of the arrests was carried around the world. Alfonso Caruana, the man who couldn't be caught, the elusive "Ghost" who'd confounded police in several countries, had run his global drug empire from his home near Toronto. Now he'd finally been arrested. Media calls from a dozen countries poured into the CFSEU.

Some of the top lawyers in Canada were hired to defend the accused.

Initially Alfonso Caruana retained John Rosen, one of Canada's most high-profile criminal lawyers, famed for his unsuccessful but blistering defense of sex-killer Paul Bernardo. Rosen, who had defended several organized crime figures in the past, later dropped out of the case. His place was taken by Pierre Morneau, a top Montreal lawyer.

Pasquale Caruana hired Marlys Edwardh, a criminal lawyer who is looked upon with a combination of fear and respect by police officers who have faced her in court. Ms. Edwardh doggedly blitzed the court with challenges, as well as requests for translations, tapes, documents, and all manner of items for disclosure. So aggressive and meticulous were her demands for disclosure that an amusing memo in Larry Tronstad's file wryly notes: "I wonder, does she know she forgot to get DNA samples from all the officers involved?" Pasquale Caruana, who reportedly paid as much for legal services as his brother, Alfonso, got his money's worth.

Gerlando Caruana was represented by Pierre L'Ecuyer of Montreal.

Months and months of wrangling ensued. Accusations flew that Oreste Pagano had in effect been very illegally kidnapped in Mexico. Defense requests for disclosure of information, of original surveillance notes, of original tapes of recorded conversations—a whole host of demands bogged down the Caruana case. Meanwhile, in Houston, Texas, drug- and money-smugglers John Hill and Richard Court made full statements and worked out deals with the U.S. government.

The end was in sight for the Caruanas when Oreste Pagano, the man with too many names, became a number: 0.5171.

During his four months in custody, Pagano tried to get enough money to hire a decent lawyer. In letters to his beloved Milagros, he urged her to use "any means possible" to prevent his extradition to Italy; he was, he said, facing only three or four years of incarceration in Canada before he'd be free.

But his financial difficulties were his more immediate concern. By November, the Caruanas still owed him for the 500-kilogram shipment to Montreal.

Pasquale Caruana told Pagano he still hadn't heard anything about the arrival of the Montreal shipment. Pagano knew better: in a telephone call the day before the arrests, Gerlando Caruana had confirmed the arrival.

When Pagano protested, Pasquale Caruana told him to relax. "Don't worry about it. We will [see] if we can get something to arrive."

"What do you mean, let's look into getting something to arrive?" an angry Pagano asked him. "There are still 500 kilos you owe me for." He knew other members of the Caruana-Cuntrera in Toronto and Montreal were distributing the shipment and collecting the money.

Gerlando Caruana continually talked to him about bringing in more shipments. "We'll bring in more and make it all back."

"We are not talking about 500 grams," Pagano said. "We are talking about 500 kilos."

Later, Pagano said he knew then that they were going to clean him out. "They were already talking about taking everything," he said. "I had invested the money for the capital, I had put up the money for the 200 kilos [seized in Houston], and now I find myself without any money."

Pagano knew he was one of the group's strongest sources of income. The Caruanas often discussed helping him escape, Pagano said. "In fact, they said first of all they would try to get me out of there as soon as possible and I would be able to continue working."

But Pagano was becoming increasingly disillusioned. Adding in the money he'd put up for Alfonso Caruana's portion of the shipment, Pagano was owed a total of us$7 million. He'd also become convinced that his arrest four months earlier had come as no surprise to Alfonso Caruana. "I'd tried to call him a few times but he'd no longer answer the phone," Pagano said. "I don't doubt that he was in touch with important police people from Mexico City, he found out about the fact that my arrest was underway."

On the morning of November 5, 1998, Oreste Pagano approached the Caruana brothers at the Toronto East Detention Centre, where they were being held. They shunned him. He knew they believed he was talking to police. In fact, Larry Tronstad later said, he believed that Pagano could be turned, if anyone could.

At 11:35 a.m., Detective-Sergeant Steve Perrow got a telephone call from Shelina Shivji, operations manager at the Toronto East Detention Centre. Shivji told Perrow that an inmate named Oreste Pagano wanted to speak to him right away.

Perrow and Tony Saldutto arrived at the Toronto East Detention Centre at 12:50 p.m. and were ushered into an office. Pagano was shown in and introductions were made.

With Saldutto translating, Pagano said he wanted to make a deal, "a patch." He could give police the entire organization. In return, he wanted his common-law wife, Milagros, to be brought under guard from Venezuela; he wanted a new identity and a place to live with his family; he wanted the money and assets seized by Mexican authorities; and he wanted to be moved from Toronto East. He wanted his sister and her children in Italy to be protected, and, he added, Alberto Minelli to be "excluded" from prosecution. "He was just doing what he was told to do," Pagano said.

"What information, in general, can you give us?" Perrow asked.

"I can give you Caruana, Cuntrera, Vella, Rizzuto and Napoli." He added that he could provide narcotics networks in Italy, the United States, Canada, and Colombia.

Perrow told him he could make no commitments.

Pagano replied that he could show that a total of 10 tons of cocaine had been moved through Alfonso and Gerlando Caruana's network. He told them about a 7,500-kilogram shipment that had gone to Italy. He told them about how containers were used to smuggle cocaine into the United States, who his contacts were in the Mexican cocaine cartel, how 50,000 kilograms were shipped each year to California, and how tons of cocaine were being brought into Canada.

By four o'clock that afternoon, Oreste Pagano was out of the jail and hidden at another facility. It would take several months to negotiate an agreement that was acceptable to both the Justice Department and Pagano.

The crafty old Camorra boss took pains, whenever he could, to dirty up Alfonso Caruana, who he felt had used him, robbed him, abandoned him and was about to eliminate him. Assistant Crown Attorney Rick Visca, in a videotaped statement, asked about the 200-kilogram cocaine shipment seized from Hill and Court in Houston. Pagano smiled. "I organized this shipment of 200—always by the word of Alfonso Caruana—by his command."

Pagano was of concern to the other accused, and to some defense counsel. Police officers attending several court hearings at which Pagano had appeared—under heavy guard—had noted men idling around the courthouse, some with flesh-colored plastic two-way radio devices plugged into their ears.

Arrangements were made for the CFSEU to set up an ambush for anyone following the police convoy ferrying Pagano between the courthouse and the detention facility. But the RCMP Emergency Response Team, responsible for Pagano's security, got spooked and sped through red lights to escape the followers instead. The followers turned out to be private investigators hired by one of the defense lawyers, who badly wanted to get a statement from Pagano before he testified.

Oreste Pagano underwent months of negotiating with government lawyers. The CFSEU agreed to "lend" him $25,000 to get legal representation. He hired criminal lawyer Fred Fedorson, who cut him a deal: $100,000, protection for his family,

Alfonso Caruana had faithfully paid his back-tax installments until his arrest. In an interview with the newspaper *La Presse*, auditor Rejean Boudreau of Revenue Canada said there was nothing the government could do while Caruana was in custody. "We have no chance to recoup the money Alfonso Caruana owes us," he told veteran crime journalist André Cédilot.

and a place in Italy's witness protection program after he finished testifying before Italian courts. On December 7, 1999, Pagano quickly entered a plea of guilty in a Toronto courthouse, was sentenced to one day in jail, and was on a plane to Italy the following day. He had indicated that he was willing to cooperate with Italian authorities about his drug-trafficking and money-laundering activities. He would also, he said, testify as to his involvement in several murders in Italy. And if needed, he would be brought back to Canada to testify against the Omertà suspects.

But a call to bring Pagano back was never needed. An avalanche of guilty pleas began.

On February 25, 2000, Alfonso Caruana, faced with the evidence of thousands of pages of wiretapped conversations, the betrayal of Oreste Pagano, and the prospect of being extradited to Italy even if he beat the Canadian charges, pleaded guilty. He was sentenced to eighteen years in prison. His dream of buying a farm in Canada, like the one he'd had to abandon in Venezuela, was dead.

Cocaine deals were still in the works. The Siculiana family would continue without his leadership; there was younger blood to run the organization. For Alfonso Caruana, the priorities of his life would be to serve the shortest sentence possible and avoid extradition to Italy.

Gerlando Caruana pleaded guilty to conspiracy to import and traffic cocaine. Already on parole for heroin trafficking, he was sentenced to 18 years.

Pasquale Caruana pleaded guilty to the same charge. Between finishing his sentence in Italy for drug trafficking and being arrested by the

Omertà team, he'd been a free man for only eight months. He was sentenced to ten years in prison.

Giuseppe Caruana, Gerlando's son—who had counted the $1.5 million shipment of cash sent from Alfonso Caruana to Montreal in which $100,000 was missing—was sentenced to four years. His main role had been to transfer drug payments from Toronto to Montreal, and eventually to Miami.

The evidence against Domenic Rossi and Ignazio Genua was the weakest. Rossi's sole involvement had been to drive to Montreal with a bag given to him by Ignazio Genua. Police speculated that the bag contained money to be delivered to the Caruanas in Montreal. His story, which was defensible, was that, as a contractor, he'd helped build Genua's mid-town Toronto restaurant. Business financing had required him to travel to Montreal to get some papers signed. He was to have returned with restaurant supplies. It was, he would say, a part-time job for an elderly man in ill health.

Lead lawyer for the federal Justice Department, Beverly Wilton, allowed the charges against Rossi and Genua to be stayed. Minutes after he was released, Rossi's ill health improved significantly; he energetically shook hands with police and reporters and talked about his future plans. "I plan to get back in the construction business," he said. "The brains behind it—the managing end."

"Ah, Rossi's an old dog in the heroin business," an officer later said. "He got done once in a heroin case with Nicola Genua, Ignazio's old man. He needed a break and he got it."

Gerlando Caruana's lover, Anna Staniscia-Zaino, emerged from court with more dignity than most of the defendants. Charges against her were withdrawn; privately, sources close to the case say they never had much hope of convicting Ms. Staniscia-Zaino, that her arrest was leverage to turn an informant close to the family. "It was a long shot, but the way Gerlando felt about her, it was worth a try."

During their months in custody, Alfonso, Pasquale, and Gerlando Caruana had watched Staniscia-Zaino with a mixture of dread and admiration.

"They were taking an interest in her because they told me that the police were pressuring her. They wanted to know something in exchange for letting her out," Oreste Pagano said. "But that woman had handled herself well and they were getting ready to pay, I believe, one hundred thousand dollars to bail her out."

Although she was not taken to trial, Staniscia-Zaino's fairy-tale dream of moving with her Gerlando to Belize was dead.

Seven months after he was arrested, charges were withdrawn against Alberto Minelli. He was immediately arrested again on a provisional warrant from the Italian authorities. Offered the chance to provide information to the Omertà team, Minelli declined. He was sent back to Italy to face money-laundering charges. Minelli was later released, and again arrested on money-laundering charges by Italian authorities.

Canadian charges were dropped against Nunzio LaRosa and his gofer, Marcel Bureau. Both were ordered extradited to Houston, Texas, to face drug charges.

Antonio LaRosa, like Giuseppe Caruana, was fast-tracked for early release from prison; he served only nine months. Under the automatic parole review process, a first offender who was sentenced for a non-violent crime was eligible. Although a parole board member wrote LaRosa's links to organized crime were "very disturbing", he was freed anyway. Vic Toews, justice critic for the Canadian Alliance, was angered at the release. "These organizations thrive on violence, so it seems the reasoning of the parole board is somewhat suspect," he told the *National Post*. "Knowing the type of organization this individual was involved in, why would they put him on that kind of accelerated program?"

Antonio LaRosa pleaded guilty and was sentenced to four years for importing and conspiracy to traffic cocaine.

Richard Court and John Hill pleaded guilty to federal drug charges in Texas. Both were sentenced to eleven years.

Milagros, Oreste Pagano's common-law wife, was jailed in Venezuela after the Mexicans arrested him. She was held in custody while complex negotiations were underway between Pagano and the Canadian police. She was released, in keeping with Pagano's demands in return for his cooperation.

Enrica Pagano and her brother, Massimiliano, managed to evade capture by Venezuelan authorities. The CFSEU located a telephone number for Enrica and arranged a phone call with her father. She and her brother again disappeared a short time later, perhaps having acquired documentation for a new identity. Pagano told the Omertà squad they would never catch his kids. "They learned from the best," he said proudly, touching his chest.

Italy

Throughout Project Omertà, police in Italy were conducting a parallel investigation into the Italian side of the Caruana-Cuntrera organization. In addition to unraveling the international travel and financial dealings of Alberto Minelli and Enrica Pagano, the ROS had targeted Vito and Vincenzo Triassi, both of whom had married into the Mafia family of Santo Caldarella. The ROS had uncovered a scheme to ship a 250-ton load of hashish from Spain to the Italian-French border.

In November 1998, both Triassis were charged in Rome with several drug offences, along with Fabio Di Francesco—who had rented the hideout apartment in Spain for Pasquale Cuntrera—and three others.

Germany/Liechtenstein

The full extent of Giuseppe Cuffaro's activities in Germany in the 1980s became clear fifteen years later, in 1999. While the Siciliana family's master corrupter set up the European Pizza Connection, planting "sleeper" contacts through the country's Sicilian Mafia members, he was also setting in motion a financial pipeline. Aware that the European connection would generate huge heroin profits, Cuffaro also knew that without a strategy to launder the money, the venture would eventually collapse.

Throughout the 1980s, German police intelligence reports had warned that the Sicilian Mafia, particularly the Siciliana family, were operating a drug and money laundering network based in several German cities, but the reports were largely ignored. Rumors abounded that the Caruana-Cuntrera had penetrated financial sectors in Switzerland, Austria, Germany and Liechtenstein. It was no surprise—the families, wherever they set up shop, persistently assaulted the legitimate financial sector, taking advantage of bank confidentiality laws and corrupting people at all levels of politics and commerce. As banking laws were changed to restrict the flow of criminal money in one jurisdiction, the traffickers would simply shift their efforts to another.

Even though the government had refused to admit it, Germany was hit particularly hard in the 1980s, mostly by the drug side of the Caruana-Cuntrera operations. Thousands of Sicilian immigrants had flooded into the country in the 1950s and 1970s. Among them were several Mafiosi from the Palermo families and towns in the Agrigento area, including Siculiana. Outwardly hardworking pizzeria operators and shop workers, they replicated the American Pizza Connection, as they had at the same time in Canada.

Among them was Alfonso Caruana, who operated a pizza restaurant which he used to launder his drug profits. In Germany, as in Canada, he dealt whenever possible with Italian-born bank staff. Caruana formed businesses with the leaders of the Sicilian Mafia families controlling the international drug trade, opening front companies and making joint investments. Using contacts in banking systems in nearby countries, Caruana also facilitated the laundering of other traffickers' profits as well as his own.

The blood lust of the Corleonesi followed these expatriate Mafia families into western Europe. Outcast boss Gaetano Badalamenti's son was shot dead in Solingen, his body cut into pieces and disposed of. Giovanni Caruana, Alfonso's uncle, narrowly escaped death in the mid-1970s when he was gunned down in Germany. Several others vanished, either into South America or into the *lupara bianca*. Throughout the 1970s and 1980s, German authorities were confused and disconcerted by the discovery of several bodies.

By the late 1980s and early 1990s, the German intelligence service estimated that there were almost five hundred Sicilians suspected of being Mafiosi in their country; they also found members of more than sixty Italian organized crime cells, including Calabrians and Neapolitans. Dozens of business had been purchased with drug profits—either legitimate concerns, such as hotels, or front businesses that facilitated the heroin or money-laundering initiatives.

Criminal profits also found their way to Switzerland. Swiss banks were accessible by automobile or train and body-packers carried millions of dollars out of Germany. As the cocaine trade came on-stream in the 1990s—an estimated 200 tons were shipped in 1992 alone—those profits had to be repatriated, no longer to the suppliers in Turkey and Asia, but to the suppliers in Colombia.

Liechtenstein, strategically located between Switzerland on the west and Austria on the east, was an ideal venue for launderers. It had no natural resources to speak of, but it did have a free-enterprise economy with what is called "a vital financial services sector." Border controls were close to nonexistent. This meant that money from any source could be put through the principality. From there it could be sent anywhere in the world, quickly and anonymously.

The importance of Liechtenstein to the Caruana-Cuntrera became clear in March 2000. A report—a long overdue wakeup call—by the Bundesnachrichtendienst (BND), the German intelligence service, linked some of Liechtenstein's prominent businessmen to the Sicilian Mafia. (The BND report was sparked by a story published one year earlier by *Der Spiegel*, a German newspaper, in which the German finance minister likened Liechtenstein's financial system to "maggots in meat.") The 2000 report by the BND's Department 2, specializing in counter-narcotics and counter-money-laundering efforts, focused on several prominent financiers.

Dr. Herbert Batliner, an internationally known lawyer and trustee and close friend of former German chancellor Helmut Kohl, was named in the report. "[He] specialized in the creation and administration of foundations and trusts. . . . [He] supposedly administers over 10,000 letterbox companies and foundations," the report said. Citing an earlier *Der Spiegel* article, the BND report said that Batliner "is prepared to take large amounts of cash without asking for its origin from client with a reputation. He also keeps accounts for drug barons and dictators and to have cared for a 'Russian clientele' for some time."

The alleged money laundering, BND said, was carried out via the Verwaltungs- und Privatbank, which has branches in the Caribbean. The Verwaltungs- und Privatbank's Caribbean subsidiary allegedly maintained accounts for Colombian cartel leader Pablo Escobar, for the Medellin and Cali cartels, and for flight capital of Zairian dictator Mobuto and Philippine dictator Marcos.

Engelbert Schreiber and Peter G. Frommelt were also named. Both were described as trustees in Liechtenstein and as business partners. Frommelt had been arrested in 1997 for money laundering and fraud; Schreiber had also been arrested, but was later released. Schreiber was accused of having used a private jet to carry cash from Milan to Zurich, or via Switzerland to Liechtenstein. And, the BND noted, he owned a large number of companies with alleged contacts with Italian, Russian, and Latin American crime cartels.

Prominently mentioned is the Caruana-Cuntrera-Cardarella, described as a "large clan of Mafia groups [that] has been dominating drug traffic between North–South America and Italy since the 1970s. The range of their action reaches from the United States, Canada, and Venezuela to Great Britain, Switzerland and Italy."

According to the report, money from the Juarez Mexican cartel—the group Oreste Pagano dealt with—also went through Schreiber and Frommelt: "[They] are supposed to have negotiated an entry into the Russian market between the Mexican drug cartels and a Russian organized crime group."

Two banks, the Liechtensteinische Landesbank and Verwaltungs- und Privatbank, were named as money-laundering vehicles. Using Recona AG, a company based in Liechtenstein, criminal money from the Caruana-Cuntrera-Caldarella family was used to finance a power station in northern Italy. Engelbert Schreiber was reportedly a consultant to Recona AG.

The BND said Recona AG had for fifteen years offered money-laundering services, going back to the days when Giuseppe Cuffaro was setting up the European Pizza Connection.

Toronto, Ontario

Six months after the close of Project Omertà, the Combined Forces Special Enforcement Unit was reorganized into teams specializing in Italian, Asian, and Eastern European organized crime. Inspector Ben Soave was promoted first to Superintendent and then, in 2001, to Chief Superintendent. Under Soave, the CFSEU, in quick order, took out two Eastern European crime groups and one of the largest Asian heroin-importation rings in Canadian history. When, in September 2000,

RCMP Deputy Commissioner of Organized Crime Giuliano Zaccardelli was named Commissioner of the force, Soave was among those who praised the move, hoping that Canada's efforts against crime syndicates would improve. The appointment of Julian Fantino, another prominent fighter against organized crime, as chief of the Toronto Police Service, was also seen as a move in the direction of more focused targeting of criminal organizations.

Bill Sciammarella and Tony Saldutto remain with the CFSEU. Both were nominated for police officer of the month for their work on the Caruana project. Sciammarella praises Ben Soave's support for the Omertà project. "He was important, crucial; he believed in our investigation, and did everything possible to carry it to conclusion. He understood the importance of the people we were after."

Detective-Constable Mike Harvey is still with the CFSEU and still driving behind people who, he hopes, don't know he's there.

Larry "Tromper" Tronstad has several major cases underway. Still an RCMP staff-sergeant, he says: "Two guys in this job ain't going any higher. Me and the commissioner. And that's okay with me."

Winston Churchill, when asked in 1942 about an Allied victory in Egypt, said: "Now this is not the end. It is not even the beginning of the end. But it is, perhaps, the end of the beginning."

So it is with Project Omertà.

Dozens of suspected traffickers and money launderers in several countries were identified but not charged. Hundreds of telephone numbers led to more criminal connections and criminal organizations. Intelligence flowed through the tapped telephones, vital information that was never followed up. Political connections were found, but not exposed. None of this was necessary to the singular vision of jailing Alfonso Caruana and his brothers.

In all, there were almost fifty people—main targets or associates—under investigation in Project Omertà. Police admit that they knew of 7,500 kilograms of cocaine moved by the Caruana-Cuntrera—and yet they seized only 200 kilos.

Project Omertà cost an estimated $8.8 million to conduct. It took thousands of man-hours, plus the wiring of dozens of private telephones, pay phones, pagers, cellular phones, offices, fax machines, and hotel rooms in several countries. The financial returns were relatively small: $623,578 in jewelry, $622,000 in cash of mixed currencies, and $585,000 in U.S. investment bonds. That just about covered the costs of translators in the case. Financially, Omertà was a failure.

"You know, people accuse the police of wanting ever more money, ever more powers, but if you look at the Omertà project you'll see it wasn't about money," Ben Soave said. "It was about having the right people in the right time in the right place. As far as money is concerned, think about this: a kidnapping case that ran eleven days cost $200,000 in overtime. Omertà, over three years—and we're talking mostly around the clock—cost the same amount. I had guys working on their own time, not even putting in for overtime. They easily gave an equal amount of time for nothing."

Perhaps the most contentious asset is the 400,000 hectares (880,000 acres) of land in Bolivar State owned by Oreste Pagano. The land, which boasts literally billions of dollars' worth of natural resources, was acquired by Pagano through complex means. There was, he said, an Arab man who owed him $600,000 because a promised money transfer didn't go through. "He said he had a territorial property of four hundred thousand hectares," Pagano said. "But he was in need of a lot more money for his own purposes."

Pagano checked into the property and was told "it was priceless." Experts found that the land, which included two volcanos, two diamond mines, and hundreds of millions of dollars in raw materials, was worth at least US$20 billion in extractables.

Pagano gave the Arab US$2.5 million and received in return a mortgage made out to his financial front man, Alberto Minelli. When a collapse hit the Venezuelan banking system, the Arab fled to London, England. By then he owed Pagano US$7 million. Pagano had meanwhile managed to get sole possession of the land, spending a total of about US$5 million.

When he was arrested, he said, he was in the midst of selling it to an unnamed Canadian mining company. When making his deal with the Justice Department, he signed the property over to the Canadian government. Currently, negotiations are underway between the Canadian and Venezuelan governments over ownership.

All major criminal investigations have spinoffs, and Project Omertà is no different. Investigations in several countries are currently underway. A telephone number in Thailand believed to have been dialed several times by either Oreste Pagano or his daughter, Enrica, during and after Project Omertà may have uncovered an initiative to activate a new heroin pipeline. The number, subscribed to a residential telephone on the island of Phuket, was dialed on five occasions and is expected to lead to an international investigation into further expansion by the Siciliana family into Asia. Review of the numbers called from the Thailand subscriber showed several contacts with suspects listed in either Italian anti-Mafia files or in drug trafficking files. A faxed message from the Coordinator of the Far East Region noted: "Our Italian colleague advises that he had previously obtained rumors to the effect that Italian traffickers had been establishing themselves in the Phuket region, but this is his first lead."

And intelligence information—ranging from telephone records to bank account information—is being examined by Swiss authorities who are continuing to unravel the flood of Caruana-Cuntrera profits that flowed through accounts into that country. Documents seized during the raid at Alfonso Caruana's home have led to the possibility of a resurgence in activity in the United Kingdom by the Siciliana Family. References to "direct flights to London," the name of a Venezuelan-Colombian shipping company, and a "receiving company" in England, as well as references to some item being "well-concealed in fruits" may point to yet another undetected shipping route into Europe. As well, links to several other countries, including the U.S., Greece, France, and Germany, are under investigation.

Oreste Pagano is providing information in Italy that should lead to the resolution of several homicides, including the murders of police officials. He has already turned over his Colombian drug supplier, Erman Rubio, who in turn is cooperating with authorities. Rubio will have a lot to testify about: the circumstance of his marriage to the daughter of a prominent Colombian armed forces general is expected to reveal a network of drug trafficking as far away as Russia and official protection of cartel members. Rubio claims he himself provided 75 tons of cocaine from Colombia, much of it to the Siculiana family, much of it through Oreste Pagano, over a twelve-year period. Italian magistrates visited Colombia in 2001 to interview Rubio.

In January 2001, Alfonso Caruana was notified by the prosecutor in Italy that his acquittal on charges arising from Operation Cartagine, the South America-Italy cocaine pipeline, was being appealed. Armed with new evidence and testimony provided by Oreste Pagano, the Court of Assizes at Turin said the case would be re-heard against several accused.

Caruana was served the notice at Fenbrook Institution, a medium security facility in Gravenhurst, north of Toronto. Even with sixteen years left on his sentence in Canada, ongoing criminal investigations in several countries, and the prospect of an even heavier sentence in Italy if convicted at Turin, Canadian prison officials clearly believe he isn't a flight risk. His brothers, Gerlando and Pasquale, were also placed in medium-security prisons after serving a minimum portion of their sentences.

And there was fallout in Italy for Oreste Pagano. In spite of an agreement that he would serve minimum time—as little as one year—for Italian criminal charges, he was told in late 2000 that because of changes to the laws governing informants, he'd be required to serve more than ten years, one quarter of his outstanding sentences.

The new leadership of the Caruana-Cuntrera/Siculiana family isn't known. Traditionally, or perhaps by coincidence, the family is alternately governed by a Cuntrera, then a Caruana, then a Cuntrera, and so on. If this pattern is followed, the next powerhouse to come out of the family will be led by the Cuntreras, men in their late thirties and early forties.

Project Omertà effectively removed a generation from the equation, but several younger members of the organization have already moved into place to stake their claim to power. It'll be an orderly transition: the Caruana-Cuntrera isn't, after all, a family of cutthroats and thieves.

Endnotes

Prologue

1 "The Mafia's Rothschilds": this description was first applied to the Caruana-Cuntrera family by journalist Giuseppe D'Avanzo in "I Rothschild della Mafia," *la Repubblica*, December 17, 1989.
2 Alberto Maritati, in an interview with the authors, April 22, 1999.

Chapter 1

1 Quotes from Enio Mora in this book were obtained through several informal interviews with the authors (1988–1994).
2 Author interview with underworld sources; confirmed by CFSEU investigators.
3 *Legione dei Carabinieri di Palermo, Stazione di Siculiana*, Rapporto 6646/19P, Siculiana: October 17, 1981.
4 Paolo Iacono, in a 1992 interview with authors, following the extradition of the Cuntrera brothers to Italy.
5 Tom Blickman, "The Rothschilds of the Mafia on Aruba" in *Transnational Organized Crime*, Volume 3, Number 2; published by Frank Cass, London.
6 Jean Pierre Charbonneau, *La Filiere Canadienne* (Montreal: Les Editions de L'Homme, 1975) pp. 87, 142, 146, 461.
7 Blickman.
8 Source note: Disclosure regarding: Statement of Oreste Pagano, Superior Court of Justice, Toronto, court file number F0383.

Chapter Two

1 This quote is from a 1998 conversation that actor Tony Nardi, who portrayed Joe Bonanno in the movie *Bonanno: A Godfather's Story*, had with the aging Mafia boss.

2 Tommaso Buscetta, in a 1991 interview with the authors.

3 Adrian Humphreys, *The Enforcer: John Papalia: A Life and Death in the Mafia* (Toronto: HarperCollins, 1999).

4 Pino Arlacchi, *Men of Dishonor: Inside the Sicilian Mafia—An Account of Antonino Calderone* (New York: William Morrow and Company, Inc., 1992), p. 139.

5 Authors' interview with a Montreal police intelligence expert, 1999.

6 Source: Operation Benoit, RCMP wiretap, Montreal, 1974.

7 Ibid.

8 Authors' interview with a Montreal underworld figure, 1995

9 Project Pilgrim: Gerlando Caruana et al.; Conspiracy to import and traffic in narcotics and possession of assets derived from the commission of crime, RCMP, May 18, 1985, at page 11.

10 Reasons for Judgment, *The State* vs. *Pasquale Caruana and Giuseppe Cuffaro*, May 31, 1991, Tribunal of Palermo, at page 109.

11 Tommaso Buscetta debriefing, 1984.

12 Sentencing Report, *Beddia + 12*, Tribunal of Palermo, January 18, 1996, at pages 50 to 57; a conversation taped at the Reggio Bar, Montreal, on April 22, 1974.

13 Authors' interview with a Montreal underworld source, 1995.

14 Peter Edwards, *Blood Brothers: How Canada's Most Powerful Mafia Family Runs Its Business* (Toronto: Key Porter Books, 1990), pp. 145–46.

15 André Cédilot and Lakshmi Nguon, research for a documentary produced by Sovimage Productions, Montreal, on the Caruana-Cuntrera, directed by Daniel Creusot.

16 This story by Michel Auger was published in *Le Journal de Montréal*, on April 27, 1997.

17 Project Pilgrim Report at page 11.

18 U.S. Department of Justice/Federal Bureau of Investigation report, *The Caruana-Cuntrera Sicilian Mafia Organization Racketeering Enterprise Investigation Intelligence Profile*, March 20, 1991, at page 20.

19 U.S. Department of Justice/Federal Bureau of Investigation Report, *La Cosa Nostra in Canada*, March 1985.

20 U.S. Department of Justice, *Report on the Caruana-Cuntrera Organization*, 1991.

21 Ibid.

22 *Beddia + 12* at page 254.

23 Ibid. at page 295.

24 Ibid. at pages 75–76.

25 Ibid. at page 249.

26 U.S. Department of Justice Report, *The Caruana-Cuntrera Sicilian Mafia Organization Racketeering Enterprise Investigation Intelligence Profile*, 1991.

27 Project Pilgrim Report at page 1.

Chapter Three

1 Attilio Bolzoni, "Sul loro narco-impero non tramontava il sole," *la Repubblica*, September 13–14, 1992, p. 4.

2 Authors' interview with an organized crime figure in Canada, in 1995.

3 "Rapporto giudiziario di denuncia a carico di Bono Giuseppe + 159 (Bono plus 159); ritenuti responsabili di associazione per delinquere di stampo mafioso e finalizzata al traffico delle sostanze stupefacenti. Questura di Roma, Squadra narcotici," February 7, 1983, volume 1 at page 199.

4 This quote of Di Carlo is taken from the CTV network program "w5," whose reporter, Tom Clark, interviewed Di Carlo for a story on the Caruana-Cuntrera in October 2000.

5 Goffredo Buccini and Peter Gomez, *O mia Bedda Madonnina* (Milan: Rizzoli, 1993), p. 152.

6 *Beddia* + 12 at page 154.

7 Verbale dell'interrogatorio di Francesco DiCarlo, September 5, 1996, Procura di Roma. The Camorra is the Neapolitan version of the Sicilian Mafia.

8 Interview with Di Carlo on CTV program "w5," October 2000.

9 A third-party interview with the authors, 1999.

Chapter Four

1 Italian magistrates' indictment "Giuseppe Bono + 151."

2 This information and that subsequent is from interviews with RCMP officers, including Mark Bourque, and two reports filed on the Caruana-Cuntrera money-laundering and drug-trafficking investigations.

3 Testimony before Judge Natoli, December 4 and 5, 1990.

4 Sentenza contro Caruana, Pasquale e Cuffaro, Giuseppe. Tribunale di Palermo, May 31, 1991.

5 RCMP Canadian Mafia Update, 1990, internal document.

6 U.S. Justice Department Report, *La Cosa Nostra in Canada*, 1985.

Chapter Five

1 U.S. Justice Department Criminal Intelligence Review.

2 Ibid.

3 Ibid.

4 Ibid.

5 Royal Canadian Mounted Police Criminal Intelligence Files.

6 U.S. Justice Department Criminal Intelligence Review.

7 U.S. Justice Department Criminal Intelligence Review.

8 Quoted from a speech given by President Andres Perez on March 12, 1974, at his swearing-in ceremony.

9 Alessandro Pansa, in an interview with the authors, 1999.

10 *Beddia* + 12 at page 295.

11 U.S. Justice Department Report: *La Cosa Nostra in Canada*, 1985.

12 Authors' interview with retired U.S. DEA agent John Costanzo, 2000.

13 A drug trafficker in a 1995 interview with the authors.

14 Oreste Pagano's videotaped statements to the Combined Forces Special Enforcement Unit, Canada, in 1998 provide the quotations in this section of the book.

15 Oreste Pagano's disclosure statement.

Chapter Six

1 *Corriere della Sera*, March 4, 1993: "M. Antonietta Calabrò, Nei Caraibi il primo stato comprato dai boss di Cosa Nostra."

2 A former government minister of Aruba, in an interview with the authors in 1999.

3 Magistrate Giovanni Falcone, in an interview with the authors at Palermo in 1989.

4 Oreste Pagano's disclosure statement.

5 Ibid.

6 Ibid.

7 Ibid.

8 Ibid.

9   Ibid.

10   Ibid.

11   *Giornale di Sicilia*, October 21, 1997.

12   "Operation Zama" press release by ROS, November 28, 1998, in Rome, Italy.

13   *Ultima Noticias Recife*, online edition, July 16, 1998.

Chapter Seven

1   Bourque, Project Pellerin, November 1986; U.S. Justice Department report: "The Caruana-Cuntrera Sicilian Mafia Organization Racketeering Enterprise Investigation Intelligence Profile; Interpol Ottawa "urgent fax" 94MTL/SCO/075, May 17, 1994.

2   Richard Dickins, who retired from the RCMP as an assistant commissioner, was later seconded to the United Nations Drug Control Program as a law-enforcement adviser in Thailand. He was interviewed by the authors in 1998 in Rangoon, Burma, where he was UNDCP resident country director.

3   Canadian and American intelligence reports.

4   RCMP criminal intelligence files.

5   U.S. Justice Department criminal intelligence profile of the Caruana/Cuntrera Sicilian Mafia Organization.

Chapter Eight

1   The full story of Green Ice and DEA agent Heidi Landgraf can be found in *Global Mafia: The New World Order of Organized Crime* by Antonio Nicaso and Lee Lamothe (Toronto: Macmillan Canada, 1995).

Chapter Nine

1   This and subsequent quotations from Oreste Pagano are drawn from the Oreste Pagano debriefing.

2   Oreste Pagano debriefing.

3   From testimony at Alfonso Caruana's Revenue Canada hearing in Montreal on February 12 and 27, 1997.

Chapter Ten

1 Maria Cuntrera's unpublished letter was provided to the authors by a confidential source.

2 Adrian Humphreys, *The Enforcer*.

Chapter Eleven

1 The events surrounding Nunzio LaRosa and Marcel Bureau are based on the Agreed Statement of Fact. At time of writing, Nunzio LaRosa hasn't been extradited to the United States to face narcotics charges. Sources: Hill/Court debriefings in Houston, Texas; RCMP fax regarding Hill/Court debriefing, and transcript; Hill/Court (videotaped) statements/interviews provided prior to their sentencing in the U.S.; Canadian and U.S. surveillance reports.

Chapter Twelve

1 Report of RCMP Liaison Officer Dennis Fiorido.

2 Oreste Pagano debriefing.

2 Ibid.

Acknowledgements

There are literally a hundred people who assisted in researching and writing this book. Some we already knew from writing previous books, others we still haven't met—they're email impulses that appear with alarming regularity or fax machine printouts that arrive without warning. We would like to first thank the two men who made the case in the first place, and that led to us making the book in the second:

Detective-Constables Bill Sciammarella and Tony Saldutto, of the Combined Forces Special Enforcement Unit. They successfully pushed a large rock up a steep hill.

And to: RCMP Staff-Sgt. Larry Tronstad, RCMP Sgt. Marc Bourque, Ontario Provincial Police Detective Ron Seaver, RCMP Commissioner Giuliano Zaccardelli, Montreal Police Det. Sgt. Pietro Poletti, RCMP Sgt. Reg King and RCMP Sgt. George Capra, Toronto Police Services Det.-Constable Mike Harvey, Ontario Provincial Police Staff Sgt. Steve Perrow, RCMP Sgt. Glenn Hanna, Prefetto Alessandro Pansa (Rome), ROS Capt. Andrea Carpani (Perugia), Retired DEA Special Agent John Costanzo, former RCMP Assistant Commissioner Richard Dickins, former RCMP Sgt. Gabriel Marion, Criminal Intelligence Service Analyst Pierre de Champlain, CFSEU Det. Dave Stilo and RCMP Investigator Luigi Vaccaro, English-Italian translator Emanuele Oriano, Montreal veteran crime reporter Michel Auger, Crown Attorney Beverly Wilton, "the lawyer"—whoever you are—and the members of the Omertà team. And: Salvo Palazzolo (Palermo), Sergio Casagrande (Perugia), Pietro Del Re (Rome), Alessandro Cancian (Toronto), Alfonso Bugea (Agrigento), Daniel Creusot (Montreal), Lanshmi Nguon (Montreal), Anna Cocca (Toronto), Adrian Humphreys (Toronto), Paul Cherry (Montreal), Dale

Ann Freed (Toronto), Rob Benzie (Toronto), Scot Magnish (Toronto), Eric Mayne (Windsor), Bruce Bowie (Vancouver) and all the colleagues at *Corriere Canadese*, the Italian daily newspaper in Toronto. Finally: Don Loney and the crew at HarperCanada for the suggestions, advice, and patience; and Catherine Marjoribanks.

Special thanks: Mario and Deborah Possamai, RCMP Chief Superintendent Ben Soave, Toronto Police Service Chief Julian Fantino, Alan Cairns, and Montreal veteran crime reporter André Cédilot.

Personal thanks: To Lucy White

To Antonella and Massimo

Index